The Psychology of P~~ol~~

Ashley Weinberg

The Psychology of Politicians explores a topic which fuels public and media debate yet is under-researched and has potentially far-reaching consequences for the success of our political systems. Focusing on research with democratically elected representatives from the UK, Poland and Italy, and on the political behaviour of a former US President and voters' perceptions in the emerging democracy of Ukraine, this book is packed with psychological insights. Using quantitative and qualitative methodologies, the contributors chart the progress of the individual politician from selection as a candidate to becoming established in Parliament, examining their qualities as communicators, thinkers and leaders. The impact of work and non-work pressures on their mental well-being and capacity to handle a crisis are probed, and the roles of personality traits in politicians' values and in public perceptions of our elected representatives are highlighted.

Dr Ashley Weinberg is a Chartered Psychologist and senior lecturer in psychology who conducted the first study of stress in UK Members of Parliament as a postgraduate Masters' student and has been researching the impact of the job on national politicians for twenty years. Ashley has published books, academic articles and chapters on the importance of psychological health in a range of public-sector occupations – including his Ph.D. on *Sources of Stress in the UK National Health Service* – as well as politicians, social workers and academics. He is co-author of *Organizational Stress Management* with Val Sutherland and Cary Cooper (2010) and *Surviving the Workplace* with Cary Cooper (2007). From 2000 to 2006 Ashley led the establishment of the psychology department at the University of Salford, where he continues to work, also holding an honorary lectureship in psychology at Manchester University.

The Psychology of Politicians

Edited by

Ashley Weinberg

CAMBRIDGE
UNIVERSITY PRESS

CAMBRIDGE UNIVERSITY PRESS
Cambridge, New York, Melbourne, Madrid, Cape Town,
Singapore, São Paulo, Delhi, Tokyo, Mexico City

Cambridge University Press
The Edinburgh Building, Cambridge CB2 8RU, UK

Published in the United States of America by Cambridge University Press,
New York

www.cambridge.org
Information on this title: www.cambridge.org/9780521130660

© Cambridge University Press 2012

First published 2012

Printed in the United Kingdom at the University Press, Cambridge

A catalogue record for this publication is available from the British Library

Library of Congress Cataloging in Publication data
The psychology of politicians / edited by Ashley Weinberg.
    p.   cm.
Includes index.
ISBN 978-0-521-11372-4 (hbk.) – ISBN 978-0-521-13066-0 (pbk.)
1. Politicians – Psychology.   2. Politicians – Psychology – Case
studies.   3. Political leadership – Psychological aspects.   4. Political
leadership – Psychological aspects – Case studies.   I. Weinberg,
Ashley.   II. Title.
JC330.3.P8   2011
324.01'9–dc23
                                                            2011017981

ISBN 978-0-521-11372-4 Hardback
ISBN 978-0-521-13066-0 Paperback

Contents

Figures

Tables

Acknowledgements

Ever since early political discussions with my dad about times of great political upheaval, I have been keen to understand the behaviour of those holding power. To produce a book on this topic has been an ambition of mine for twenty years and so I am especially grateful to my family for their help: my wife, Anne, for her love and support, my children, James and Lottie, for their ideas and enthusiasm and my parents, Martin and Risha, for their encouragement. I would like to thank Andrew Peart for commissioning this work and to his successor, Hetty Marx, as well as Jo Lane for all her help (including finding the image for the front cover) and Carrie Parkinson at Cambridge University Press. I am hugely grateful to all of the contributors, who have demonstrated both dedication and patience in the preparation of their chapters and whose commitment to their research into national politicians has helped to make this volume possible. I would particularly like to acknowledge the contribution of Professor Hugh Freeman to this field. I would like to thank my colleagues in the Psychology Department at the University of Salford, whose support for my sabbatical helped me to lay the foundations for this book, as well as my friend and colleague Professor Cary Cooper for his support for research into politicians over the years. I am indebted to the hundreds of national politicians who have participated in my research, as well as the handful who aroused my curiosity with their refusals. The relationship between psychological functioning and political work may not seem a fashionable topic for research, but where political decisions carry high stakes, I argue that it needs to be. I hope this book provides convincing evidence for this.

I dedicate this book to all students of the human political condition, who include James from an historical perspective and Lottie through the lens of psychology:

May your reading of the past and present inform all of our futures!

Contributors

CLAUDIO BARBARANELLI, Professor of Psychometry, 'Sapienza' University of Rome.

PETER BULL, Reader in Psychology, University of York.

GIANVITTORIO CAPRARA, Professor of Psychology, 'Sapienza' University of Rome.

PAVLO D. FROLOV, Senior Research Fellow, Institute for Social and Political Psychology, Academy of Pedagogic Sciences of Ukraine, Kiev, Ukraine.

AGNIESZKA GOLEC DE ZAVALA, Senior Lecturer in Psychology, Middlesex University.

JEAN HARTLEY, Professor of Organisational Analysis, Warwick Business School, University of Warwick.

RICHARD KWIATKOWSKI, Senior Lecturer in Organisational Psychology, Cranfield University.

MAX V. METSELAAR, Senior Researcher, Department of Defence, Netherlands.

OLHA V. PETRUNKO, Senior Research Fellow, Institute for Social and Political Psychology, Academy of Pedagogic Sciences of Ukraine, Kiev, Ukraine.

DIMITRIY V. POZNYAK, Senior Research Fellow, Institute for Social and Political Psychology, Academy of Pedagogic Sciences of Ukraine.

JO SILVESTER, Professor of Organisational Psychology, City University, London.

MICHELE VECCHIONE, Assistant Professor of Psychometry, 'Sapienza' University of Rome.

ASHLEY WEINBERG, Senior Lecturer in Psychology, University of Salford.

1   The psychology of politicians

Ashley Weinberg

Politics is living history. It is about people and their ideas, desires, needs and their striving to debate, negotiate, protest, fight and even die in pursuit of their goals over thousands of years. Political activity has evolved to take place within institutions, punctuated with crises when peoples and nations have taken matters into their own hands and demonstrated their will through public protest and revolution. In such ways, history tends to show that our species likes to exercise control over events. Accordingly we are fascinated by civilisations that no longer exist and the reasons they ended in ruins. If something of their history is known, it is the names of their leaders, for great efforts have been made to preserve such information, perhaps as their way to ensure everlasting glory. We marvel at objects dedicated to them: pyramids, decorative statues and columns, art and artefacts. Then we ask, where did it all go wrong for those who seemed to have the world at their feet? Why did they fail?

Of course, nature has had its part to play and in time global warming might ensure that it is not only the Danish King Canute who is famed for his attempts to turn back the tide. So is it learning or luck, design or fate which has thus far ensured our survival? Recent history recognises the steady hand of leaders such as Gorbachev in ending the Cold War and Churchill in leading Britain to victory in the Second World War, but we are also aware there have been many calamitous leaders, highlighted by the rise of grisly dictators (there are many from which to choose) and ill-fated decisions to pursue this or that doomed course of action. Since the Second World War, the Suez Crisis, the Bay of Pigs invasion and the Vietnam War are high-profile reminders of such events, yet in one way these represent comparatively recent landmarks in the evolution of political thought and action. In other words, failures in governments are commonplace and occasionally such mistakes lead to the fall of a state or the birth of another.

Indeed it is thought that democracy was born out of Athenian rebellion against Spartan invasion in 507 BC (Holland, 2005). Standing on the slopes of the Acropolis in Athens, the ancient seat of democratic thought, one can imagine that the white-stone columns of the Agora provided a glorious setting for early political debate and the evolution of political process. However, events on these grounds inspired Plato to conclude, 'Until philosophers are kings and the princes of this world have the spirit and power of philosophy, and political greatness and wisdom meet in one ... then only will our state have a possibility of life, and see the light of day.' On reading these words almost 2,500 years on, we are acutely aware of the political realities of the world around us and like Plato we are tempted to conclude that such ideals are not easily realised. Is this the view of the cynic or the realist? After all, is it not the nature of ideals that they represent the fleetingly attainable or the unsustainable? Perhaps the answer is this. Within the equation by which we might calculate how best to conduct politics lies one crucial variable: the human factor. This source of constant variability transcends time and is the reason why in fifty, let alone another twenty-five, centuries' time, our species will still be striving for the ideal form of government. However, this need not be a cause for despair. Given the dependence of our survival on adaptability, perhaps this is as it should be. Even if the perfect political system is to be developed, it is unlikely to remain so for too long as the needs of individuals, groups and nations change. History shows that every regime, however imperious, eventually falls – some more quickly than others and occasionally with less bloodshed than before.

As a species, humans have evolved at a far slower pace than the comparatively hectic history of recorded events. The resulting tension between our biology and history means that limitations in our capabilities are readily apparent, as hindsight reveals that things could have been enacted differently, but the systems of thought by which we derive our actions are naturally slow to adapt. Hence a typical national response to provocation is retaliation, undaunted by the human and financial costs of previous wars. In efforts to match the challenges of our environment, human behaviour is naturally geared to solving problems, but with varying degrees of success. Technology may provide a semblance of progress on the outside, but inside the brain we are still processing stimuli from our surroundings at a rate dictated by our biological hard-wiring (Freeman, 1991). In the realms of government things are no different: fallibility is ever-present. There have been major advances in our understanding of science, engineering and medicine, which in theory should raise the baseline from which we start to solve problems in these fields, yet we continue to make mistakes. In comparison, disciplines which rely so much more on the application of social principles, such as politics or organisational management, have fewer universal truths and concrete assumptions from which to begin. The changing nature of our moods, thoughts and emotional states leads to variation in human behaviour and means that lessons of social progress have often to be learned and relearned by successive generations. The science of psychology and its rigorous study of human behaviour have shown that many insights can be gained which inform our habits, social practices and well-being. However, politicians remain one group relatively unstudied by psychologists – there are those who would argue that this is so much the better, but after twenty-five centuries of awaiting the ideal form of government, there seems little to be lost and much to be gained in subjecting those who hold power to scientific study. There are also those who would claim that in order to blend political greatness with wisdom as Plato hoped, insights into the psychological workings of those engaged in government are not so much fanciful, as rather the next essential stage in the political evolution of our species!

Are politicians necessary?

If we accept that political processes have developed to varying degrees, perhaps it is worth asking whether we need politicians at all. Once again history suggests an answer, for we know that humans have survived for tens of thousands of years and have evolved to function in groups. Where there are groups, there tend to be levels of organisation for achieving important goals, not least those of securing food and shelter. Who decides the processes involved depends on the nature and size of the group, as well as the constituent personalities. For example, this might mean one, some or all members having a say before a decision is made. On a much larger scale, modern democracy attempts to organise decision making in relation to a panoply of issues, based on the election of political representatives who to some degree convey the wishes of their constituents. Even in such an example of representative democracy, the processes are already relatively fixed, but there is acknowledgement of the need for debate, and this is centred on deciding which goals are given priority. In societies which describe themselves as democratic, politicians have a necessary role to play, for without the reduction of the numbers of people involved in the debate to a manageable size, decisions would be hard, if not impossible, to achieve.

Of course there are many forms of political system, in which the role of a politician will be quite different, but in some sense he or she is likely to be representing the views of a particular interest, whether openly declared and accountable or not. In short, if we concur with the idea that groups consisting of thousands and millions need some level of organisation in order to best ensure their survival, then the answer is that we do need politicians. Whether we like their decisions or indeed them as individuals is quite another matter!

Who are the politicians?

As organisations of any size are about the people they comprise and the use of their collective power to achieve common goals, we are in a position to accept that groups cannot avoid political activity and are likely to benefit from it as part of everyday functioning. In other words, family units, voluntary groups, work organisations, etc. bear daily witness to politics at the micro-level and beyond. As such any group can give rise to politicians, ranging from the child who wishes to get their own way to the corporate leader who wants a certain image for their company. Whatever the role of the individual within these formal or informal contexts, influence of some sort is exercised, but this political behaviour is unlikely to mark him/her out as different from others. Family members naturally seek to influence behaviour, often accompanied by considerable debate and, if we are fortunate, decisions will arise to which we have contributed. In essence the process of voting at a general election represents a much more diluted contribution to a far larger debate. For many of us this might be the extent of our own political influence and even the limit of our aspirations to change the world around us. At the individual level, political actions are part of the norm, as we jostle for position to achieve our chosen aims, however, if we define these in terms of politics, the same activities are viewed somewhat differently. Actions which many would find worthy of praise are viewed with scepticism when we acknowledge that the role played by the individual concerned is a 'political' one.

This perception may in turn shape our view of politicians whose sphere of influence is perceived by citizens as far greater. For some this can breed resentment that we are the ones without power or, alternatively, we may be quite content as we are – at least until things go wrong. This could lead one to conclude that there can be no such thing as a well-liked politician, yet there are community and national representatives who have earned the respect of those across the political spectrum. From the panoply of political behaviour, it might be that the strutting and fretting across the political stage appeals least to the voters, whereas perceived similarities between voters' and politicians' behaviour in other areas are more likely to generate positive evaluations. Perhaps this assessment of 'having something in common' is at the root of our view of politicians which in turn evokes strong emotions in response to their very public actions.

Politicians as employees of the people

There tend to be five things which promote animated discussion about national politicians: (a) how much they earn, (b) the quality of their decisions, (c) their speech making, (d) that they reply to us when we have taken the trouble to contact them, and e) that they do not engage in personal relationships or dealings likely to arouse indignation or condemnation. In other words, if a politician is very lucky, he or she may please some of the people most of the time. So who are these individuals who thrust themselves forward into the public eye and what do they hope to achieve? What are they like as people and how much have we got it right when we make our pronouncements on them? At best we hope that they get on with the job and meet at least some of the expectations we had of them on election day, and at worst we may not care, 'because they're all as bad as each other'. There have been many attempts to probe the amalgam of qualities and characteristics which contribute to the individual we call the 'politician'. Furthermore in the field of social science, political psychologists and analysts have tried to shed light on how they affect us.

It is the aim of this text, using research into politicians themselves, to gain an insight into their own experience. Could it be they are in a job which garners apparent power, requires higher ambition than most of us have, but carries the low levels of control over their working lives with which many of us are all too familiar? Or is the perception of privilege and wealth justified?

In many jobs, we are accustomed to seeing someone who has done well in a particular task gaining promotion to be in charge of others or shouldering greater responsibility which turns out to be quite unrelated to the original job. However, wonderful doctors and teachers do not always make such great heads of services and schools. This process of promotion continues to produce mismatches despite leadership and management development courses devised to prepare them for the task. In politics there is also little way of knowing how well an individual will do in leading a party or a country before they are given that opportunity. The difference here is that it is much less a matter of standardised selection procedures and rather more a question of who the majority of the political party is likely to support in winning or retaining power. Indeed there may be fear that what is seen as a sanitised selection procedure may even rob us of a great and visionary leader. However there is also an argument for doing everything possible to ensure that our leaders are, and remain, in possession of the qualities best suited to political office and to exercise power appropriately in making life-changing decisions on behalf of all. As we take steps to ensure this with those responsible for the lives of others, such as doctors and teachers, why should those taking charge of whole nations be exempt?

Political philosophy in the democratic tradition

Until John Locke's *Second Treatise on Civil Government*, political philosophers had considered the notion of political decision making and activity as resting in the hands of an elite. This comprised either groups or individuals, based on Plato's concept of intellectual aristocracy or Hobbes' version of absolute rule by the sovereign. Alongside these variants, ran Machiavelli's advice on securing and maintaining power at all costs. Locke's departure from this tradition featured the 'law of nature', which provided that 'no one ought to harm another in his life, health, liberty or possessions', encapsulating the priority given to human rights and the maintenance of appropriately deliberated laws. As such he became the 'theoretical architect' of Western-style democracy, directly influencing French and American revolutionaries alike, with his writings quoted and paraphrased in the American Declaration of Independence and Constitution. However it was left to John Stuart Mill to emphasise that, while majority rule was essential, so too was the protection of the rights of minorities. In other words, the denial of the rights of others to express their opinion is to assume one's own infallibility (Mill, 1859). Whilst this can be clearly harnessed to criticise the authoritarian approach to government, it also proves difficult in practice to predict when the actions of the minority may be harmful to the majority. Thus Mill recognised that certain limitations should be placed upon governmental powers, facilitated by the requirement to elect 'in a democratic society . . . enlightened individuals who will be mature and responsible because they reflect upon the issues which face them'.

Marx contended that this opportunity was denied by the existence of political and economic constrictions, such as the class system, although these could be overcome through the conflict borne out of the Hegelian dialectic, in which a thesis is opposed (antithesis) and a new solution, or indeed social order, is produced (synthesis). Notwithstanding the widespread influence of Marxism, the Utilitarian philosophy of the 'greatest happiness for the greatest number' seems to have provided the motivation for the continuous improvement of laws and other societal processes in Western-style democracies. However, this is not the approach adopted by all governments worldwide and indeed is not universally seen as desirable.

Such differences in the approach to government stem from many factors including history, religion, cultural expectations, as well as prevailing political and economic conditions. None of this implies that one system is right and another one wrong, rather that political traditions vary and the history of Europe and the United States over recent times has demonstrated that democratic principles have tended to prevail over those of despotism. This has led to both successful and unsuccessful attempts by Western nations to export their version of democracy across the world. However a non-partisan view would likely detect the combined influence of Machiavelli and Mill in the behaviour of any political system, not least democracy. Whether 'true' democracy exists is a bigger issue than this book has scope to address, but it does seem appropriate to focus on the territories which have devoted most of the last 200 years contesting it: Europe and the United States. In order to fully grasp the challenges facing politicians in democratic systems, it is important to acknowledge the influence of their environment, both in terms of relevant political tradition and the shift from continental to global political considerations.

A democratic tradition?

Many European history courses take the French Revolution of 1789 and the ensuing Napoleonic Wars as a hinge from which to focus on a new era in the continent's development. From this point on the reasons for conflict in Europe – and elsewhere – invariably stemmed from attempts by nations and peoples to assert their right to self-determination. The United States' proclamation of independence from Britain in 1776 had already signalled both economic and political change. After this period the main European powers sought to guarantee the national sovereignty of smaller European countries, whilst beginning their scramble for imperial gains in Africa and jostling for influence in the New World. In the 'Year of Revolutions' which gripped Europe in 1848, the seeds of the new nations of Germany and Italy were sown, as the Hapsburg Empire of Austria-Hungary began to crumble. Within sixty years Near- and Middle-Eastern nations evolved from the remains of the Turkish Ottoman Empire, while Russia and its satellites exchanged the despotic rule of the Tsars for the turmoil of Bolshevik revolution in 1917. The Second World War heralded a reshuffle in world order, German and Italian dictators were halted, the decline of British and French imperial interests accelerated and the West and the former USSR began their Cold War tussle for supremacy. Since the collapse of the Soviet Union in 1990, democratic systems of government have spread to Eastern Europe, yet attempts to transport this tradition further east in recent years by Western-led alliances have met with varying levels of success.

In short, to the accompaniment of the writings of Locke, Mill, de Tocqueville and Marx, the modern history of Europe has been played out on a global stage with many countries taking turns to aspire to dominate the continent and beyond, including Spain, the Netherlands, Austria-Hungary, France, the United Kingdom, Germany and Russia (and arguably the United States of America). This jockeying for position has also seen European countries forming blocs of political power, which have emerged, flourished and in their time failed. Indeed it is argued by eminent historians, that the global standing of Europe as a political power is in decline. Despite two hundred years during which major European powers have sought to defend the sovereignty of their neighbours, current efforts to exert such influence have met with stiff resistance and indeed diplomatic defeat at the United Nations (UN). An examination of European and American-led votes at the UN in the ten years since 1998 reveals a 'fading power to set the rules' (*Guardian*, 18 September 2008). Writing at the approach to the new century, Hobsbawm asserted that 'the uncertainties surrounding political democracy no longer seemed quite so remote' (1994, p. 141). Support for EU-sponsored human rights policies dropped from 72 to 48 per cent of UN members and US-led policies received the support of only 30 per cent of UN countries compared to 77 per cent at the start of the millennium. The balance of international power appears to be shifting towards China, India and the Islamic coalitions (*Guardian*, 18 September 2008), in the wake of Western attempts to alter the political systems of Iraq and Afghanistan. For example, China – with a population in excess of one billion – has positioned itself as a global influence, boasting strong economic ties with Africa and its own contribution to space exploration, while India – with the world's second-largest population – is similarly poised to dominate the world's service sector.

The significance of these trends for political psychology lies within the need for a greater understanding of the impact and functioning of a range of political systems and the political players within them. For example, China retains its communist-style political system and a number of emerging nations are governed by unelected royal families in the old European mould. This book takes a step towards examining the functioning of politicians from a cross-section of modern and mainly European political systems, including those with communist and royalist backgrounds, thus embracing both new and more established democracies in order to encompass modes of government which can be considered broadly comparable. Inevitably, national, cultural and political differences are evident, but the focus on Europe (alongside a European view of a United States foreign policy in crisis) also offers natural diversity. The scrutiny of political behaviour in democratic systems in this book is based on two real-world factors which have direct implications for methodology. Firstly there is the greater potential for data collection than in totalitarian states, as democratic systems accustom their politicians to some level of accountability, which tends to ease researcher access; and secondly there is the increased likelihood of such politicians being representative of a range of perspectives in national politics, rather than comprising a smaller, self-selected and relatively unaccountable sample.

Theoretical perspectives, methodology and ethics in political psychology research

Whatever the nature of the prevailing political system, political behaviour is traditionally conducted away from public view, as leaders and their advisors, parliaments and government cabinets meet to take key decisions. As a discipline political psychology has attempted to illuminate the processes involved and one emphasis has been on scrutinising the roles of cognitive and social phenomena within decision making and belief systems (McGuire, 2004). However, research into political behaviour has often been tied to secondary data analysis or laboratory studies of participants drawn from non-political samples. It should be recorded that there have been some notable exceptions, such as Tetlock's (1984) study of cognitive style and belief systems among UK MPs. Meanwhile excellent texts such as *Political Psychology* by Jost and Sidanius (2004) have attempted to bring together the highlights of a fifty-year period of research in the field of political psychology, while others, such as Kuklinski's (2002) 'Thinking about Political Psychology', have urged researchers to consider the full range of perspectives at their disposal.

The origins of modern political psychology date back to the Second World War and attempts to understand the link between personality and political behaviour in prominent leaders. Case studies of many world leaders have endeavoured to shed light on their motivations and actions (see Freeman, 1991). Indeed the psycho-biographical approach inspired by advocates of Freudian psychoanalytical thinking, such as Lasswell, sought to explain a wide range of political outcomes, from Woodrow Wilson's failure to obtain US Senate ratification of the League of Nations Treaty (George and George, 1964) to Josef Stalin's systematic destruction of sections of the Russian population. Whilst the interpretation of individual actions in the light of deduced motivations provides a fascinating commentary, it does however raise the issue of the subjectivity of the writers, unsurprisingly influenced by their own context and motivation (Carr, 1987) and has also been criticised by some for its lack of 'political sophistication' (Sullivan, Rahn and Rudolf, 2002) as clearly, 'not all psychological predispositions are acted out in the same way in different political contexts' (Sullivan *et al.*, 2002, p. 29). Barber's (1992) development of this is evident from his emphasis on political context, whereby individual psychological factors are seen to interact with political factors at the time. Nonetheless psychobiography seeks 'to explain political actions that we have difficulty comprehending if we rely solely on conventional political explanations and theories' (Sullivan *et al.*, 2002, p. 29). Some political psychologists realise this is not an easy task (e.g. Greenstein, 1992), indeed the limited generalisability of this knowledge base is compounded by the relative rarity of psychological studies of large numbers of individuals involved in political processes at a national level. In order to maximise the chances of understanding political activity, there remains scope for deploying both quantitative and qualitative approaches which gather data from far larger numbers of national politicians and, notwithstanding the limitations of such methodologies, make possible more generalisable conclusions.

The popularity of a range of media news-streams suggests that there is a ready demand for psychological knowledge about political figures, yet one might be forgiven for sensing a reticence on the part of psychologists for dealing with them directly in order to gather the necessary data. Of course this may well stem from the limited time which busy public figures can commit to contributing to such research, although this does not seem to prevent the steady flow of market-research studies desperate to attract the participation of politicians. Reluctance may also be engendered by the limited funding opportunities for work with what many see as a privileged occupational group therefore undeserving of detailed scrutiny. Additionally psychologists may perceive risks in working with high-profile individuals and the collection of potentially sensitive data which are at odds with any personal preference for 'quieter' professional lives. The supposition of a power dynamic likely to favour the politician may undermine the confidence of a researcher, whose position in their employment institution may be destabilised by a well-aimed objection from a disgruntled participant. Whichever, or however many, of these and other potential difficulties, are actually responsible for the dearth of studies carried out on national politicians, the outcomes in terms of the existing body of academic knowledge are clear: comparatively little has been published in books or journals by psychologists highlighting the psychological issues reported by national politicians. Therefore our understanding of political acts tends to rely on deductions about relatively few key individuals who tend to have been prominent leaders and where the direct impact of psychological factors is harder to verify.

It would seem that we are only beginning to lift the lid and peer into what many academics have hitherto considered a Pandora's Box. This fear may have promulgated a lack of research, but the realisation which often startles is that politicians are keen to talk about their work, their reasons for doing it and the problems associated with it. This is not uncommon in any occupational group and should not of itself be surprising. The issue of sensitive data relates to many organisational contexts and so the maintenance of ethical propriety should not be too difficult for the careful researcher to address. Similarly consideration of the time required of national politicians to participate in research is the same as one would give to engaging any busy individual. The sensitive issues of difficulties in obtaining funding, potentially unwelcome publicity and warding off negative fallout from a powerful and unhappy participant are more likely to test the resolve of individual researchers and their employers. However, in a supportive research environment and with due respect to protocol these issues should not of themselves be insurmountable.

Taking each of these factors into account, there remains a sizeable gap in existing data about those who take decisions at national and global levels. This is clearly a major omission in a society committed to its improvement and the advancement of knowledge. Just as there is a responsibility of governments to answer to its supporters – particularly those which are democratically elected – it is incumbent on the proponents, functionaries and observers of these systems (including psychologists) to encourage as wide an understanding as possible of how they work.

This book represents proof that the potential pitfalls need not turn this area of research into a Pandora's Box. Instead the contributors have unearthed a veritable trove of psychological insights into the functioning of individuals who operate our national political systems at the highest level. *The Psychology of Politicians* brings together those whose empirical research with national politicians informs each chapter. In a field where the majority of publications are US-based, it is significant that the contributors are European and the focus is mainly on European politicians. This emphasises both the level of this kind of research activity across the continent as well as its ability to complement the predominantly theoretical, sociological and laboratory-based perspectives hitherto available. Thus it is not the intention of this book to set itself above other approaches, rather to add to the current literature through its perspective on politicians as individuals. In this way, *The Psychology of Politicians* is the first book written by psychologists about national politicians utilising empirical methods among others to provide insights into their behaviour, functioning and health. It is hoped that this research-based guide will further our understanding of politicians' behaviour as the salience of their decisions is unlikely to diminish, nor is the fascination with the capabilities and limitations of global power-holders who emerge to take the lead in things.

The focus of this book

The Psychology of Politicians uses first-hand psychological research with national politicians to reveal what really lies beneath the surface and seeks to set an agenda for future research in this field. This book is subdivided into four sections consistent with the overarching themes outlined below:

- 'Becoming politicians': the processes of political selection and socialisation in UK politics are explored, including the skills and psychological adjustments which individual politicians bring to their job.
- 'Being at the centre of things': how national politicians function in their job roles comes under scrutiny, examining political communication, leadership skills and their cognitive abilities. The social and cognitive processes which underlie politicians' daily behaviour are scrutinised.
- 'Coping with the pressure?': the nature and prevalence of psychological strain (commonly referred to as 'stress') among politicians is scrutinised, alongside the main sources of pressure – such as workload and work-life balance – and the relative impact of organisational events and reforms on individual well-being. The impact of multiple factors on politicians' preparedness for a crisis situation is considered.
- 'People as politicians': the personality traits and values of politicians and those who elect them are compared and the ways in which people conceptualise their politicians are examined, shedding light on what voters are seeking and what they can expect to find.

'Becoming politicians'

The first section of the book examines the rites of passage for potential and elected national politicians in the United Kingdom. Beginning with quantitative research by Jo Silvester on the competencies the politician requires, this highlights aspects of the selection process which are linked to electoral success. Drawing on comparison with wider employee recruitment practices, Silvester examines the advantages and disadvantages of transferring the 'knowledge, skills and attributes' approach commonly assessed in everyday job selection into the political arena. The implementation of standardised selection procedures for parliamentary candidates in two of the three main political parties is described and there is a clear acknowledgement of the 'political' nature of the processes involved. Perhaps the most intriguing finding is that competencies such as critical thinking have been linked with improved election results.

Having overcome the hurdles of selection and election, it would be possible for politicians, particularly the vast majority who serve on the backbenches, to fade from the scrutiny of all but those who inhabit their constituencies. Richard Kwiatkowski's interviews with those seeking power and influence provides a unique insight into the strategies and organisational processes which translate into everyday political behaviour in parliament. Examining the early years of the newly elected UK government of 1997, Kwiatkowski finds resonance with the functioning of organisations in which many of us work. Culture, loyalties and simply 'getting ahead' are concepts familiar to most employees, although it is here argued that the key difference in parliament is the pursuit of power as a necessary means 'to achieve a "higher purpose"'.

'Being at the centre of things'

Having arrived and survived, what do politicians actually do? There are three main areas of activity which arguably define the occupational category under scrutiny: communication, leadership and political judgement. Discussing the first of these, Peter Bull applies a Social Skills Model to observed political communication, highlighting the features of effective social performance and taking into account a range of factors including timing, feedback and the context of the communication. The familiar ploys seen in speech making and interviews are considered, ranging from equivocation (there are thirty-five ways of not answering a question) to timing and responding to interruption. All of these contribute to the politician's 'face' (attempts to convey desirability and competence) and his/her manipulation of it for political benefit, with advantages literally clear for all to see.

By contrast, what is not immediately apparent to the public is the hidden dimension of cognitive skills and abilities. These are explored by Agnieszka Golec de Zavala through her studies conducted with national politicians in Poland. It is widely assumed that politicians have considerable prowess in cognitive sophistication, hence it is a cause of public comment when this is shown not to be apparent! Through the use of standardised interview schedules and scales, the cognitive styles of Polish national politicians are assessed and levels of complexity in their thinking found to vary across the political spectrum. Golec de Zavala highlights potentially startling links between political leanings and styles of cognitive functioning. Furthermore she underlines the importance of flexibility in political thinking and opinions in reflecting politicians' tolerance of uncertainty on the political landscape. The fascinating implications of these findings for democratic discourse are considered in a post-communist context.

Politics is inevitably about power and this is perhaps most obviously expressed through leadership – whether in terms of personal qualities, or as a means of proposing a vision of how society and political organisations should be shaped. There are differences between political and other forms of leadership, most obviously in that the former is founded on the source of legitimacy, which is largely derived from a mandate provided by the voting public. In light of this, Jean Hartley's chapter considers the types and functions of political leadership, the contexts and arenas in which it operates and the inherent challenges therein. Based on data collected at UK local and regional level, Hartley demonstrates how effective leadership capacities in national government may be identified in order that they should be enhanced, detailing the development of the Warwick Political Leadership Questionnaire and the utility of 360-degree feedback.

'Coping with the pressure?'

Stress is often seen as a modern epidemic which has swept through working lives, registering a negative impact on employees' health, job performance and personal relationships. The editor's chapter on psychological strain highlights that politicians are no different from other occupational groups in this respect; a conclusion based on a number of quantitative studies with UK national politicians. No doubt it is of concern to politicians that the job takes a psychological toll, but it is also of wider concern to the electorate that resulting poor mental and physical health may impair optimal job performance. Despite the litany of poor decisions made by politicians who have become ill after taking office, there has been an unwillingness to recognise what might be considered the sum of all fears: one or more leaders bent on a dubious political goal from which their psychological health or inability to cope prevents them from deviating. This chapter underlines the importance of supporting politicians accordingly and appropriately, whilst ensuring that the design of the political job is well considered. Ranging from long working hours and the difficulties in managing work–life balance to evaluating the impact of reforms to working hours and of critical events such as an election landslide or a major scandal (i.e., UK politicians' expenses), the psychological health of UK MPs is placed under the spotlight.

If electorates expect automatic value from their politicians, there are words of warning from those who seek to understand the human brain by comparison with computers: 'the constantly increasing volumes of information being received by ... political leaders may be placing too great a burden on the relevant processing machinery' and 'when over-aroused for long, the ability of the brain to integrate data into a meaningful whole is adversely affected, and judgement is likely to be impaired' (Freeman, 1991, p. 20). With cognitive overload in mind, Max Metselaar applies his Political Coping Theory to one case study, namely the behaviour of US leaders in the period preceding the Tet Offensive of January, 1968 during the Vietnam War. In particular the chapter focuses on the role of inappropriate cognitive coping via denial and avoidance of information which clearly showed that an attack was building. This ineffective approach to unfolding events is scrutinised with reference to autobiographical accounts, archives and political analyses. Metselaar asserts that the likelihood of denial and avoidance is increased by fear among politicians of having insufficient resources to deal with a given crisis, dilemmas created by conflicting political demands, as well as the limitations of operating in a way which discourages critical debate – even within a democratic system. The outcomes are evident from the lack of preparedness of policy-makers and consequently those expected to handle conflict situations on the ground. Parallels with scenarios in more recent conflicts may be readily drawn.

'People as politicians'

Harking back to an understanding of where politicians come from, the final section of this book focuses on the psychological origins of political attitudes. The penultimate chapter by Gianvittorio Caprara, Michele Vecchione and Claudio Barbaranelli examines the role of personality in determining political preference in both national politicians and voters. Using the Five Factor Model as the basis for their analyses, Caprara *et al.* review their own and others' studies from Italy and abroad, highlighting the relationship between values and personality traits, in relation to presidential and party political preferences. As in Golec de Zavala's earlier chapter, similarities and comparisons are drawn from across the political spectrum. The nature and stability of the perceptions of politicians' personalities are also noted, together with the relative importance of traits and values in voters' decisions. Furthermore it is suggested that voters relate their perceptions of politicians' traits to their own, in simplifying their path through the vast quantity of information available to them towards a decision about who to support.

Such mental short-cuts are evident in how Ukrainian voters perceive their politicians too. Pavlo Frolov, Olha Petrunko and Dmitriy Poznyak provide an insight into the development of voters' cognitive representations of politicians in a country experiencing democratic systems for the first time, following the end of communist rule in 1990–1. Under these circumstances, all but one of the political parties were new and the absence of any conceptual distance between politicians and their electors is evident from the proliferation of candidates – in other words, the politicians in a new system of government are mainly without any previous experience and at least in terms of power may be regarded as little different from those who have decided not to stand for election. From this perspective the voters and politicians may be considered as one. This is a situation which may be deemed a precursor to that outlined in an established democratic system by Caprara *et al.*, whereby voters seek similarities in their politicians who have 'grown apart' from their electorate. In this chapter, Frolov *et al.* use qualitative techniques to examine the development and measurement of political cognitions, particularly schemas of leadership, in an electorate with limited experience of making choices between political candidates. It is not surprising that the issues of trust and competence in leadership are common themes to both chapters in this final section of the book.

Where next? The potential consequences of psychological insight into politicians

Perhaps the time is well overdue to ask that the process by which leaders are selected, and their functioning monitored, is one which includes assessments of their suitability against more objective criteria than if they can win power. To some this may only appear to be a 'luxury' afforded to democratic systems, but at the heart of its intention is the optimal functioning of democracy and public accountability. Regardless of political system, any individuals and groups hoping to see their priorities championed would be well advised to consider carefully how to choose both representatives and leaders 'fit to govern'. This is not to say that there is such a thing as an ideal set of psychological attributes for politicians, as the arguments over what constitute the amalgam of qualities, personality characteristics and skills best suited for political office are intricate. However, the problems this raises are not reason enough to avoid improving the process of recruiting, training and supporting elected representatives from whom our leaders are chosen.

Doubtless there are dangers in attempts to rationalise political processes which might result in the exclusion of highly talented people and this would be undesirable. Nevertheless there are advantages to regular and reliable health screening of serving politicians, which could help to flag up serious misgivings about the behaviour of a leader. As history shows, only in major crises does the question begin to be asked audibly, 'Should this person be in charge?' As with selection, health screening of politicians is likely to be challenging to introduce, but constitutes a necessary precaution against political abuse.

However, there are a number of facets of political activity which are not on public view and which are positive in their nature. What is often not seen, unless one follows the newscasts of presidential or prime ministerial campaign trails, is the physical commitment of those engaged in political activity at any level, often embedded in rigorous travel schedules, challenging campaigns, debates and rallies and participation in community events, to name but a few. While it is possible to measure such behaviour, the overarching aspect of political endeavour which is less easily assessed, but must be present in some form to drive these observable actions, is the commitment, perseverance and purpose to pursue agreed political goals. Accompanying these are the cognitive and social skills which enable the politician to grapple with the complexities of varying perspectives, legislative change and mass communication. Once again the public would want to be reassured that the politicians are suitably equipped – and where appropriate trained – to deal with challenges in these areas and above all that they are giving of their best.

It is perhaps not surprising that there are many colourful phrases describing those engaged in politics on the national stage, ranging from 'career politician' to 'political animal' and worse. Such epithets are often accompanied by a knowing look or wink, as though recognising that dealing with political individuals is likely to require a healthy scepticism about what they say, however convincingly it is expressed. The need for such caution may stem from politicians' need to calculate the impact of what they are conveying, for without doing so, they run the real risk of upsetting those upon whose support they depend. In a democratic system, failure to assess such risks could cost crucial votes and with it the opportunity to enact what they believe to be the common good. Just how committed politicians are to acting in the public interest is readily questioned by the electorate. Many people do not engage in high-profile political processes, so it can be hard to understand the motivation of those who do, and herein lie the seeds of distrust. Politics is after all about power and, as Lord Acton famously stated, 'power corrupts; absolute power corrupts absolutely'. This need not mean that the politician's role is redundant, as the systems of government in which they operate do contribute to achieving the goals of society. After all, life is about survival and alongside it attaining a reasonable quality of existence. Therefore those who seek to govern are worthy of scrutiny and if we are not convinced of the probity of their motives, then we are justified in feeling they are also worthy of our contempt! In other words, politicians are important in our lives, whether we like them as individuals or not, so it is incumbent on all of us to play our part in choosing and supporting those suited for the purpose. It is time for political psychology to step up!

References

Barber, J. D. (1992). *The Presidential Character: Predicting Performance in the White House*, 4th edn. Englewood Cliffs, N.J.: Prentice-Hall.

Carr, E. H. (1987). *What Is history?* Harlow: Penguin.

Freeman, H. (1991). The human brain and political behaviour. *British Journal of Psychiatry*, 159 (1991), 19–32.

Guardian (2008). Western influence at UN wanes as power balance shifts. 18 September. George, G. A. L. and George, J. L. (1964) *Woodrow Wilson and Colonel House: A Personality Study*. New York: Dover Press.

Greenstein, F. (1992). Can personality and politics be studied systematically? *Political Psychology*, 13, 105–28.

Hobsbawm, E. (1994). *The Age of Extremes: The Short Twentieth Century 1914–1991*. London: Abacus.

Holland, T. (2005). *Persian Fire*. London: Abacus.

Jost, J. T. and Sidanius, J. S. (eds.) (2004). *Political Psychology*. New York: Psychology Press.

Kuklinski, J. H. (ed.) (2002). *Thinking about Political Psychology*. Cambridge University Press.

McGuire, W. J. (2004). The poly-psy relationship: three phases of a long affair. In J. T. Jost and J. Sidanius (eds.), *Political Psychology* (pp. 22–32). New York: Psychology Press.

Mill, J. S. (1859). *On Liberty*, 2nd edn. West Strand: John W. Parker and Son.

Sullivan, J. L., Rahn, W. M. and Rudolf, T. J. (2002). The contours of political psychology: Situating research on political information processing. In J. H. Kuklinski (ed.), *Thinking about Political Psychology* (pp. 23–47). Cambridge University Press.

Tetlock, P. E. (1984). Cognitive style and political belief systems in the British House of Commons. *Journal of Personality and Social Psychology*, 46, 365–75.

Part I

Becoming politicians

2   Recruiting politicians: designing
     competency-based selection for
     UK parliamentary candidates

Jo Silvester

According to George Bernard Shaw, 'democracy substitutes election by the incompetent many for appointment by the corrupt few' (1903), yet selection and election decisions both play an important part in determining who will ultimately become a politician. Most politicians represent a political party, and successful democratic elections in the UK and a majority of other Western countries[1] depend on the ability of political parties to *attract* and *select* the best possible candidates. In fact, recruiting individuals to legislative office is seen as a core function of political systems, with the quality of candidates selected impacting ultimately on the quality of government delivered (Gallagher and Marsh, 1988; Katz, 2001). As gatekeepers to political roles political parties therefore bear an important responsibility to their members, and the public they hope to represent, to identify the best possible candidates through fair and effective selection procedures (Lovenduski, 2005).

Despite clear parallels between political recruitment and employee selection, there has been surprisingly little exploration of how selection research might inform our understanding of how and why certain individuals become politicians (Silvester and Dykes, 2007). Indeed, industrial and organisational (I/O) psychologists have paid remarkably little attention to politics and political work in general (Bar-Tal, 2002; Silvester, 2008). This chapter sets out to redress this situation by exploring how knowledge and practice relevant to employee selection research might be usefully applied to the political context. More specifically, it considers whether such knowledge and practice might be used to improve how political parties select candidates and identify those individuals likely to perform well in government. Beginning with a review of

---

[1] The US is unique in that the two political parties that dominate do not control who can run (and be elected) for political office. These individuals are therefore comparatively independent of party discipline, policy and finance. This makes US politics unlike that of most countries and particularly unlike that of the European countries with which it is usually classed (Stokes, 2005, p. 121).

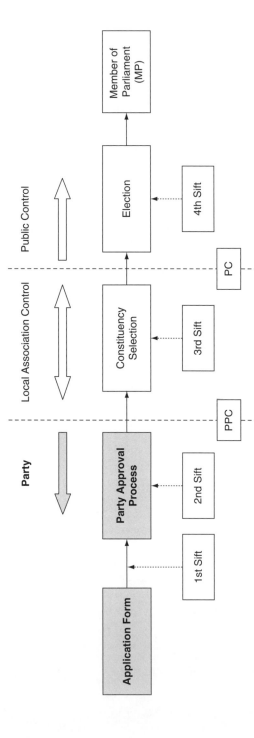

Figure 2.1. Key decision points (sifts) in the selection and election of UK parliamentary candidates

existing research on political recruitment (conducted mostly by political scientists), the chapter considers potential advantages and disadvantages of applying traditional employee selection methods to political recruitment. Finally, two examples of competency-based selection procedures for approving prospective UK parliamentary candidates are described; one with the Conservative Party and one with the Liberal Democrat Party. Although the chapter takes a predominantly UK perspective, focusing on the role of Member of Parliament (MP), similarities with political recruitment and implications for practice in other countries are discussed.

Political selection

Candidate selection is one of the most important functions of a democratic organisation (Katz, 2001). It is the primary mechanism by which a political party decides whether an individual has the qualities needed to become an elected representative and perform the role well. Historically, decisions about who could or could not become an MP in the UK were in the control of aristocratic families and the monarch, who between them controlled patronage of most constituencies. Although the 1832 Reform Bill reduced this influence, it was not until Prime Minister Disraeli introduced a further Reform Bill in 1867, allowing men who did not own land to become MPs, that the pool of individuals eligible to become a parliamentary candidate significantly increased. A challenge to the power of patronage, it resulted in a need for political parties to adopt tighter forms of organisation and exert more influence over the choice of political candidates (Weber, 1918).

Nearly 150 years later the process of becoming an MP can still be a complex and protracted affair. In their comparison of political selection practices in three Western democracies (Canada, Australia and the UK), Norris, Carty, Erikson, Lovenduski and Simms (1990) identify five common steps to becoming a national politician. Firstly, individuals must be eligible to stand for election. Next, they need to be approved as a prospective candidate by a political party. Thirdly, once a local constituency announces a vacancy for a candidate, individuals must apply and be shortlisted by a constituency committee. Shortlisted applicants are then invited to participate in a selection process that can involve speaking at a public meeting and being interviewed by a panel of local members. Finally, if successful in being selected, the candidate begins campaigning within the constituency in the hope of being elected to parliament at the next election. Figure 2.1 illustrates this process, together with key decision points (sifts) and the groups that have most influence over them.

Selection procedures are broadly similar for each of the three main UK political parties, although there are some differences in the level of influence that the party's national executive can exert (or is willing to exert) over later selection stages. In the case of the Labour Party, for example, there is no strict requirement that applicants for constituency selection should be approved. For all political parties, however, local candidate selection in particular is the setting for attempts at influence from different groups, each competing to get their preferred candidate selected. Shepherd-Robinson and Lovenduski (2002) describe how senior party members frequently seek to improve the chances of 'favourite sons' (and daughters) by publicly supporting their campaign efforts. Yet there are also efforts to influence selection decisions that are sanctioned by the parties, for example strategies such as A-lists (Conservative Party), all-women shortlists, 'twinning' and 'zipping'[2] have all been adopted at different times in an effort to improve the diversity of the pool of candidates. These strategies are generally unpopular with local selection panels, where members are likely to vigorously defend their right to choose a candidate. As Norris *et al.* (1990, p. 229) point out, candidate selection is 'one of the few areas of party life in which local parties continue to exert their independence'. This means that whilst national party executives retain the power to veto a local association's choice of candidate, most are very reluctant to do so in practice.

Figure 2.1 makes clear the fact that local association selection is only one stage of a more extensive selection process, which can take longer for some prospective MPs than others. Seats vary widely in terms of their 'win-ability' for a particular party and therefore in terms of their attractiveness to potential candidates. The most sought after are 'safe' seats, where there has been strong historical support for a party and the likelihood of a candidate being elected to parliament is therefore high. However, new prospective parliamentary candidates are usually expected to first 'cut their teeth' as the candidate for a marginal seat. This means that they can learn how to campaign effectively and also demonstrate their level of commitment to the political party. It also means that with general elections taking place on average every four years an individual may have to wait many years before becoming an MP; if indeed they ever do. A good example of this is former Prime Minister Margaret Thatcher, who, whilst initially selected as parliamentary candidate for Dartford in 1949, had to wait a further ten years before

---

[2] 'Twinning' and 'zipping' are strategies that have been used to encourage equal representation in politics. Twinning involves neighbouring seats selecting a man and a woman candidate, and in zipping male and female candidates are alternated on local association candidate lists.

securing the safe Conservative seat of Finchley and being elected as MP. The journey was much shorter for Tony Blair, but he too fought and lost a by-election in Beaconsfield in 1982 before being adopted as parliamentary candidate for Sedgefield in May 1983. Blair was elected to parliament as MP in the general election that followed five weeks later (Rentoul, 2001).

Local candidate selection is the most visible and easily accessed stage of political recruitment, and perhaps not surprisingly has been the focus of most research into political selection. Yet, arguably the most important part of the selection process, and the point at which political parties can exert greatest influence over who will become an MP, involves decision making about whom to approve or not as prospective parliamentary candidates. Described as the 'secret garden' of politics (Lovenduski, 2009), these processes take place far from the glare of public scrutiny and as such have received little attention from researchers (Lundell, 2004). This constitutes an important gap in our understanding of how individuals become politicians for two reasons. Firstly, approval decisions determine the pool of candidates eligible for local party selection (and therefore those able to become MPs), and secondly decisions made earlier in a selection process remove a greater proportion of individuals from the talent pool, with potentially important consequences for political diversity.

Employee selection and political recruitment

So how can employee selection research help us to understand political selection processes and highlight particular challenges? In broad terms, employee selection practices are concerned with identifying the most suitable individual for a position on the basis of person-job fit. This usually involves selecting individuals who possess the knowledge, skills and abilities (KSAs) that a particular role requires on the basis that a better match between job requirements and individual capabilities will result in higher levels of performance. Developing a selection process involves five stages: (1) a job analysis to establish the tasks and activities that are expected of a job incumbent; (2) a person-needs analysis to determine the KSAs a person will need in order to perform the job effectively; (3) identification of discrete selection criteria to guide decision making about applicants; (4) recruitment activities to attract the widest possible pool of applicants; and (5) design of standardised assessment methods (e.g., assessment centres and psychometric tests) to evaluate reliably whether applicants possess the necessary KSAs and differentiate those likely to perform better or worse in the role (Anderson and Cunningham-Snell, 2000). In short, selection procedures should discriminate between individuals on the basis of job-relevant characteristics: selection decisions are deemed 'good' if they demonstrate high criterion-related validity, that is, they reliably identify those individuals who perform well in the role and reject individuals who would perform poorly. Similarly, decisions are considered 'fair' if they are based on role-relevant criteria, such as skills, as opposed to non-role-relevant criteria such as patronage or membership of particular groups (Arvey and Faley, 1988).

Although employee selection provides a useful lens through which to examine political selection, any attempt to apply selection practices used in the public or private sectors to the political context is unlikely to be straightforward. In particular, the democratic nature of political roles presents several challenges. Despite the fact that, arguably, politicians perform 'political work' few parallels have been drawn between this and the work undertaken by individuals in other types of employment. In fact, for many people political roles are fundamentally different to other types of work roles and should not be treated as equivalent (Phillips, 1998). The most obvious difference between politicians and other workers is that the former are elected rather than selected and it is the democratic legitimacy of political roles, which derives from being elected, that is central to claims of non-equivalence. Elected by constituents, politicians have a democratic mandate to wield power, govern, and take decisions on behalf of others (Morrell and Hartley, 2006). This power is limited by their election for a fixed term (up to five years in the case of UK MPs), meaning that they must face the electorate again and be accountable for their actions before they can secure a further period in power.

Yet, for many people the very idea that politicians can be 'selected' appears to run counter to democracy, because it undermines the belief that political roles should be open to people from all sections of society. Selection based on pre-specified criteria risks perpetuating those powerful elites who are responsible for shaping selection criteria, and 'cloning' individuals who share characteristics with existing MPs or powerful party members. Although similar fears often exist in employee selection (Schneider, 1987), politics is potentially more vulnerable because restricting access to political roles can result in less diversity and fewer elected representatives who can understand and act on the needs of different sections of the electorate (Norris and Lovenduski, 1993).

Additional practical challenges to the application of employee selection processes to political selection may be easier to address. For example, it is possible that characteristics such as role-related knowledge and skills traditionally used in employee selection are less relevant for political roles than, for example, knowing why an individual wants to become a politician. Do they want to secure power to serve their own needs or the needs of others? Understanding an individual's motivation or 'calling' to become an MP and whether their values fit with those of the political party might be more useful indicators of how they will act once in power and where they will invest their time and energy. Another important difference between selection and election is that the selection decisions are usually made by a small number of senior managers on the basis of agreed criteria. In contrast election decisions result from the individual judgements of large numbers of voters who are free to base their decisions on whatever criteria they believe to be important. This means that in an election each voter has 'a voice' to decide who they perceive to be the most suitable political candidate. Unlike recruiters, however, voters do not usually have information about a candidate's competence to perform the role and typically base their decisions on different criteria, including whether a political candidate shares similar interests (Moskowitz and Stroh, 1996). Interestingly, it seems that increased media exposure may be leading voters to pay more attention to the personalities of political candidates (Caprara and Zimbardo, 2004). Perhaps we may see this exposure leading to more public questioning about whether political candidates also have the competence to perform the roles expected of them (Silvester, 2008).

Fundamentally, however, there are two basic requirements of employee selection: knowing what the job requires the job incumbent to do (which is usually derived from a job analysis), and knowing what a person requires in order to perform the role well (the KSAs, normally identified from a person analysis). Yet, in reality, we know very little about what the role of an MP entails and there has been no investigation of the knowledge, skills and abilities required to perform the role well. These are the two most important areas that need to be addressed if political selection practices are to become more like those used for selection in other work contexts.

What is the MP role?

There has been surprisingly little systematic study of the role of an MP and the closest approximation to a job description is the Code of Conduct for MPs (Parliament, 2009a), the purpose of which is 'to assist Members in the discharge of their obligations to the House, their constituents and the public at large' (House of Commons Information Office, 2009, p. 7). According to the UK Parliament website, MPs are elected by members of the public to 'represent their interests and concerns in the House of Commons' (Parliament, 2009b). The site goes on to describe MPs normally splitting their time between working in parliament, within their constituency and for their political party. In parliament MPs attend debates, vote on new laws and join committees that scrutinise government policy. In their constituency, MPs hold 'surgeries', where local people can come along to discuss any matters that concern them, they also attend functions, visit schools and businesses and generally try to meet as many people to understand the needs of their constituency.

Although there are rules and regulations about how MPs should behave, in reality politicians have considerable independence to pursue the goals they consider important in the way they want (March and Olsen, 1999). As an MP commented to the author in a recent interview 'you have total autonomy, you are essentially self-employed and can do the role in whatever way you choose'. This means that the experience of being an MP can vary considerably from person to person. The nature of the role also varies depending on whether a politician belongs to the party in government or opposition, and on their additional responsibilities within their party or parliament (e.g., member of a select committee, party whip, minister or backbencher). To make things more complicated MPs are accountable to multiple stakeholders including their constituents, their party and government. All of these factors complicate matters for those developing selection procedures, because prospective parliamentary candidates are not selected for a single role, but a multitude of different roles within government over the course of a political career. Therefore, whilst there may be a core set of responsibilities for MPs (e.g., representing people, holding government to account and legislating), political selection decisions need a greater focus on criteria such as an individual's ability to learn and adapt quickly to changing circumstances and different roles.

What qualities and skills do MPs require?

The second important question asks what are the KSAs that MPs require in order to perform these roles and responsibilities effectively? Selection decisions are usually based on whether or not individuals possess these necessary characteristics, but in the case of political roles there has been very little study of how individual KSAs impact on political performance. Indeed, many political scientists argue that individual differences among political actors will matter little given the multitude of other factors that can influence both political performance and outcomes like elections (Hargrove, 1993; Moe, 1993). For example, Greenstein (1992) argues that group behaviour will be a more dominant influence in political environments than the actions of any individual political actor. Similarly, electoral performance is influenced by a range of contextual factors such as historical patterns of voting, the performance of a political party nationally, levels of campaign resources available to a candidate and the strength of their political opponents. That said, if individual differences do not play a part in determining political outcomes there would be little need to select political candidates in the first place.

In fact, most active campaigners believe that the personal vote (i.e., votes attributable to the actions of a particular candidate) is important. When interviewed about her campaign efforts in the previous general election Kate Hoey, Labour MP for Vauxhall, commented 'it would be miserable if there were no correlation between all that work, effort and support' (Norris, Vallance and Lovenduski, 1992). In support of this, other researchers (mainly psychologists) have argued that the personal characteristics of politicians are important in politics (e.g., Hargrove, 1993; Rubenzer, Faschingbauer and Ones, 2002; Simonton, 1988). Neustadt (1990) argues that as the constitutional power base of the US presidency is so narrow, effective leadership will depend more on personality-related factors such as reputation, persuasiveness, political skills and self-confidence of the office-holder. Yet, once again there has been little systematic study of politicians' characteristics and their job performance, although a growing body of research concerned with political skill in organisational contexts may have relevance for future studies (Ferris et al., 2005).

Developing competency-based selection processes for political parties

Despite the lack of an evidence base to support decisions about suitability and competence for political roles, there have been growing calls for improved political selection processes across all political parties and areas of government. In his report for the Electoral Commission, Riddell (2003) argues for greater transparency about how political parties attract and select prospective parliamentary candidates, and identifies seven principles of good candidate selection that political parties should demonstrate:

1. *Inclusiveness*: by adopting and publishing policies to encourage selection of a broad range of candidates for all levels of elected representation.
2. *Diversity*: by encouraging a balance of gender, ages, ethnic groups and occupations among individuals on their approved lists.
3. *Community Activity*: by aiming to recruit people who are active in their localities, for example in community groups or as volunteers.
4. *Transparency*: by taking a professional approach to candidate selection that specifies the skills sought, and the responsibilities of the elected representative.
5. *Suitability*: by looking beyond political activity to the skills needed to hold elected office and give effective representation to their constituents.
6. *Collegiality*: by offering candidates full support and training.
7. *Participation*: by enabling as many party members as possible to participate in the selection process.

Two of these (transparency and suitability) are relevant to employee selection, because they relate to the premise that roles demand particular qualities, and that political parties should communicate publicly what they consider to be the qualities that are important for their candidates. Suitability also relates to criterion-related validity and the assumption that selection systems should reliably differentiate between those individuals capable of performing well in political roles and those who will not. Yet, political parties rarely change their selection processes (Norris and Lovenduski, 2004). Like other large-scale institutions, bureaucratic entrenchment can lead to difficulties in adapting quickly to changing circumstances and the ability to foster effective organisational learning. Decision making in political parties is also far less centralised than in other types of work organisation (Norris, 2004). Whereas most large private and public sector organisations have human resource (HR) departments that take responsibility for selecting and developing staff, political parties do not. This can mean that political parties lack the capacity and resources required to create and manage new selection systems. Responsibility for political selection procedures can also lie with several committees, made up of representatives from different groups within the party. As such no one person is responsible for strategic decisions, and any changes to selection practices will require the collective agreement of many people and groups, each with potentially conflicting views.

However, political parties are most likely to change and innovate when they are in opposition and seeking new ways to build power. This can include identifying new ways to attract and recruit candidates likely to be popular with the electorate and capable of winning back control. This is what happened in the following two examples, each of which describes a separate project by the author with the Conservative Party (2002) and the Liberal Democrat Party (2008). Both involved the redesign of party approval processes for prospective parliamentary candidates, using methods and practice from traditional selection procedures.

The Conservative Party

In 2001 the Conservative Party lost its second consecutive general election following a period of seventeen years in power. At that time 15 per cent of Conservative MPs were women, and there was a perceived need within the party to attract and select a more diverse group of political candidates to better engage with and reflect the needs of the general population. Part of the solution to this was recognised as a need to re-examine the party selection process for approving prospective parliamentary candidates. After initial discussions with Christina Dykes, Director of

Candidates and Development for the party, and other senior politicians a decision was taken to adopt modern selection practices and redesign the approvals process based upon an agreed set of competencies to perform the role of MP. This meant that the Candidates Committee maintained control over the list of approved candidates, but a rigorous assessment procedure ensured that all candidates on the list and therefore eligible to apply to local selection panels would already have been assessed as having the qualities necessary to become an MP.

Development of this system began with an analysis of the MP role to identify shared beliefs about the competencies and skills associated with being effective and behavioural indicators of good and poor performance. Competency models are common in organisational settings; they make explicit important role-related behaviour and enable organisations to facilitate a shared understanding and common language around what is required of role incumbents (Schippmann *et al.* 2000). The MP role analysis involved Silvester and Dykes undertaking critical incident interviews and focus groups with representatives from different stakeholder groups, including current and past MPs, prospective parliamentary candidates, senior party members, party volunteers and party agents. By involving people from all sectors of the party it was possible to capture the views of people with different experiences and perspectives on MPs and their work. In addition, participants were asked to describe how the role had changed, how it might change in future and the skills and abilities that were likely to be relevant. A visionary approach was considered important, because like most other work roles the MP role is continually changing (Silvester and Dykes, 2007). The six competencies that emerged from an analysis of the interviews and focus groups were:

1. *Communication Skills*: the capacity to communicate messages clearly and persuasively across a variety of audiences and media contexts.
2. *Intellectual skills*: the ability to understand, learn and prioritise complex information quickly and present ideas in a transparent manner.
3. *Relating to People*: the capacity to relate easily to people from all backgrounds, demonstrate tolerance, approachability and the ability to inspire trust in others.
4. *Leading and Motivating*: the capacity for leading and motivating people by recognising their contribution and providing support when required.
5. *Resilience and Drive*: an ability to cope effectively and positively with and remain persistent in the face of challenge, setbacks and criticism.
6. *Political Conviction*: a commitment to party principles and public service, including integrity and courage in disseminating and defending beliefs.

Each of these competencies was further defined by using four positive and four negative behavioural indicators, which could be used as anchors for rating prospective parliamentary candidates during selection procedures. All competencies and indicators were discussed and further refined in consultation with the Party's candidates department.

The second stage of the process involved using the competencies and interview material to develop an assessment centre (AC). Assessment centres are a popular selection method for management level positions, which generally demonstrate good levels of criterion-related validity and face validity (Hough and Oswald, 2000). A process not a place, ACs involve different assessment methods (e.g., work sample measures, group discussion, interviews and psychometric tests) and exercises that reflect different aspects of the role. Participants are observed and rated by different assessors in different exercises, and assessors are trained to use the same standardised criteria based on the competency framework. The AC developed for the candidate approvals process involved a competency-based interview, a group exercise, a public speaking exercise, an in-tray exercise and a critical thinking questionnaire. Each AC involved four assessors: two MPs and two Conservative Association members, all of whom were trained in fair and objective assessment practices, including awareness of the potential for bias. Efforts were also made to ensure that assessors had no prior knowledge of applicants' experience or background before observing them during the AC, to minimise the influence of factors such as prior links with key party members.

The new approvals process was evaluated in two ways. First, as it was intended to reduce potential bias against women and minority applicants, performance across competencies and exercises was compared for male and female applicants for the first 400 participants in the AC. There were no significant differences between men and women either for different competencies or exercises, providing support for the argument that men and women are equally suited to political roles. Secondly, as 106 participants in the AC were successful in being selected to stand as parliamentary candidates in local selection, their AC performance could be compared with performance in the 2001 UK general election (see figure 2.2). Two criteria were used: 'percentage votes' – the proportion of votes secured by a candidate – and the 'percentage swing' in votes to their political party achieved by the candidate in that constituency. Regression analyses revealed that critical thinking raw scores and competency interview ratings were significantly associated with 'percentage swing'. The relationship between 'percentage votes' achieved by a candidate and critical thinking scores also approached significance (Silvester and Dykes, 2007). These findings provide evidence that individual

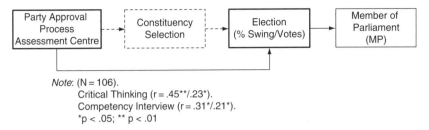

Note: (N = 106).
Critical Thinking (r = .45**/.23*).
Competency Interview (r = .31*/.21*).
*p < .05; ** p < .01

Figure 2.2. Predicting political performance in the 2005 UK general election

differences can impact on electoral success, over and above factors such as local issues, national performance of the political party and the perform-ance of other political parties. The revised approvals process continues to be used by the Conservative Party.

The Liberal Democrat Party

A similar project to redevelop the candidate approval process for the Liberal Democrat Party was undertaken by the author between 2007 and 2008. The Liberal Democrat Party is the third-largest party in UK politics and formed a coalition government with the Conservatives in 2010. It has a much smaller base of sitting MPs than either Conservatives or Labour. Yet the Liberal Democrats maintain a policy of fielding a candidate in each constituency eligible to return an MP (650 in the 2010 general election). This presents the party with the challenge of attracting and selecting a greater proportion of individuals who are willing to stand for election in marginal seats. Whilst the ultimate aim of a selection process is to select a candidate capable of winning, in marginal seats it is also important to select individuals capable of building support and developing the party's profile in that area.

In order to understand how the approvals process could be developed interviews were first conducted with representatives of groups involved in the former assessment process (assessors, facilitators, candidates depart-ment, regional chairs and senior party members) to identify those aspects most in need of change. Perhaps the most important issue related to flexibility. The former approvals system was seen as too unwieldy and resource intensive, requiring substantial time investment from those involved in setting up and running assessment days, as well as people providing follow-up support and development for applicants. This made it difficult to respond quickly and flexibly when there was a need to approve candidates, which in turn could mean that at times applicants had to wait a long period before being able to attend an assessment day. There was also some concern that the former assessment process was more complicated than it needed to be. The main challenge was therefore to produce a flexible and fair system that was comparatively easy to implement. As with the Conservative Party project, a decision was taken to undertake a role analysis and develop an assessment centre based on a competency framework. The six competencies were:

1. *Communication Skills*: Communicates clearly and persuasively with a variety of audiences and in a variety of contexts, generates opportunities for communication for self and others.
2. *Leadership*: Motivates self and others, delegates and provides support as appropriate, demonstrates flexibility, accepts responsibility for outcomes and has integrity.
3. *Strategic Thinking and Judgement*: Understands and prioritises complex information; looks at the bigger picture and promotes overall team and campaign objectives.
4. *Representing People*: Relates well to people from all backgrounds by being aware of their effects on others, demonstrating tolerance, approachability and by inspiring trust.
5. *Resilience*: Copes effectively with pressure and remains positive and proactive in the face of challenge, setbacks and criticism.
6. *Values in Action*: Works hard to develop a campaign team, secure resources, promote Liberal Democrat values and maximise party profile.

Not surprisingly there were many similarities between the projects, particularly as the same procedures were adopted for the role analysis and designing the AC. However, certain differences demonstrate the importance of political context in determining the shape and content of political selection procedures. For example, whilst the competencies, skills and knowledge required for MP work may be the same irrespective of party, the two role analyses revealed the importance of capturing political values and incorporating these into selection exercises. In the case of the Liberal Democrats, this involved creating an exercise that asked AC participants to describe what their values were and how these impacted on their political activities.

Another difference that influenced development of the new approvals process was the fact that the Liberal Democrat Party is a federal party, and decisions are delegated to the local level wherever possible. Responsibility for approval decisions for English seats lies with the English Candidates Committee, and there are separate committees for Scotland and Wales. Regional groups also have an important say in deciding whether changes can be made to the overall approval process. This meant that a much longer consultation process was required in order to accommodate different views and perspectives. A survey was also undertaken with all party chairs to check the validity of the competencies and behavioural indicators and to gain commitment to the process.

Although involving different groups in deciding and agreeing changes takes longer, it also makes the process more democratic ensuring that a majority of stakeholders understand what changes are being made and are more engaged in the new process. The Liberal Democrat Party is also keen to encourage more people to become prospective parliamentary candidates by rendering the approvals process more open and transparent.

Discussion

These two examples show that, whilst Norris and Lovenduski (2004) suggest that political parties rarely alter their selection processes, at times fundamental changes are possible. To conclude, it is worth considering why these changes may have occurred now rather than at any other point in time. One obvious reason may be that standardised selection practices have become so much part of the normal work experience for the general public that political parties cannot remain immune to the need for more objective processes. However, in recent years the media has also become increasingly important in shaping public perceptions of politicians and challenging assumptions about political practices (Katwala, Whitford and Ottery, 2003). Lobbyists have continued to be vocal in advocating the need for more diversity and greater efforts to tackle the under-representation of certain groups, and as such have done much to raise public awareness of the lack of fairness in selecting who becomes a politician. There have also been an increasing number of questions about the relative competence of individuals to perform as politicians and the types of support they might need in order to be effective (see Pickard, 2009). Therefore, this may herald the beginning of a period of greater interest in the demands of political work.

That said, there is also a need for caution before we embrace wholeheartedly the idea of HR practices in politics. Decision making in political organisations may appear overly protracted, inefficient and frustrating, but this may simply be an inevitable feature of more democratic forms of organisation. We may have to accept that, if we want democracy, it takes longer to persuade people to commit to a particular course of action, or to make organisational changes, than it would do in other types of organisations. Equally, we need to be aware that HR practices themselves are political (Ferris and King, 1991) and can serve to institutionalise power relationships through organisational members' acceptance of the way in which they are governed and led (Novicevic and Harvey, 2004). Therefore unthinking application of HR processes, like selection, may act to undermine rather than enhance democracy. The challenge will be for industrial/organisational psychologists to create systems that accommodate the unique needs of political environments, and support politicians in their efforts to govern more successfully on behalf of the people they represent.

References

Anderson, N. and Cunningham-Snell, N. (2000). Personnel selection. In N. Chmiel (ed.), *Introduction to Work and Organizational Psychology: A European Perspective* (pp. 69–99). Oxford: Blackwell.

Arvey, R. D. and Faley, R. H. (1988). *Fairness in Selecting Employees.* Reading, Mass.: Addison-Wesley.

Bar-Tal, D. (2002). The (social) psychological legacy for political psychology. In K. R. Monroe (ed.), *Political Psychology* (pp. 173–92). Mahwah, N.J.: Lawrence Erlbaum Associates.

Caprara, G. V. and Zimbardo, P. G. (2004). Personalizing politics: a Congruency Model of political preference. *American Psychologist*, 59, 581–94.

Costantini, E. and Craik, K. H. (1980). Personality and politicians: California party leaders, 1960–1976. *Journal of Personality and Social Psychology*, 38, 641–61.

Elgood, J., Vinter, L. and Williams, R. (2002). *Man Enough for the Job? A Study of Parliamentary Candidates.* Manchester: EOC Discussion Series, Equal Opportunities Commission.

Fawcett Society (2005). Record numbers of women MPs. Retrieved 20 November from: www.fawcettsociety.org.uk/documents/May05electionWomenMPs.pdf.

Ferris, G. R. and King, T. R. (1991). Politics in human resources decisions: a walk on the dark side. *Organizational Dynamics*, 20, 59–71.

Ferris, G. R., Treadway, D. C., Kolodinsky, R. W., Hochwarter, W. A., Kacmar, C. J., Douglas, C. and Frink, D. D. (2005). Development and validation of the political skill inventory. *Journal of Management*, 31, 126–52.

Gallagher, M. and Marsh, M. (1988). *Candidate Selection in Comparative Perspective: The Secret Garden of Politics.* London: Sage.

Greenstein, F. (1992). Can personality and politics be studied systematically? *Political Psychology*, 13, 47–91.

Hargrove, E. C. (1993). Presidential personality and leadership style. In G. C. Edwards, J. H. Kessel and B. A. Rockman (eds.), *Researching the Presidency* (pp. 69–109). University of Pittsburgh Press.

Hough, L. M. and Oswald, F. L. (2000). Personnel selection: looking toward the future – remembering the past. *Annual Review of Psychology*, 51, 631–64.

House of Commons Information Office (2009). You and your MP. Factsheet M1 Members Series. Retrieved 20 November 2009 from: www.parliament.uk/documents/upload/m01.pdf.

Kamp, A. (2000). Breaking up old marriages: the political process of change and continuity at work. *Technology Analysis and Strategic Management*, 12, 75–90.

Katwala, S., Whitford, B. and Ottery, C. (2003). Politics and the media: is it time for change? *Observer*, 27 July.

Katz, R. S. (2001). The problem of candidate selection and models of party democracy. *Party Politics*, 7, 277–96.

Lovenduski, J. (2005). *Feminizing Politics*. Cambridge: Polity Press.

  (2009). Political recruitment research. Paper presented as part of Political Careers Seminar, 9 September, City University London.

Lovenduski, J. and Norris, P. (2003). Westminster women: The politics of presence. *Political Studies*, 51 (1), 84–102.

Lundell, K. (2004). Determinants of candidate selection: The degree of centralization in comparative perspective. *Party Politics*, 10, 25–47.

Maidment, R. and Tappin, M. (1994). *American Politics Today*. Manchester University Press.

March, J. G. and Olsen, J. P. (1999). Institutional perspectives on political institutions. In J. G. March (ed.), *The Pursuit of Organizational Intelligence* (pp. 52–72). London: Blackwell.

Moe, T. M. (1993). Presidents, institutions and leadership. In G. C. Edwards, J. H. Kessel and B. A. Rockman (eds.), *Researching the presidency* (pp. 337–85). University of Pittsburgh Press.

Morrell, K. and Hartley, J. (2006). A model of political leadership. *Human Relations*, 59, 483–504.

Moskowitz, D. and Stroh, P. (1996). Expectation-driven assessments of political candidates. *Political Psychology*, 17, 695–712.

Neustadt (1990). *Presidential Power and the Modern Presidents: The Politics of Leadership*. New York: Free Press; London: Collier Macmillan.

Norris, P. (2002). *Democratic Phoenix: Reinventing Political Activism*. Cambridge University Press.

  (2004). *Electoral Engineering: Voting Rules and Political behavior*. Cambridge University Press.

Norris, P., Carty, L. K., Erikson, L., Lovenduski, J. and Simms, M. (1990). Party selectorates in Australia, Britain and Canada: Prolegomena for research in the 1990s. *Commonwealth and Comparative Politics*, 28, 219–45.

Norris, P. and Lovenduski, L. (1993). *Political Recruitment: Gender, Race and Class in the British Parliament*. Cambridge Universtity Press.

  (2004). Why parties fail to learn: Electoral defeat, selective perception and British party politics. *Party Politics*, 10, 85–104.

Norris, P., Vallance, E. and Lovenduski, J. (1992). Do candidates make a difference? Gender, race, ideology and incumbency. *Parliamentary Affairs* 45 (2) (October 1992), 496–517.

Novicevic, M. M. and Harvey, M. G. (2004). The political role of corporate human resource management in strategic global leadership development. *The Leadership Quarterly*, 15, 569–88.

Parliament (2009a). House of Commons: The Code of Conduct and Guide to Rules. Retrieved 20 November 2009 from: www.publications.parliament.uk/pa/cm/cmcode.htm.

Parliament (2009b). What MPs Do. Retrieved 11 November 2009 from www. parliament.uk/about/how/members/mps.cfm.

Phillips, A. (1998). Democracy and representation: or, why should it matter who our representatives are? In A. Phillips (ed.), *Feminism and Politics* (pp. 224–41). Oxford University Press.

Pickard, J. (2009). What every MP should know. *Financial Times Weekend Magazine*, 14 November, 32–7.

Rentoul, J. (2001). *Tony Blair: Prime Minister*. London: Time Warner.

Riddell, P. (2003). *Candidate Selection: The Report of the Commission on Candidate Selection*. London: Electoral Reform Society.

Rubenzer, S. J., Faschingbauer, T. R. and Ones, D. S. (2002). Assessments of America's Chief Executives: insights from biographers and objective personality measures. In L. Valenty and O. Feldman (eds.), *Political Leadership for the New Century* (pp. 105–34). London: Praeger.

Schippmann, J. S., Ash, R. A., Battista, N., Carr, L., Eyde, L. D., Hesketh, B., Kehoe, J., Pearlman, K., Prien, E. P. and Sanchez, J. I. (2000). The practice of competency modelling. *Personnel Psychology*, 53, 703–40.

Schneider, B. (1987). The people make the place. *Personnel Psychology*, 40, 437–53.

Shaw, G. B. (1903). *Man and Superman*. Westmister: Archibald Constable and Co. Ltd.

Shepherd-Robinson, L. and Lovenduski, J. (2002). *Women and Candidate Selection in British Political Parties*. London: The Fawcett Society.

Silvester, J. (2008). The good, the bad, and the ugly: politics and politicians at work. In G. P. Hodgkinson and J. K. Ford (eds.), *International Review of Industrial and Organizational Psychology*, vol. 23 (pp. 107–48). Chichester: John Wiley and Sons.

Silvester, J. and Dykes, C. (2007). Selecting political candidates: a longitudinal study of assessment centre performance and political success in the 2005 UK General Election. *Journal of Occupational and Organizational Psychology*, 80, 11–25.

Simonton, D. K. (1988). Presidential style: personality, biography and performance. *Personality Processes and Individual Differences*, 55, 928–36.

Stokes, W. (2005). *Women in Contemporary Politics*. Cambridge: Polity Press.

Weber, M. (1918). Politics as a vocation. Reprinted in M. L. Morgan (ed.), *Classics of Moral and Political Theory*, pp. 1213–49. 4th edn. Cambridge: Hackett Publishing Company.

3   Politicians and power: MPs in the UK parliament

Richard Kwiatkowski

This chapter is about power and how it is gained by Members of Parliament (MPs). It shows that, despite the rather unusual nature of the parliamentary workplace, typical organisational political behaviours and mechanisms are clearly recognisable. Politicians are not necessarily more adept at 'doing organisational politics' by virtue of their unquestionable familiarity with large-scale political thought and behaviour – though some seem to be. However, parliament is not an ordinary organisation, because on a day-to-day level it has the power to profoundly affect the lives of millions of people, and so behaviour within it may be disproportionately important.

The data presented here are part of a longitudinal project using an interview panel study of government Members of Parliament involving backbenchers, whips, parliamentary private secretaries (PPSs), ministers and cabinet members which has been ongoing since 1997. The findings are based on interviews undertaken between 1997 and 2003. The theoretical approach employed is best described as thematic semi-grounded, with areas of discussion remaining constant, e.g. 'how would you currently describe the job of MP?' The respondents were free to reply in any way, and ample opportunity was given for matters of current concern to be raised (e.g., the Gulf War, demonstrations, expenses). Findings are illustrated throughout with quotes from MPs and a variety of psychological mechanisms are indicated that may link to the thinking, feeling and enacting of political processes. Factors emerging in the House of Commons are compared to political factors present in organisations outside of Parliament.

What is power for?

At the outset, and embedded in what follows, it needs to be emphasised that the majority of government MPs interviewed wanted to be elected because of a set of deeply held beliefs around such issues as 'social justice', 'equality', 'fairness', 'redistribution' and 'socialism'. They clearly, consistently and repeatedly articulated these views. For some, through extended periods in opposition, serving on councils, or working with the disadvantaged, these beliefs and values were reinforced – in some cases this provided the motivation for them to become personally involved in politics. Many had been members of the Labour Party for a significant time.

The role of MP, and membership of any political party, are almost invariably predicated on formal party membership, carrying with it a shared set of beliefs and values and a desire to influence or change society to reflect those beliefs and values. Without this important caveat it may seem that some of what follows is an egocentric focus on individual power and its acquisition, and whilst that may exist, for most MPs interviewed there is a greater purpose in acquiring power, namely the 'betterment' of society according to specific beliefs and principles, with oneself as an agent (or perhaps even a leader) of that change. For example, in response to a query about why they wanted to become an MP, one newly elected member stated:

As, for me, ... justice certainly, justice which is for everybody, which is fair and which recognises that all we have – in terms of resources and energy and so on – has to be shared amongst the whole population . . . it's a philosophy . . . of ensuring that the country's resources are well used for the benefit of the whole population.[1]

Getting selected

The first hurdle for the putative MP is finding a seat to contest – assuming that they have already found a party, and have been permitted onto the party's national list. Favoured party members are found safer seats, though every seat – with the traditional exception of that of the Speaker (see below) – is contested. Silvester in this book and elsewhere (2007) discusses the complex process of selection, showing how modern methods can be profitably applied to the process. Notwithstanding the 'scientific' and evidence-based approach adopted, Schneider's work on the Attraction-Selection-Attrition cycle (1987) cautions that implicit notions such as 'fit' are often tacitly used in selection decisions. For example work by the Fawcett Society indicates that the number of women who moved from the Conservative A-List to actually becoming candidates is relatively

---

[1] For issues of confidentiality individual MPs are not identified. Quotes are based on transcripts of interviews. Any omitted material is indicated by three dots '...', any inserted words are indicated using square brackets '[]', ems. ahs and other markers may be edited out, longer pauses are indicated with a hyphen '-', punctuation may be added to clarify meaning.

small. (This is noteworthy since the A-List, which prioritises preferred candidates, received unusually rigorous professional psychological input – for instance using assessment centres). Additionally, this A-List has been 'topped up' using criteria other than those originally specified (Fawcett Society, 2006). But this is not a party political issue, as this first hurdle is notoriously difficult to leap in all parties, and was reflected in the creation in 2008 of a 'Speaker's Conference' seeking to address the under-representation of women, ethnic minorities and the disabled in the House of Commons. For instance, at the time of writing, even with A-lists and all-women shortlists in the two main parties, only 19 per cent of UK MPs are women, and the situation is even less representative for other groups. The Speaker of the House of Commons has a pivotal role to play in reform as s(he) is, outside the visible chairing of debates, the de facto administrative lead and parliament's representative to external authorities. This role became the focus of intense debate in 2009 following investigations into MPs' expenses when the then Speaker, Michael Martin, resigned and became the first holder of this office in 300 years to be, in effect, removed from office.

To return to the selection process itself, potential candidates of whatever party have to put themselves up for local selection. At a minimum, candidates (and often their spouses, partners and even children) are traditionally examined through several rounds of interviews and meetings, are frequently expected to make some form of presentation or engage in a debate, and meet members of the local party. They will have to demonstrate their credentials, skills and style, their ability to listen, communicate and persuade, their enthusiasm, dynamism and knowledge of local issues. Selection decisions are usually made behind closed doors and seem only marginally subject to normal employment legislation. Most MPs will have had the experience of undertaking this process several times; and this fact itself does indicate that a good deal of individual resilience is required by people seeking to become MPs (Rutter, 1993). Once they have been selected as a candidate, Cognitive Dissonance Theory (Festinger, 1957) suggests that membership of a club that is hard to join will make membership of that club more valued. The MPs interviewed were all pleased, and sometimes extremely grateful to have been selected by their local party. Prior to the 'Expenses scandal' they clearly valued being an MP, and for some this was the summit of their political life; though for others higher office was now the new target.

There's a mixture of optimism and hope and a sense of loss as well [of the previous life] and feeling that, well you know actually I do have a contribution to make which is beyond the role you can fulfil as a backbencher. It's a different role, I'm not denigrating those who want to make their names as good parliamentarians, but ... I also do want to do a ministerial job and be part of the government. I've got to be honest with myself about that.

In 1997 the political calculations made by some people suggested that working for the party and 'showing willing' in standing for election in an 'impossible' seat might induce future party gratitude and lead to a more winnable seat in subsequent contests. For example, 'Ivan Henderson, the docker who took Harwich ... admitted that some regarded his candidacy more as a "tester" than as one with a chance of winning' (*Independent*, 1997). The result of the 1997 election was a landside victory, with Labour winning many more seats than thought possible, and achieving a majority of 179. This background is important because some of the experiences of the 1997 intake were unique due to the unusual circumstances and enormous numbers of new MPs, whilst others were shared with the 'intakes' of 2001 and in particular 2005, which were much more typical, more closely representing 'business as usual' in the House of Commons. Additionally, some of the 1997 intake were relatively inexperienced, and perhaps more characteristic of the population as a whole rather than being 'career politicians'.

Getting elected

The process of becoming an MP, once one has been selected to represent a party, involves a very public selection process that few 'ordinary' people would care to face (Paxman, 2003, p. 70–84). All registered voters in a constituency can vote, and whilst some MPs continue to hope for an incumbency factor, the evidence is that swings to or against a party can sweep candidates and sitting MPs in or out of power. This can be regardless of the hard work, skills, qualities or performance of that individual in the years prior to the general election. MPs are therefore largely dependent on the performance of their party and particularly of their leaders, and this leads to certain party-related behaviours before election and once election is achieved. This includes publicly and enthusiastically supporting policies, professing support for senior party members, working in adjoining constituencies if a by-election is called, canvassing at local and European elections, being involved in regional groups, etc. Believing in the 'incumbency factor' may be a way of dealing with the anxiety of the situation (Bion, 1961) or retaining some measure of Internal Locus of Control (Rotter, Chance and Phares, 1972). However, given the 2009 expenses scandal, incumbency is now seem by some MPs as a negative factor, and if they have given of their best, and worked hard, it can deal quite a blow to their self-worth and even their self-esteem.

There are numerous differences to a normal job selection process – several of which are described by Silvester and Dykes (2007). For example, most of a normal selection process is carried out privately in organisations, and the candidate frequently does not even announce the fact of their entry into the selection process, for reasons of negotiating advantage, face saving and the possibility of remaining in their current job. In a parliamentary election the candidate faces selection in public, and has to manifest a range of expected behaviours. For example, they must be seen to really want the post and to expect to win, even if privately they are fairly sure that the seat is unwinnable and that they are acting the part of confident candidate:

'Actually, and I wouldn't say this to the [party] workers, I think I have less than a fifty-fifty chance.'

Thus a great deal of emotional labour can be involved in the process (Ashforth and Humphrey, 1993) and, more than that, the candidate is always on show, and has to exercise a great deal of control for the time they are in the public gaze (Lacan, 1979). In this regard they can be said to be 'performing' in a particular role (Clark and Mangham, 2004), taking part in a recognisable, almost theatrical activity: visiting schools and hospitals, setting up stalls in shopping centres, canvassing door to door and in many ways doing what MPs described as 'kissing babies' (referring to the tactic of complimenting a parent on their child in order to gain goodwill, or better still a photograph in the local paper). However, as with any skilled performance, all these behaviours need to look natural; as after all, this is what the audience expects.

Consequently when a seat seems marginal or even unwinnable, cognitive dissonance emerges perhaps as a form of defence mechanism, with some MPs stating that to be re-elected is what they want not for themselves, but rather for the party. Whilst this is a genuine belief, it may additionally help to enhance the resilience necessary for performance in the psychologically threatening situation of publicly standing for election, particularly if the contest is predicted to be 'nasty' or 'personal'.

The House of Commons

The stage of action (Morgan, 2006) within which the organisational process examined here takes place is the House of Commons, so before turning to the notion of how power is accrued it is useful to know something about the institution within which MPs work, its organisational culture and the scope of the work role involved. There is limited space here to examine each component of an MP's role, however an emerging list (as supplied by MPs) would include the following: work within, as well as at, the crucial interface with the constituency;

representing constituents in parliament, representing the government in the constituency, an ever-increasing constituency caseload, parliamentary private secretary (PPS) or ministerial roles, negotiating and managing relations within and between departments, campaigning, juggling competing demands, working with civil servants, relations with local councillors or Welsh Assembly and Scottish Parliament members (especially complex if they are from other parties), seeking to influence or at least cope with the media and finally managing the 'small business' that is their office including accommodation, staff and equipment. Our focus will be on the MP in Westminster. A more detailed view is provided by the work of Michael Rush, who for many years has been a significant and clear-sighted observer of the parliamentary process (e.g Rush, 2005).

Culture

Context is all important and before examining power we shall briefly look at some aspects of the culture of the House of Commons. There are numerous rules and conventions that an entrant to any organisation needs to learn. These may be explicit rules such as relevant laws, or a code of conduct, or the staff handbook; or they may be implicit rules linked to the culture of the organisation, such as the sort of clothes to wear, how to refer to each other, how to treat customers, and how one 'gets on' or succeeds. Deal and Kennedy (1982) applied anthropological ideas to organisations, and pointed out that it is possible to 'read' cultures using a range of methods; noting how an organisation presents itself, how strangers are treated, what official publications say (and how they are written) and what is valued as opposed to what *should* be valued (Argyris, 1999). The House of Commons has a long history and numerous rituals and complex rules for the newcomer to learn, aided by a regularly updated handbook called 'Erskine May'. For example, when Tony Blair entered the House of Commons for the first time after the 1997 election new MPs clapped. However, this was not considered proper parliamentary behaviour, and the practice of clapping was extinguished within a short while. 'I recall, when I was first elected, a period of confusion and muddle [in relation to the procedures]' (MacTaggart, 2001).

Many Labour MPs expressed surprise, joy and even awe at arriving at the House of Commons; 'I still can't quite believe it, but I'm getting used to saying MP when I phone someone, but I'm still the teacher from x.' All sorts of unusual rituals and behaviours were noted, but whereas at the beginning these were often described in a somewhat surprised manner, two years later the process of socialisation (Watson, 1995) had taken place for many MPs. As an example one MP commented,

'The staff here call you sir – some are old enough to be my grandfather – and have to wear these [ridiculous] clothes and can't sit in your presence [said disapprovingly]', but two years later the same MP stated, 'In such a complex organisation it's important that we all have our roles.'

The culture was examined in the interviews using the Analogies Similies Metaphors and Images (ASMI) model, asking MPs to describe the House of Commons in these terms and then discuss them in detail. In 1997 the descriptions of the culture were similar to those of a 'lay' group at the time: 'an old boys club', 'a public school', 'theatre on the floor of the House', 'a dinosaur', 'a temple', 'a creaking, lumbering Victorian machine', 'a boxing ring', 'a market place', 'as fascinating as a kaleidoscope', 'as noisy as the dawn chorus and as dangerous as eagles', and 'like the Roman forum'. Interestingly MPs became rather less willing over time to engage with the process of describing the House of Commons using the ASMI approach, variously adopting explanations such as the importance of the institution and that this question was akin to 'market research' (not psychology) or that it was simply too complex an institution to summarise so tritely.

Betty Boothroyd (the Speaker prior to Michael Martin) was identified as a strong supporter of parliamentary traditions and was able to use her powers to enforce these rituals and rules, many of which dated back centuries. It may be supposed that they all served an ostensible purpose once, but it is often hard to know what genuine administrative purpose they serve in a modern parliament. Some MPs, at least initially, are well aware of the dangers inherent in working within an institution which seeks to mould its inhabitants in these ways.

architecturally magnificent and an extraordinary pleasant and comfortable place to be in ... it absorbs change very easily ... it's terribly easy and convenient for people to forget what they're here for ... when you walk around the corridors you suddenly for no very good reason come across corridors which you can only go down if you're a member – not if you're a stranger as it's called and that's very typical of symbols and rituals ... all this actually performs a very straightforward anthropological function, making you feel you belong – you know you belong – others are excluded ... you're the priesthood – others are the laity – now this is putting up barriers [which] in a modern democracy I think should not be there.

Having said that, a few MPs actually rather liked the markers of power and status, though they were careful to express this as important because it conveys respect for the role rather than the individual occupant and not any sort of personal desire for status, which might perhaps be seen as aggrandisement or egocentrism.

Political skills: acquiring power

A number of skills are important for 'getting on' in parliament and these may be rather different from those necessary for getting selected or elected. Many of these factors are present in any organisation and are summarised in Table 3.1, which compares them with the work of Morgan (2006) on sources of power identified within organisations, and 'common

Table 3.1. *Advancement in parliament compared with other organisations*

Key Factors in Advancement in Parliament	'Common Tactics' (Buchanan and Badham)	'Sources of power' (Morgan)
Loyalty to / party / Policy / beliefs		Control of counter organisations
Personal history / Known membership of 'groupings'	Making friends with power brokers	
Understanding the politics of the workplace	Implicit in 'skilled' political behaviour	Implicit in 'skilled' political behaviour
Understanding Parliamentary procedure, rules, protocols		Use of structure, rules, regulations and structural factors that define the stage of action
Gaining a range of experience / Stretching yourself		
Being 'useful' / being 'expert' / 'contributing something' / reading the political mood / being 'lucky'		Control of knowledge and information
Performing under pressure / delivering / managing / making difficult decisions / being respected for getting things done/ being clever enough		Ability to cope with uncertainty
Being noticed, being visible, being known (including speaking and communication)	Self promotion, publicising success	Symbolisms and management of meaning
Gaining support and networking	Building a network of useful contacts	Interpersonal alliances, networks, and 'informal organisation'
Getting a mentor and a champion	Using key players to support initiatives	

tactics' used in the organisational domain as identified by Buchanan and Badham (2008). Each factor in turn will be elaborated and examples provided.

Comparing the findings from this study with the work of Morgan (2006, p. 167) and of Buchanan and Badham (2008, p. 22) there are clear overlaps between what happens in everyday workplaces and the House of Commons. Interestingly, some of the 'less common' political tactics that Buchanan and Badham identify as infrequently used in organisations are more frequently, and indeed openly, used in the House of Commons:

- 'finding someone else to blame or highlighting other peoples errors and flaws' (e.g. the previous government's policy, the local council's action, the inadequacies of a rival party's leader);
- 'conceding minor issues to win major goals' (e.g., in a Bill's progress, in a committee, in pairing arrangements, in agreeing amendments to Bills or instruments);
- 'using social settings to discover opinions' (informal discussion in the bar, employing the 'usual channels' [secret communications involving party whips] to sort something out confidentially behind the scenes, attending informal meetings or all party groups);
- 'deliberately withholding useful information' (e.g., placing information in the Commons library just before a debate, springing a surprise vote, not calling an expected vote, introducing an unexpected topic at Prime Minister's Questions);
- 'Using delaying tactics' (e.g., delaying legislation, introducing unexpected or complex amendments in the House of Lords which exist to 'amend and approve' legislation, raising points of order, using parliamentary procedures, helping bills to 'die' at the end of a session, filibustering).

These appear to be seen as legitimate tactics within the House of Commons, especially to be deployed against political opponents, and there are few private complaints about them, except amongst newer MPs. Such strategies seem to established MPs a legitimate part of the political 'game', and long-standing government MPs recalled using them whilst in opposition. Indeed, for many years there was palpable disappointment amongst some Labour MPs that the opposition at the time was ineffectual, partly because it was demoralised, and partly in that it did not properly deploy the available weapons of opposition. Prior to the election of a coalition government in 2010, some of these tactics were once again effectively deployed. Despite their use against one's political opponents (who by definition will not help one acquire power) these 'less frequently used tactics' do not seem to be differentiators in determining who 'gets on' in the House of Commons.

Loyalties

In the UK parliamentary system the political party is crucial (Wright, 2003, pp. 22, 50). To be an independent voice is to limit one's chance of election, and, if one is unelected, ministerial office only rarely beckons via the House of Lords (Peter Mandelson being a prominent recent exception). Thus an MP has to keep the party happy and this is a complex task: not only must the party at national and parliamentary level be satisfied, but also the local constituency party, whose members will canvas support, stuff envelopes, deliver material, organise fundraising, provide voluntary support and act as the 'eyes and ears' of the MP. In marginal seats a few hundred votes can make the difference between winning and losing and the rise of websites such as Theyworkforyou.com and the publicwhip.com brings to public attention the attendance, performance and voting record of MPs. This is in addition to other publicity such as expense claims, details of which were revealed by a national newspaper in 2009, leading to the resignation, or a promise not to stand for re-election, of a number of MPs from all parties.

Winning the seat is crucial. For some MPs in marginal seats the demands of parliament, e.g., being chair of a committee, a PPS or a minister, seem to have taken up much of their energy and focus; some have known that they were in unsafe seats, but have not somehow been able to act on that knowledge on a day-to-day basis. In contrast, other MPs have focused very deliberately on the local party and campaigned almost constantly, regardless of other duties, and retained seats that were just as marginal. Again the complexity of the route to power is highlighted. One may have done all the 'right things' at Westminster, and have been very effective and successful, but this counts for nothing if the voters fail to support a candidate on election day. In the House of Commons the view was that loyalty was valued, as was a lack of public dissent, a willingness to serve on boring or unpopular committees, asking helpful although obviously planted questions during oral question time or debates and regular and reliable attendance (for example, during quiet or unpopular periods).

Most MPs realised this:

The government and the whips value loyalty, obedience, discipline and possible sycophancy.

There is performance rating going on by the whips and there's that whole thing of – are you loyal? Are you a trouble-maker?

People who are ambitious knew that they had to juggle demands, had to remain loyal and to visibly work for the party, for example, by helping during European, local and other elections, visiting other constituencies, becoming involved in policy-making groups or in fundraising. Yet this was a necessary, but not sufficient, condition for advancement.

Personal history

Linking to, but predating, networks within the House of Commons and the parliamentary party, the myriad of links and contacts relating to an MP's personal political history were considered powerful.

I do come with an advantage, just 'cause I've ... been in politics for donkey's years.

A lot of those people have known each other for quite a long time and you know they've been involved in different activities and struggles [together] over the years.

But this can have negative as well as positive consequences:

What I think happens is sometimes minds are made up about a person and sometimes it's very difficult to then shift that and it may be something they've come in with, it's an assumption or a perception about them.

The same process happens in organisations where some people in a team are favoured or trusted because of their history (Gratton and Erickson, 2007) and this can contribute to effective and collaborative functioning. However, there is often a small temporal 'window' where someone may legitimately join a group for what are seen as genuine reasons rather than to capriciously assist advancement.

You know, there are certain groupings within this place which act as a sort of travelator really through the system – I think to try to join them [now] and sort of hustle in ... it's just a bit demeaning really ... that's something which I just couldn't bring myself to do, not because I don't like those people, I admire those people ... I'm sure if one were really determined that's what you would do.

Understanding the politics of the workplace

All workplaces have a political element to them. Some members of parliament view this organisation in much the same way as they view previous organisations, and understand and act within what they perceive to be a political context.

Before I came here, when I was a candidate, I went to see the then Chief Whip [and] I've made a point of seeking people out. I haven't done enough of it, I need to do more, but seeking out older members ... you know just getting advice. Quite apart from anything else, it builds up people who take an interest in you, because you ask their advice ... but I mean you should do it anyway ... it's how you should behave in any established organisation.

You do have a lot of freedom as a Member of Parliament to pursue issues and again your name has been associated with particular issues or causes ... yes, people come here and they are able people and they are intelligent people and they are people with a drive and a motivation to change things and clearly the more senior you are the more opportunity there is to have your version of social justice or whatever it might be [enacted].

Others seemed to be genuinely surprised that organisations had a political dimension and their frustration, linked to core beliefs, caused them some discomfort, as illustrated by this quote from a new MP in 1997:

The thing that has really upset me most is that I have been on the doorstep saying, yes, we will democratise the country because we have democratised the party, the thing that is totally undemocratic is here [the House of Commons]. There is no ... I can see no hint of democracy here at all.

Gaining experience

In the absence of a formal talent management program those MPs who wanted to succeed tended to be quite proactive, and to ensure that they had a range of experiences which were valued by the organisation.

If I get bored with something then I look for more challenges, I don't sit back and complain about it; well, I complain about [it] but I actually do something about it ... I've still got a long way to go before I reach the stage of thinking this is routine.

There are some Members who've got [deliberate] tick boxes, like putting down motions, like doing an adjournment debate ... doing a ten-minute rule bill, making sure you get up and get involved in some of the debates.

Performing well in the chamber and just being seen a lot, reminding people that you exist, popping up at questions a lot, putting down questions on a regular basis is what we [*sic*] are looking for'

Being 'useful' and 'lucky'

There are a number of ways that individuals can contribute and in an arena where no job description exists, MPs have to decide what sort of MP they are and what their professional parliamentary focus is going to be. For some Members of Parliament it was clear from an early stage that they were going to focus their energy on legislation, or holding the executive to account, or becoming a parliamentary private secretary, or being a back-bencher, or being a good constituency MP.

You may decide you want to be a Dennis Skinner or a Dale Campbell Savours [MPs with reputations for plain speaking] and we need those people. I do not intend to be one but we need them.

If you want to be a leading backbencher then I think it is perfectly open to specialise in something and it could be a department through a select committee ... or it could be a particular thing that you make your own and whenever the media needs someone to talk on whatever it is then they automatically think of you and you start to become the country's spokesperson for that thing ... one day it will become important.

This is reminiscent of Primo Levi's comment: 'One of the most important things I have learnt ... was that one must always avoid being a nobody. All roads are closed to a person who appears useless, or are open to a person who has a function, even the most fatuous' (1999 [1963], p. 235). In parliament, as in most organisations, it seems that, to have value, one requires a function. A number of successful MPs spoke of being in the right place at the right time, and of being lucky; however, it was noticeable that these people also exhibited a number of the characteristics identified by Wiseman (2004) as typical of lucky people: they networked, had an external focus and were alert to opportunities. Indeed, they embodied many of the political factors that differentiate those who are successful from those who are not.

Performing under pressure

Taking on extra responsibilities was frequently seen as a way of demonstrating one's competence. Being an effective PPS, whip or junior minister was seen as a route to demonstrating to those more senior in the party that one has the ability, or at least the potential, to make a contribution at a higher level. Furthermore, there was a perception that performance was *actively monitored:*

I am told, although I haven't seen it ... that yesterday in the Chamber or the day before, one of the whips was standing at the bar of the House with a piece of paper and the names of everyone who was down to ask a question and a whole series of categories and they were being rated and I said to the person who'd seen this, I said 'Oh, performance ratings.'

The Prime Minister sat and said you've got all these issues, we've got to be bold, how do we do it, what are the priorities, what do you think they are and so one after the other [they] said 'Delivery'; 'Delivery, we've got to focus on delivery now.'

Being 'clever enough' was considered important. There was suspicion of people who were seen as too cerebral and intellectual, and instead practical intelligence was more valued. However, at a ministerial level it was acknowledged that to succeed you had to be both bright and flexible in your thinking in order to understand, to absorb and appropriately act on a mass of data and initiatives, to see the bigger picture and not to be bulldozed by the seemingly reasonable demands of other departments or be bamboozled into making a hasty or politically inept decision, particularly when new in the post.

Being visible

Being noticed and being visible is a factor that differentiates those who are successful in rising up the hierarchy from those who are not. One minister stated, 'It's not what you do that matters, it's what people think you do.' As already said, one could be noticed, in a positive way, for all sorts of behaviours:

I think being a good constituency MP is actually noticed and valued. It's very interesting, So many people have already said to me, 'God, he is amazing with his immigration casework,' ... He would be sitting in the Chamber or in one of the restaurants or sitting around the lobby with piles of gruesome immigration cases and people saw him working, they knew what he was doing and that's how he turned his seat into a safe one ... All that stuff gets around, so that's important.

Being good in the Chamber, you know being quick on your feet, asking sharp questions, that's valued.

The chief whip said, 'You know we want you to be effective, we obviously don't want you to cause trouble but the worst, one of the worst things we can say about anybody is 'He's fine, he never gives us any trouble,' because he's not making his mark, you know, there's nothing there.

I think if you want to end up on the front bench then you're judged on performance in the chamber ... so when you have the opportunities to speak you speak well – you make good interventions ... you deal with interventions on your own speaking well, so they have then got confidence that you could speak from a despatch box and also you can build up expertise.

However, whilst realising that these processes were taking place, some MPs (in particular some of the 1997 intake) were not at all clear as to how these worked:

My impression at the moment is that the only way you get ahead is by being known in the Whips' office. I am amazed at the way in which people have had a phone call from the Whip to be a member of a committee or to go on a foreign trip or to do this, that and the other.

Gaining support

In common with most organisations, in order to succeed it is necessary to build a positive network of contacts within the organisation; to have access to the informal power structures and ways of getting things done that coexist alongside formal and sometimes bureaucratic processes (Child, 2004). Many MPs were well aware of the necessity to build up positive and strong networks, for professional, political and personal reasons. These consisted of contacts with parliamentary peers in their own and other parties, officials in the House of Commons and their own party, and sometimes members of other groups such as journalists, lobbyists, and representatives of non-governmental organisations (NGOs), pressure groups and unions.

When you are in the office at nine in the morning and go through to midnight, it gives you a lot of time to bond with your colleagues ... we are in this pressure cooker for many, many hours ... this is a great bonding pressure cooker.

Listening very carefully, which a lot of MPs are very bad at doing ... listening in the Chamber, listening at meetings, like the regional groups and the PLP [Parliamentary Labour Party] ... if you're wise you listen.

You can go to a [private] meeting ... learn something from a discussion, be invited to a symposium, be in the inner circle really ... be seen and be able to talk to people ... there might be a Christmas party somewhere and certain people gravitate to that party ... [this is one example of the] subtle ways of getting noticed.

Getting a mentor and a champion

In many organisations mentoring is now an accepted part of talent management (Lewis and Heckman, 2006). In the first eight years of the 1997 Labour government, three power blocks were identified: the first, and most powerful, was related to the prime minister, Tony Blair, the second to the chancellor, Gordon Brown, and the third to the deputy prime minister, John Prescott. One had to ally oneself with one of the 'barons' (a metaphor that was used by some MPs, which linked to their notion of Tony Blair presiding at a 'court') or with one of their key lieutenants to have a serious chance of speedy advancement. Whips were seen as representatives of these barons, and particularly as agents of the prime minister. MPs who had identified this route as a way to enhance progression made themselves useful to more senior colleagues, and sometimes acquired a mentor to help them make sense of the organisation.

People ask certain questions to give a good impression to a minister so that they can help [them in the future] – all that goes on in politics.

It's still based on patronage, and very often your advancement or lack of advancement can be down to one thing that may have been said, or one misconstrued perception ... and yet others [people with a strong champion] who get advancement can say all sorts of things that you would normally think were wrong but it doesn't seem to affect their advancement.

People on the ladder of success ... are being helped to climb that ladder with a bit of advice [and] get put into certain positions that can benefit them.

Politicians do not necessarily display the same political skills regarding their own careers that they do outside the House of Commons or even in relation to their behaviour in the Chamber. Some MPs noticed what was happening but were resentful. These quotes are taken from the first years of the Labour administration, and, intriguingly, the speakers did actually achieve advancement or became part of bodies (e.g. committees) that they wished to join:

I shall be very interested to see how people are chosen to go on the various ... committees. I don't understand ... I've been asked to put my list in but I already have the feeling that it's beginning to be sewn up.

There are favoured sons and I suspect there are favoured daughters now, now how you become one of those, I don't know ... I really still haven't worked out how it works, and why some people are listened to and others are just dismissed.

I honestly don't know [why some people advance], well I suspect a lot of it may actually be down to personality rather than anything that you actually sort of do or don't do ... it's just [as] if there is such a thing as a ladder of success.

I think there are things that you can do. There are hoops that you can jump through and I suspect that I haven't jumped through those hoops and it's partly because I don't know what they are some of the time ... you just don't know they are there ... you know you wouldn't necessarily know where to find them if you were looking for them.

Not having power

Some people, inevitably, do not rise to ministerial office; some are philosophical about this, while others seem to be genuinely disappointed.

I've seen too many people who've become fairly sad, I suppose by thinking that they should be there, and they're not there, and if you are offered a ministerial career it is fairly short in terms of most parliamentary careers and, therefore, it is a peak.

I don't really have the feeling that there's a coherent approach being taken in trying to evaluate the skills of who are here and in terms of an organisation ... of this size ... you'd be quite keen to know what skills, experience and so on we have.

I'm sure it's true for everybody, when they first enter this place, it's full of expectations about being able to progress through to a position where you really are a key player and ... actually if this is going to happen it's going to take a lot longer than you would have hoped.

I guess I'm just sort of being a bit philosophical about it, really, if it happens it happens, but the longer in this place and it hasn't happened, the less likely it is to happen really.

Despite the impression often given of MPs as being obsessed by power, and wanting advancement at any cost, there are a number of MPs who are known not to have sought to climb that 'greasy pole'. Examples included well-known backbenchers such as Dennis Skinner or Austin Mitchell, or chairs of committees such as Tony Wright and Gwyneth Dunwoody (the UK's longest-serving woman MP, now deceased). However, not having status or power can have an impact on an MP's ability to influence the political process. For example, to the chagrin of many new MPs there is a clear order of precedence that the Speaker seems to follow in calling members to speak in debates.

It's frustrating ... for a relatively new MP like me, there's an order people are called ... it's Privy Counsellors and time servers that get called before us ... I had to spend seven hours bobbing up and down before I was called – seven hours!'

Conclusions

The House of Commons is a unique workplace, but the people within it are subject to the same psychological forces as those working in any organisation. Similarly, some people are better at understanding the political aspects of the workplace, and are able to use the ties produced by past personal history to facilitate entry into powerful groups, to utilise arcane parliamentary procedures to their and their colleagues' advantage, to be 'useful' or 'expert', to contribute something important and to be lucky. They have gained respect, managed and delivered, become visible and known, gained support, networked effectively and perhaps had the advantage of having a mentor and a 'champion at court'. As they rise, as in any organisation, it becomes their turn to be courted, to mentor and provide help to colleagues, who, in their turn are gaining power. Some people are better than others at 'doing' organisational politics.

However, this is not an ordinary organisation. The House of Commons operates under bizarre nineteenth-century procedures; the trauma of public election and equally public dismissal – by vote – is unusual else-where; and whether 'UK plc' is doing well or badly, a shadow workforce (including a very visible Board) is desperate to get into power, convinced that they can do your job better than you, and which is constantly, loudly and publicly knocking on the door. Political processes that would be seen as unusual, maladaptive and unnecessarily energy-sapping in ordinary organisations are routinely, openly and deliberately used against one's political opponents. Finally, an MP's private life is curtailed as their behaviour is publicly scrutinised. All this is important because this organisation makes laws, raises and spends taxes, and affects the lives of every-one in the country, in often profound ways.

Given all this, there are factors that actually are unusual in the psychology of politicians that may differentiate them from other political players in other more typical organisations. They do wish to have power, but in general, they believe, at least in part, this power is necessary to achieve a 'higher purpose', as noted at the beginning of this chapter. They perhaps aspire to be 'wise' in their political behaviour and where there is awareness of organisational politics, they aspire to use this with integrity (Baddeley and James, 1987). The public perception of late, perhaps unfairly, is not congruent with this view. Despite being politicians some MPs are rather naive when it comes to organisational politics; others, however, are experts. In either case the fact that they are members of powerful in-groups sharing profound beliefs means that there is an overlay of values to any quest for power.

Finally it is perhaps apposite to remember that one of the founders of applied psychology in the UK believed that psychology should have a role in politics: 'the practical object of . . . psychology [is] to promote the art of living, to improve intra- and inter-social relations, to establish better principles and methods of education, work and leisure, and to prevent social maladjustments and misgovernment' (Myers, 1937, p. 133). By bringing to bear known psychological principles and techniques to the study of politicians, perhaps we can contribute to that worthy aim by demonstrating politicians are equally subject to organisational politics and that awareness and insight are precursors of adaptive action. In a democracy it is ethically important that we understand as much as possible about those with power over us, and, as shown here, the mechanisms underlying the pursuit of that power.

Reflective note

The researcher and author is present in any piece of work, and there is an increasing realisation in psychology that it is both appropriate and necessary to 'show one's hand' and at least to be reflective, if not reflexive. My contact with politicians over more than ten years has influenced how I see them – as people doing a job and constantly fearing that Enoch Powell may be right: 'all political careers . . . end in failure, because that is the nature of politics and of human affairs' (1977, p. 151). For MPs change is seen as hard to achieve, the job increasingly difficult, and time as an enemy. Yet they do it, although after the 2009 'expenses scandal' many are wondering if it is worth it. That key episode is a topic for another paper. Personally, I have enjoyed the research, which is to say I have grown to know and like the participants (well, most of them) and herein is another facet of longitudinal research based on human contact. To an extent one runs the risk of inevitably losing the 'objectivity' to which a scientist practitioner aspires (Kwiatkowski and Winter, 2006). So have I pulled my punches and written this with two audiences in mind, the readers and the politicians who I now know as real people? Possibly. Perhaps that is inevitable: we are actually co-creators of this piece, and whilst I have been able to observe and write, the interviewees have acted, 'and that has made all the difference' (Frost, 1916). This account of how politicians acquire power – as part of a much wider project – is inevitably subjective and partial, but has benefited from some unusual access. My thanks go to the many busy MPs who gave so generously of their time and spoke so candidly about themselves, their work and the institution.

References

Argyris, C. (1999). *On Organizational Learning*. London: Blackwell.

Ashforth, B. E. and Humphrey, R. H. (1993). Emotional labour in service roles: The influence of identity. *Academy of Management Review*, 18 (1), 88–115.

Baddeley, S. and James, K. (1987). Owl, fox, donkey or sheep: political skills for managers. *Management Education and Development*, 18 (1), 3–19.

Bion, W. R. (1961). *Experiences in Groups*. London: Tavistock.

Buchanan, D. A. and Badham, R. J. (2008). *Power, Politics and Organizational Change: Winning the Turf War*. London: Sage.

Child, J. (2004). *Organization: Contemporary Principles and Practice*. Oxford: Blackwell.

Clark, T. and Mangham, I. (2004). Stripping to the undercoat: a review and reflections on a piece of organizational theatre. *Organization Studies*, 25, 841–52.

(1982) Culture: a new look through old lenses. *Journal of Applied Behavioral Science*, 19, 487–507.

Deal, T. E. and Kennedy, A. A. (2000). *Corporate Cultures*. London: Penguin.

Fawcett Society (2006). Fawcett warns Conservatives need to do better on women candidates. Press Release based on research accessed 2 August at www.fawcettsociety.org.uk/index.asp?PageID=345.

Festinger, L. (1957) quoted in Festinger, L. and Carlsmith, J. M. (1959). Cognitive consequences of forced compliance. *Journal of Abnormal and Social Psychology*, 58, 203–10.

Frost, R. (1916). *The Road Not Taken, in Mountain Interval*. New York: Henry Holt.

Gratton, L. and Erickson, T. J. (2007). Ways to build collaborative teams, *Harvard Business Review*, November 2007, pp. 101–9.

Independent (1997). One term wonders leave their old lives. Accessed 6 May at http://www.independent.co.uk/news/uk/home-news/oneterm-wonders-leave-their-old-lives-1260008.html.

Kwiatkowski, R. and Winter, B. (2006). Roots, relativity and realism: The occupational psychologist as 'scientist-practitioner'. In D. Lane and S. Corrie (eds.), *The Modern Scientist Practitioner: a Guide to Practice in Psychology*. London: Routledge.

Lacan, J. (1979). *The Four Fundamental Concepts of Psychoanalysis*. London: Penguin.

Levi, P. (1999 [1963]). *If This Is a Man and The Truce*, trans. S. Woolf. London: Abacus Books.

Lewis, R. E. and Heckman, R. J. (2006). Talent management: a critical review. *Human Resource Management Review*, 16, 139–54.

MacTaggart, F. (2001). *Hansard*, 6 March, Column 149–50.

Morgan, G. (2006). *Images of Organization*. Updated edn. London: Sage.

Myers, C. S. (1937). *In the Realm of Mind*. Cambridge University Press.

Paxman, J. (2003). *The Political Animal*. London: Penguin.

Powell, E. (1977). *Joseph Chamberlain*. London: Thames and Hudson.

Rotter, J. B., Chance, J. E. and Phares, E. J. (1972). *Applications of a Social Learning Theory of Personality*. New York: Holt, Rinehart, and Winston.

Rush, M. (2005). *Parliament Today*. Manchester University Press.

Rutter, M. (1993). Psychosocial resilience and protective mechanisms. In J. Rolf, A. S. Masten, D. Cicchetti, K. H. Neuechterlein and S. Weintraub (eds.), *Risk and Protective Factors in the Development of Psychopathology* (pp. 181–214). Cambridge University Press.

Schneider, B. (1987). The people make the place. *Personnel Psychology*, 40, 437–53.

Silvester, J. and Dykes, C. (2007). *Selecting Political Candidates: A Longitudinal Study of Assessment Centre Performance and Electoral Success in the 2005 UK General Election Journal of Occupational and Organizational Psychology*, 80, 11–25.

Watson, T. (1995). *Sociology, Work and Industry*. 3rd edn. London: Routledge and Kegan Paul.

Wiseman, R. (2004). *The Luck Factor: the Scientific Study of the Lucky Mind*. London: Arrow Books.

Wright, T. (2003). *British Politics; A Very Short Introduction*. Oxford University Press.

Part II

Being at the centre of things: how politicians
function in their job

4   What makes a successful politician?
The social skills of politics

Peter Bull

In 'The experimental analysis of social performance', Argyle and Kendon (1967) proposed that social behaviour can be understood as a form of skill. Social behaviour, they argued, involves processes comparable to those involved in motor skills, such as driving a car or playing a game of tennis. Given that we already know a great deal about motor skill processes, they proposed that this knowledge could be used to advance our understanding of social interaction. In recent years, the Social Skills Model has been significantly revised and updated (e.g. Hargie and Marshall, 1986; Hargie, 1997; Hargie 2006a, 2006b). Although neither version was intended to encompass political behaviour, in this chapter it will be argued that the model has significant implications for our understanding of what makes a successful politician.

Not only has the Social Skills Model contributed to our understanding of social interaction and interpersonal communication (Bull, 2002), it also has significant practical applications. If social interaction is a skill, then it should be possible for people to learn to interact more effectively, just as it is possible to improve performance on any other skill (Argyle and Kendon, 1967). This proposal was formalised in what was termed social skills training. More recently, it has more become more commonly known as communication skills training (CST), and has been used extensively in a wide variety of social contexts (e.g., Hargie, 2006c).

This narrowing of focus from social to communication skills represents a shift from the original Social Skills Model (Argyle and Kendon, 1967), which was concerned with other aspects of social interaction besides interpersonal communication. In this chapter, the significance of both social and communication skills will be considered in the context of contemporary politics. However, its particular focus is on political communication. Given the significant role of the mass media in contemporary politics, it will be argued that a politician's communication skills have become of central importance. Contemporary politics is mediated politics, politicians communicate both with each other and with the electorate especially through television. Politicians are not only seen and heard, they are seen and heard in close-up; their appearance – indeed their every action – is open to close scrutiny. As a result of the overwhelming importance of television, new communication skills come to the fore. It is not enough for a politician to be an effective orator, good conversational skills are also essential. Furthermore, what matters is not just what is said but how it is said: demeanour, tone of voice, facial expression and body movement may all affect voters' perceptions of their political representatives.

This chapter is divided into two main sections. In the first section, the Social Skills Model will be reviewed, both in its original (Argyle and Kendon, 1967) and updated versions (Hargie and Marshall, 1986; Hargie, 1997, 2006a, 2006b). In the second section, the implications of the model for the analysis of political behaviour will be considered.

The Social Skills Model

In the original Social Skills Model (Argyle and Kendon, 1967), six processes were considered to be common to motor skills and social performance: distinctive goals, selective perception of cues, central translation processes, motor responses, feedback and corrective action, and the timing of responses. Each of these processes is discussed in turn below:

1. *Distinctive goals*: these can be seen, for example, in the process of driving a car. The superordinate goal of reaching one's destination may also involve subordinate goals, such as overtaking a slow-moving vehicle, crossing a difficult junction or joining a main road in heavy traffic. In the same way, social performance can be seen as having distinctive goals. In a job interview, the superordinate goal of the interviewer (to select the right person for the job) necessitates a number of subordinate goals, such as obtaining information from the interviewee, and establishing satisfactory rapport in order to achieve those ends.

2. *The selective perception of cues*: a key process in the performance of any skill. Not all information is of equal value: that is to say, the skilled performer may pay particular attention to certain types of information relevant to achieving their objective, while ignoring irrelevant information. Indeed, one mark of skilled performance may be to learn what input can be ignored. A skilled public speaker learns to sense the interest and attention of his/her audience, and to adjust his/her performance appropriately, whereas the conversational bore completely fails to read the response of his/her listeners.

3. *Central translation processes*: prescribe what to do about any particular piece of information. The term 'translation' refers to the rule by

which a particular signal is interpreted as requiring a particular action. An important feature of skills acquisition consists of the development of such translations which, once learned, can be readily and immediately acted upon. It is in the development of new translations that a great deal of hesitancy and halting can be observed. So, for example, a novice public speaker may be thrown by an awkward question from a member of the audience, whereas an experienced speaker will over the years have developed many appropriate strategies.

4. *Motor responses*: refer to behaviours that are performed as a consequence of central translation processes. The learner driver may initially find it extremely difficult to change gear, but with practice the movements become quite automatic. This is also the case with social behaviour; initial learning may be quite awkward, but with extensive practice large chunks of behaviour can become fluent and habitual. Indeed, social behaviour can become too automatic. The monotone of museum guides who have repeated their guided tour too often is one well-known example of automatised behaviour. Similarly, there was the unfortunate case of a lecturer who reported that 'he had reached a stage where he could arise before his audience, turn his mouth loose, and go to sleep' (Lashley, 1951, p. 184).

5. *Feedback and corrective action*: refer to the ways in which an individual may modify his/her behaviour in the light of feedback from others. The term 'feedback' was derived from cybernetics. Just as in a central heating system, the information from a thermostat regulates the heating output, so too feedback is important in the context of social interaction. For example, a teacher who sees that the pupils have not understood a point may repeat it slowly in another way; again, a salesperson who realises that s/he is failing to make an impact may change his/her style of behaviour. Argyle and Kendon (1967) proposed that feedback is obtained principally from non-verbal cues, so in conversation a speaker will typically scan the other's face intermittently to check whether the listener understands, agrees or disagrees, and whether he or she is willing for the speaker to continue talking.

6. *Good timing and rhythm*: these are also important features of social skills. Without correct anticipation as to when a response will be required, interaction can be jerky and ineffective. Taking turns is the characteristic way in which conversation is structured, although turn-taking in larger groups can sometimes be problematic, because opportunities to speak can be quite restricted. Choosing the right moment to make a point in a group discussion is a useful example of the social skill of good timing.

The Social Skills Model has been revised and extended in a series of publications by Hargie (Hargie and Marshall, 1986; Hargie, 1997, 2006a, 2006b). Although Hargie fully acknowledged the value and significance of the analogy between social and motor skills, he also identified four important differences (Hargie, 2006a). Firstly, since social interaction by definition involves other people, it is necessary to consider the goals not only of one individual but of all those involved, as well as their actions and reactions towards one another. In this sense, social behaviour is often much more complex than motor performance.

Secondly, the role of feelings and emotions is neglected by the original model. Mood and emotional state can have an important bearing on responses, goals and perceptions in social interaction. Furthermore, whereas we often take into account the feelings of other people with whom we interact, this is clearly not the case in learning to perform a motor skill. The concepts of 'face' and 'facework' are also important here. According to Goffman (1967, p. 5), face is 'the positive social value a person effectively claims for himself by the line others assume he has taken during a particular contact', while facework represents the actions people take to protect threats to their own and others' face. From this perspective, face can be seen as the successful presentation of social identity (Holtgraves, 2002) and according to Brown and Levinson (1978, 1987), it is important in all cultures; face can be lost, maintained or enhanced. They argue that face preservation is a primary constraint on the achievement of goals in social interaction; thus, skilled individuals will be concerned with maintaining the esteem of both self and others.

Thirdly, the perception of individuals differs in a number of ways from the perception of objects. We perceive the responses of the other person with whom we are communicating. We may also perceive our own responses, in that we hear what we say, and can be aware of our own non-verbal behaviour. Furthermore, we can be aware of the process of perception itself, referred to as metaperception. In making judgements about how other people perceive us, we may also attempt to ascertain how they think we perceive them. Such judgements may influence our own behaviour during social interaction.

Fourthly, the social situation in which interaction occurs is important for an understanding of social skills. Significant features which may affect social interaction are the roles which people play, the rules governing the situation, the nature of the task and the physical environment. In addition, personal factors (such as age, gender and physical appearance) will be important in the way in which people behave towards one another.

In the next section, political behaviour is considered in the light of Hargie's revised version of Argyle and Kendon's (1967) model of social skills (Hargie and Marshall 1986; Hargie 1997, 2006a, 2006b).

The social skills of politics

Distinctive goals

Argyle and Kendon (1967) proposed that social interaction can be conceptualised in terms of distinctive goals. This may not be applicable to all social situations. For example, it is questionable whether the behaviour of people having an informal chat over a cup of coffee is in any sense goal-directed. But in other situations, the analysis is much more appropriate. Thus, in a job interview, the interviewer's goal is to select the right person for the job; in a medical consultation, the doctor's goal is to arrive at an accurate diagnosis in order to recommend appropriate treatment.

In the context of politics, the behaviour of politicians can undoubtedly be seen as goal-directed. For example, in a general election campaign, a political party needs a coherent set of policies to bring to the electorate. Indeed, politicians may be criticised for lacking clear vision or purpose. Thus, goals are arguably central to political behaviour. In the next subsection, it is proposed that politicians are evaluated by voters principally in terms of competence and responsiveness. From this perspective, having clear goals may contribute to a politician's favourable evaluation on both these dimensions.

Perception

According to Argyle and Kendon (1967), the selective perception of cues is integral to skilled performance. Undoubtedly, it is important for politicians to read people and situations well, since this will affect how they behave towards others. Misperceptions can have unfortunate consequences. For example, Tony Blair (Labour prime minister 1997–2007) was slow-hand-clapped and heckled in a speech delivered to the UK Women's Institute (7 June 2000); at the conclusion of the speech, many members of the audience sat stony-faced, refusing to extend the customary applause. The Women's Institute is traditionally a non-political organisation, and Blair was criticised by some members for delivering a speech that was too political. Arguably, on this occasion Blair's speech was inappropriate, because he misperceived and misconstrued the situation; as a consequence, he received a great deal of bad publicity (BBC News, 2000).

Not only do politicians need to be good at perceiving others, as public figures they need to be aware of how others perceive them. In the example above, Blair was judged unfavourably by the audience seemingly as a result of his own misperception of the situation. In a study based on the 2001 British general election, ratings of political leaders were shown to be one of the two best predictors of how people voted (Clarke, Sanders, Stewart and Whiteley, 2004). Factor analysis of these ratings showed two distinct but interrelated dimensions, labelled *competence* and *responsiveness*. Ratings of 'keeps promises', 'decisive' and 'principled' loaded on competence; ratings of 'caring', 'listens to reason' and 'not arrogant' loaded on responsiveness (Clarke *et al.*, 2004). In a previous analysis of leader ratings based on the 1987 British general election, Stewart and Clarke (1992) identified the same two factors. Accordingly, Clarke *et al.* (2004) proposed that competence and responsiveness may be regarded as two enduring dimensions of how British political leaders are perceived. Thus, politicians must endeavour to be seen as both competent and responsive, since failing on either dimension may lose them electoral support.

Mediating factors

In the original Social Skills Model (Argyle and Kendon, 1967), the term 'central translation processes' referred to the planning aspect of behaviour and to the rules by which a particular signal is interpreted as regarding a particular action. A skilled and experienced politician will have acquired many such translations which, once learned, can be readily and immediately acted upon. However, the term translation processes was widely regarded as too restrictive, and replaced with the term mediating factors (e.g. Hargie, 2006a). In the sphere of politics, an important mediating factor is impression management. As discussed above, voter perceptions are extremely important, consequently politicians must strive to create a favourable impact on the electorate, through controlling or managing the impressions or perceptions formed by others. To refer to this kind of public identity, Johansson (2008) introduced the term 'the presentation of the political self', based on Goffman's (1959/1990) *The Presentation of Self in Everyday Life*. In this seminal book, Goffman analysed social interaction as if it were part of a theatrical performance, arguing that people in everyday life are like actors on a stage, managing settings, clothing, words and non-verbal behaviour to give a particular impression to others.

In addition, Goffman (1955/1967) argued that concerns with face and facework are salient in virtually all social encounters. Drawing on Goffman's work, Brown and Levinson (1978, 1987) proposed their highly influential theory of politeness. According to Brown and Levinson, communicative actions such as commands or complaints may be performed in such a way as to minimise the threat to positive and negative face, where positive face is defined as 'the want of every member that his wants be desirable to at least some others', and negative face as 'the want of every 'competent adult member' that his actions be unimpeded by others' (Brown and Levinson, 1987, p. 62).

If positive face is essentially the need to be well regarded by others, it is undoubtedly of fundamental importance for politicians. A politician who suffers serious loss of positive face may come to be regarded as a liability by his or her political party. For example, a government minister or an opposition frontbench spokesperson may come under pressure to resign. Similarly a Member of Parliament may be defeated at the next general election, or, if deselected, may not even be allowed to stand as the party's parliamentary candidate. But negative face is also important. As Goffman (1955/1967) pointed out, people need to protect their face against even the possibility of threat; they avoid performing actions which although acceptable in the present may reflect badly upon them in the future. Hence, a politician will be careful to avoid making statements which may hamper or constrain his/her future freedom of action. This point is effectively summed up in the old political saying: 'Never say never'.

All these closely related concepts (impression management, self-presentation and face management) can be regarded as mediating factors, which play an extremely important role in political communication.

Motor responses

Motor responses refer to the performance of actual behaviour. It is not enough for a politician to be a skilled perceiver, or to be able to translate perceptions into appropriate behavioural strategies; the behaviour itself has to be performed in a convincing and effective manner.

Of particular importance for politicians are those behaviours Goffman (1955/1967) referred to as facework. A study of facework in political interviews broadcast during the 1992 British general election was conducted by the author and his colleagues (Bull, Elliott, Palmer and Walker, 1996). They developed a typology of how questions pose threats to face, identifying nineteen different types of face-threat. These were grouped into three superordinate categories: threats to the political party the politician represents, threats to self and threats to significant others.

For example, the question 'Why do you think your party is doing so badly in the opinion polls?' would threaten the face of the party the politician represents. In contrast, the question 'Do you not think the public is entitled to regard your own expenses claims as unreasonable?' would threaten the face of the individual politician. On the basis of equivocation theory (Bavelas, Black, Chovil, and Mullett, 1990), Bull *et al.* proposed and confirmed the hypothesis that politicians would typically equivocate more to those questions where all the principal forms of response posed a threat to face.

Elsewhere, the author has developed an equivocation typology (Bull and Mayer, 1993; Bull, 2003), which is divided into superordinate and subordinate categories. For example, one superordinate category is *attacks the question*. This can be further subdivided into eight subordinate categories, for example, *the question is hypothetical or speculative, the question is based on a false premise, the question includes a misquotation*. In total, there are twelve superordinate categories. When these categories are further subdivided into subordinate categories, thirty-five ways of not answering a question can be distinguished. Some of these may be seen as highly skilled, some less so and others as transparently evasive or even downright inept.

For example, Tony Blair made skilful use of the term 'modernisation' in the general election campaign of 1997 to equivocate and present the best possible face in response to awkward questions regarding the dramatic policy changes in the Labour Party which had taken place in the preceding fifteen years (Bull, 2000). In contrast, Neil Kinnock (Labour Party leader, 1983–92) made use of what were termed *negative answers*, where he stated what would not happen rather than what would happen. This was deemed an ineffectual, face-damaging form of equivocation, since interviewers would simply reiterate the question ('That is why I am asking you what you would do'), thereby drawing attention to the preceding equivocation and making Kinnock look evasive. Thus, different forms of equivocation may be seen as reflecting different levels of communicative skill, which can be understood in terms of face and face management. Politicians are frequently castigated for not replying to questions, but given that they are often placed in conflicting situations where it is not possible to answer a question directly, equivocation itself can be considered as form of communicative skill in its own right (Bull, 2010).

Feedback and corrective action

There are many different forms of feedback available to politicians. Political activity receives intense coverage through television, the internet and through newspapers. Politicians continuously monitor each other's activities, evaluating and criticising each other's performance. The electorate can also give feedback through opinion polls, focus groups, writing to their Member of Parliament and, of course, through elections.

Feedback can be explicit or implicit, verbal or non-verbal. Whereas Argyle and Kendon (1967) proposed that feedback in the context of social interaction is principally non-verbal, this is not true of politics, where feedback is typically verbal and explicit and can also be non-verbal. For example, audience responses at public meetings can be seen as a form of feedback. Through applause, audiences may explicitly endorse particular policies or sentiments expressed by the speaker. Through a standing ovation, they may show their regard for a particular politician, thus they may also send implicit messages through the quality of their applause (Bull and Wells, 2001). Interruptive applause (thus preventing the speaker getting to the end of a sentence) can indicate audience enthusiasm, while delayed applause (where there is discernible silence between the end of a sentence and the start of the applause) can indicate a distinct lack of audience enthusiasm.

In fact, so much feedback is available to politicians that their real skill lies in knowing how to respond appropriately, to avoid the twin dangers of over-reaction and under-reaction. Elections are the most important source of feedback to democratically elected politicians, yet as institutions political parties can remain remarkably resistant to change. For example, following a crushing electoral defeat in 1997, the British Conservative Party stood for election in both 2001 and 2005 with much the same right-wing agenda, resulting in further defeats. It was only with their relaunch following David Cameron's election as the new party leader (6 December, 2005) that the Conservatives made a significant impact on the opinion polls and came to be considered a serious alternative to the Labour Party, resulting in their 2010 general election victory.

Timing

The role of timing in political interaction can be illustrated through a series of studies on how politicians invite applause at political rallies. Atkinson (e.g. 1983, 1984a, 1984b) noted that the timing of audience applause is characterised by a high degree of precision; typically, it occurs either just before or immediately after a possible completion point by the speaker. Atkinson proposed that this close synchronisation between speech and applause occurs because speakers use rhetorical devices such as three-part lists and contrasts to invite applause, which enable audiences to project possible completion points, and so applaud 'on cue'. Bull and

Wells (2002) found that close synchronisation between speech and applause only occurred when rhetorical devices were accompanied by appropriate delivery (in the form of vocal and/or non-verbal cues). Whereas Atkinson argued that delivery simply increases the chance of a rhetorical device receiving applause, Bull and Wells proposed that non-verbal behaviour indicates whether or not the rhetorical device is to be taken as an applause invitation. From this perspective, the skilled use of both appropriate delivery and rhetorical devices play an important role in synchronising speaker–audience behaviour at political rallies.

Another example of timing comes from the study of broadcast political interviews. Beattie (1982) argued that Margaret Thatcher (Conservative prime minister 1979–90) was frequently interrupted by her interviewer, because she gave off what Beattie called 'misleading turn-yielding cues'. Turn-yielding cues (e.g., fall in pitch, ceasing to use hand gestures) are signals indicating that the speaker has finished an utterance, and is ready to offer the turn to another speaker (Duncan, 1972; Duncan and Fiske, 1977). According to Beattie, Thatcher would use these signals but then continue to speak, hence misleading her interviewer, who kept interrupting her. Hence, from Beattie's perspective, the poor timing and synchronisation in her interview resulted from her own lack of basic conversational skills.

Bull and Mayer (1988) took issue with Beattie's analysis, finding no evidence to support his claims. Indeed, their study of broadcast interviews during the 1987 British general election showed that the pattern of inter-ruptions received by both her and Labour Party leader Neil Kinnock correlated positively and at a high level of statistical significance. However, there was one important difference between the two party leaders. Thatcher complained a great deal about being interrupted, giving the impression that she was being badly treated by the interviewers. This impression was compounded by her tendency to personalise issues, to take questions and criticisms as accusations and frequently to address the interviewers formally by title and surname, as if they needed to be called to account for misdemeanours. In this way, she continually wrong-footed her interviewers and put them on the defensive, arguably showing a striking mastery of the arts of political competitiveness. From this per-spective, it was not her poor conversational skills but her complaints about interruptions that made the timing of speaking turns a significant issue in these interviews.

Although Argyle and Kendon (1967) were principally concerned with the role of timing in social interaction, the concept is also highly relevant to the broader political context. For example, in the British parliamentary system, the maximum period between general elections is five years, but the Prime Minister has the right to call an election before the full five-year term has ended. The timing of this decision is all important. A celebrated example of disastrous timing was Labour Prime Minister James Callaghan's failure to call an election in September 1978, which, according to opinion polls at the time, he would have won (Clark, 2008). He went on to lose the election the following year to Margaret Thatcher (3 May 1979), thereby inaugurating eighteen years of Conservative government. So politically significant was Callaghan's poor timing that, according to Clark, it changed the world: 'Labour's defeat in 1979 really was a watershed: marking the end of the collectivist, mixed economy consensus and its replacement with privatising, pro-big business neo-liberalism … It's a sobering thought that had Jim Callaghan simply done what everyone expected him to do on that fateful September day 29 years ago, "Thatcherism" is a word the world would never have heard of' (Clark, 2008).

Person–situation context

Social skills also need to be understood in terms of the person–situation context (e.g. Hargie, 1997). A good example comes again from the analysis of face and facework, which arguably varies according to situational context; examples from three contexts (speeches, broadcast interviews and parliamentary question time) are discussed below.

A political speech (monologue) gives the politician the opportunity to enhance positive face through displaying rhetorical skill, presenting new policies, celebrating past achievements and talking up his/her own political party. It also gives the politician the opportunity for face aggravation, by attacking and criticising his/her political opponents. In broadcast interviews (as discussed previously under the heading of Motor responses), politicians must defend themselves against questions which pose a threat to face (Bull *et al.*, 1996). That is to say, politicians will avoid responding to questions in ways which may make them look bad or circumscribe their future freedom of action.

Politicians also run these risks in parliamentary question time, but in addition, there is the further risk from insults and derogatory remarks from opposing politicians, who may use face aggravation as a deliberate strategy. Harris (2001) conducted an analysis of Prime Minister's Questions (PMQs), the weekly session in the House of Commons in which any Member of Parliament may put a question to the prime minister. She argued that much of PMQ discourse is composed of intentional and explicitly face-threatening acts (FTAs). For example, she identified one strategy whereby the leader of the opposition asks for some highly specific information, which the prime minister may not have to hand, or may not wish to publicise. In the event of an equivocal response, the leader of the opposition may then subsequently provide the information in order to embarrass or attack the prime minister. Bull and Law (2009) developed a typology for analysing PMQ discourse, identifying thirteen different techniques for performing FTAs. One such strategy involves asking the prime minister to perform a face-threatening act, for example, by apologising for a previous mistake, or by admitting that some aspect of government policy has been a complete failure. Such questions create a communicative conflict for the prime minister. If he apologises or admits to a mistake, then he may be seen as incompetent; if he fails to apologise or admit to a mistake, then he may be seen as arrogant. This technique was one of David Cameron's particular favourites when in opposition. According to Harris, such techniques are not only sanctioned but rewarded in accordance with expectations of Members of the House of Commons, through an adversarial and confrontational political process.

From this perspective, a successful politician will need to be skilled in different forms of facework. Thus, a skilled orator will not necessarily be a skilled debater or a skilled interviewee, nor will the politician who is skilled in face enhancement necessarily be skilled in face aggravation, or in resisting or countering face aggravation. However, by analysing these different aspects of facework, it is possible to assess different aspects of a politician's communicative skill, thereby deepening our understanding of the political process.

Communication Skills Training (CST)

There is now an extensive literature on CST (e.g., Hargie, 2006c), although there are no published studies on formal CST with politicians. However, there are plenty of anecdotal examples. Famously, Margaret Thatcher shortly after becoming prime minister underwent training to lower her voice tone, as her advisers considered that she sounded too shrill. From tape recordings of her speeches made before and after training, it appeared she achieved a reduction in pitch of 46 Hz, a figure which is almost half the average difference in pitch between male and female voices (Atkinson, 1984a, p. 113). Again, Barbara Follett (Labour MP for Stevenage elected in 1997) became so well known within the Labour Party for her pioneering work in self-presentation and media training that her techniques became familiarly known as 'Folletting'.

In principle, there is no reason why for example politicians should not receive explicit CST: in learning more effective rhetorical techniques for inviting applause (e.g., Atkinson, 1984b; Bull, 2006); in responding to

awkward conflictual questions which create pressures towards equivocation (e.g., Bavelas *et al.*, 1990; Bull, 2008); in posing awkward questions at
PMQs (e.g., Harris, 2001; Bull and Law, 2009). In practice, however,
they doubtless also learn these techniques 'on the job'. Applause can be a
powerful reward, and politicians may learn rhetorical techniques which
are effective in stirring their audience, while in interviews, they may learn
to spot contentious presuppositions in questions. In debates with their
opponents, they may learn to use or to counter-techniques of face aggravation, thus political communication skills can be learned not just through
formal training procedures, but through everyday political interaction.

Conclusions

In contemporary politics, politicians with good social skills are at a distinct
advantage. The mediated politics of the modern era expose politicians to
close scrutiny and to be a good performer on television is undoubtedly a
political asset. Arguably, the Social Skills Model provides a framework
within which to analyse politicians' communication skills. Furthermore, it
helps to specify what those skills are, for example, to be good at perceiving
others, to be aware of how one is perceived by others, to be skilled in
facework and impression management. In addition, the Social Skills
Model can be applied to the analysis of political action. For example,
good timing in making decisions and the appropriate use of feedback are
important political skills that go well beyond good communication.
Nevertheless, politicians must not only make the right decisions, they
must also communicate those decisions effectively. They need to persuade members of their own political party and the electorate as a whole of
the value of their policies. Thus, political action and political communication share a close interdependence.

In this chapter, the Social Skills Model has been extended far beyond the
original intentions of Argyle and Kendon (1967) and it is proposed that it
provides a framework for future research into political behaviour, and a
means whereby the performance of politicians can be both conceptualised
and evaluated. In the mediated world of contemporary politics, good social
skills are of central importance. Politicians ignore them at their peril.

References

Argyle, M. and Kendon A. (1967). The experimental analysis of social performance. *Advances in Experimental Social Psychology*, 3, 55–97.
Atkinson, J. M. (1983). Two devices for generating audience approval: a comparative
   study of public discourse and text. In K. Ehlich and H. van Riemsdijk (eds.),

Connectedness in Sentence, Text and Discourse (pp. 199–236). Tilburg, Netherlands: Tilburg papers in Linguistics.

(1984a). *Our Masters' Voices*. London and New York: Methuen.

(1984b). Public speaking and audience responses: some techniques for inviting applause. In J. M. Atkinson and J. C. Heritage (eds.), *Structures of Social Action: Studies in Conversation Analysis* (pp. 370–409). Cambridge and New York: Cambridge University Press.

Bavelas, J. B., Black, A., Chovil, N. and Mullett, J. (1990). *Equivocal Communication*. Newbury Park: Sage.

BBC News(2000), 7 June. WI gives Blair hostile reception. Retrieved 22 March 2009, from http://news.bbc.co.uk/1/hi/uk_politics/780486.stm.

Beattie, G. W. (1982). Turn-taking and interruption in political interviews – Margaret Thatcher and Jim Callaghan compared and contrasted. *Semiotica*, 39, 93–114.

Brown, P. and Levinson, S. C. (1978). Universals in language usage: politeness phenomena. In E. Goody (ed.), *Questions and politeness* (pp. 56–310). Cambridge University Press.

(1987). *Politeness: Some Universals in Language Use*. Cambridge University Press.

Bull, P. (2000). Equivocation and the rhetoric of modernisation: An analysis of televised interviews with Tony Blair in the 1997 British General Election. *Journal of Language and Social Psychology*, 19, 222–47.

(2002). *Communication under the Microscope: the Theory and Practice of Microanalysis*. London: Psychology Press.

(2003). *The Microanalysis of Political Communication: Claptrap and Ambiguity*. London: Psychology Press.

(2006). Invited and uninvited applause in political speeches. *British Journal of Social Psychology*, 45, 563–78.

(2008). Slipperiness, evasion and ambiguity: equivocation and facework in non-committal political discourse. *Journal of Language and Social Psychology*, 27, 324–32.

(2010). Equivocation and communicative skill. In M. B. Hinner (ed.), *Freiberger Beitraege zur interkulturellen und Wirtschaftskommunikation: A Forum for General and Intercultural Business*, pp. 69–84. Frankfurt am Main, Germany: Peter Lang GmbH.

Bull, P. E., Elliott, J., Palmer, D. and Walker, L. (1996). Why politicians are three-faced: the face model of political interviews. *British Journal of Social Psychology*, 35, 267–84.

Bull, P. and Law, H. (2009). April. Punch and Judy politics: face aggravation in Prime Minister's Question Time. Paper presented at the Annual Conference of the British Psychological Society, Brighton, UK.

Bull, P. E. and Mayer, K. (1988). Interruptions in political interviews: a study of Margaret Thatcher and Neil Kinnock. *Journal of Language and Social Psychology*, 7, 35–45.

(1993). How not to answer questions in political interviews. *Political Psychology*, 14, 651–66.

Bull, P. E. and Wells, P. (2001), July. Quality of applause and the art of oratory. Paper presented at the Annual Conference of the Social Psychology Section of the British Psychological Society, University of Surrey, Guildford, UK.

(2002). By invitation only? An analysis of invited and uninvited applause. *Journal of Language and Social Psychology*, 21, 230–44.

Clarke, H. D., Sanders, D., Stewart, M. C. and Whiteley, P. F. (2004). *Political Choice in Britain*. Oxford University Press.

Clark, N. (2008), September. How Jim Callaghan changed the world. Retrieved 22 March 2009 from http://neilclark66.blogspot.com/2008/09/how-jim-callaghan-changed-world.html.

Duncan, S. (1972). Some signals and rules for taking speaking turns in conversations. *Journal of Personality and Social Psychology*, 23, 283–92.

Duncan, S. and Fiske, D. W. (1977). *Face-to-face Interaction: Research, Methods and Theory*. Hillsdale, N.J.; Lawrence Erlbaum.

Goffman, E. (1955). On face-work: an analysis of ritual elements in social interaction. *Psychiatry*, 18, 213–31. Reprinted in E. Goffman, *Interaction Ritual: Essays on Face to Face Behaviour* (pp. 5–45). Garden City, N.Y.: Anchor, 1967.

(1959). *The Presentation of Self in Everyday Life*. Harmondsworth: Penguin. Reprinted, London: Penguin Books, 1990.

(1967). *Interaction Ritual: Essays on Face to Face Behaviour*. Garden City, N.Y.: Anchor, 1967.

Hargie, O. D. W. (1997). Interpersonal communication: a theoretical framework. In O. D. W. Hargie (ed.), *The Handbook of Communication Skills* (pp. 29–63). 2nd edn. London: Routledge.

(2006a). Skill in practice: an operational model of communicative performance. In O. Hargie (ed.), *The Handbook of Communication Skills* (pp. 37–70). 3rd edn. London: Routledge.

(2006b). Training in communication skills: research, theory and practice. In O. Hargie (ed.), *The Handbook of Communication Skills* (pp. 553–65). 3rd edn. London: Routledge.

(ed.) (2006c). *The Handbook of Communication Skills*. 3rd edn. London: Routledge.

Hargie, O. D. W. and Marshall, P. (1986). Interpersonal communication: a theoretical framework. In O. D. W. Hargie (ed.), *The Handbook of Communication Skills* (pp. 22–56). 1st edn. London: Croom Helm.

Harris, S. (2001). Being politically impolite: extending politeness theory to adversarial political discourse. *Discourse and Society*, 12, 451–72.

Holtgraves, T. M. (2002). *Language as Social Action: Social Psychology and Language Use*. Mahwah, N.J.: Erlbaum.

Johansson, M. (2008). Presentation of the political self: commitment in electoral media dialogue. *Journal of Language and Social Psychology*, 27, 397–408.

Lashley, K. S. (1951). The problem of serial order in behaviour. In L. A. Jeffress (ed.), *Cerebral Mechanisms in Behaviour* (pp. 112–46). New York: Wiley.

Stewart, M. C. and Clarke, H. D. (1992). The (un)importance of party leaders: leader images and party choice in the 1987 British election. *Journal of Politics*, 54, 447–70.

5   Cognitive skills and motivation to adapt to social change among Polish politicians

Agnieszka Golec de Zavala

For decades researchers analysing people's functioning in the domain of politics have been looking for an answer to the question whether members and supporters of different political opinions, ranging across the continuum from political left to right, also differ with respect to their cognitive complexity and the sophistication with which they approach political problems (e.g., Stone, 1980; Jost, Glaser, Kruglanski and Sulloway, 2003a, 2003b). In this chapter, it is argued that complexity of political judgement is shaped by individuals' cognitive abilities (Rosenberg, 1989; Sidanius, 1988; Sidanius and Lau, 1989) and that epistemic motivation (Kruglanski and Webster, 1996) – the will to engage with knowledge – determines the extent to which available cognitive skills are used. When analysing differences in cognitive skills the question is posed whether politicians differ with respect to their cognitive potential and when looking at differences in epistemic motivation, it is considered whether politicians differ with respect to their cognitive performance. The latter is easier to change and shape than the former, but both have consequences for the effectiveness of democratic debate.

This chapter is based on findings from two studies examining the cognitive abilities and epistemic motivations of members of the political elite in Poland, a former communist country that underwent a dramatic systemic change in the 1990s. The socio-political context of a post-communist country offers the possibility of new insights into the nature of the relationship between cognitive functioning and political preference unavailable within the context of established Western democracies (see also Golec, 2002b; Kossowska and van Hiel, 2003; McFarland, Ageyev and Abalakina-Paap, 1992; Tetlock, 1983, 1984).

Theoretical analyses of deliberative democracy – a political system that assumes and requires reasoned public discussion by citizens and their representatives for legitimate political decision making (Habermas, 1984; Lipset, 1960) – highlight the importance of constructive forms of collective communication and cooperative efforts in resolving differences of interests and opinions. Democratic forms of decision making assume that participants are able to entertain opposing points of view, withhold immediate judgement until all pertinent perspectives have been addressed and find agreements that can satisfy parties holding disparate interests and preferences. Such integrative agreements (Pruitt and Carnevale, 1982), through which diverse goals are at least partly reconciled, provide new ways of managing conflicting interests and realising core social values. In themselves they constitute new social values. Thus, adequate and effective participation in a democratic political system requires advanced cognitive skills and motivation which encourage communication capable of fostering such a consensus. Therefore cognitive complexity in approaching political problems seems to be essential for effective functioning of democratic political systems.

Numerous studies report systematic differences in the ability to exercise complex political judgements between representatives and supporters of different political opinions. One of the earliest accounts indicates that the authoritarian personality with its rigid cognitive style and limited cognitive perspective are characteristic of conservatives rather than liberals (Adorno, Frenkel-Brunswik, Levinson and Sanford, 1950). This proposition inspired a long-lasting discussion whether cognitive simplicity and rigidity are characteristic of supporters of conservative and right-wing political positions or of any 'ideologues' despite the content of the ideology they support. Subsequently it was proposed that cognitive rigidity and simplicity can also be found among representatives of the political left (Rokeach, 1960; Tetlock, 1986a, 1986b; Durrheim, 1997).

The results of personality studies on experiential openness (McCrae, 1996; Riemann, Grubich, Hempel, Mergl and Richter, 1993), the personal need for structure (Neuberg and Newsom, 1993) and many others (for a review see Stone, 1980) suggest that a simplified and emotionally laden perception of social and political reality might be the foundation for a conservative political outlook. In their seminal review, Jost et al. (2003a) conclude that most studies link cognitive motivations which elicit a simplistic cognitive style with political conservatism.

However, studies on dogmatism (Rokeach, 1960), tough- and tender-mindedness (Eysenck, 1954), as well as some analysing integrative complexity (Tetlock, 1983), suggest a curvilinear relationship. They posit that motivated cognitive simplicity can be found among representatives of both right and left political extremes. Yet another theoretical account supported by empirical evidence maintains that cognitive simplicity is related to a tendency to represent centrist and populist political positions, whereas holding extreme political views requires courage, cognitive independence, complexity and sophistication (Sidanius, 1988; Sidanius and Lau, 1989; van Hiel and Mervielde, 1996).

The models of the relationship between cognitive functioning and political preference outlined above look at differences in political preferences in relation to cognitive predispositions (e.g., limited cognitive perspective, cognitive sophistication), epistemic motivation (e.g., openness to experience, need for cognitive structure) or cognitive performance that can be shaped by both predispositions and motivation (e.g., integrative complexity). This chapter claims that individual cognitive functioning is defined by the repertoire of cognitive skills individuals possess and by the extent to which they are motivated to use and apply those skills (e.g., Kruglanski and Webster, 1996; Golec, 2002a, 2002b). The same level of cognitive functioning can be achieved by a person who has a limited range of cognitive skills but is curious, open-minded and motivated to learn as a person who enjoys a wider range of cognitive skills but is not motivated to put them to use. Thus, cognitive skills and epistemic motivations should be differentiated and analysed separately in order to achieve a comprehensive picture of cognitive functioning of representatives and supporters of different political opinions.

In empirical studies conducted in Poland in 1997–2001 cognitive skills and epistemic motivation were examined among members of political parties representing the whole political spectrum: the post-communist Social Democracy of the Republic of Poland (Socjal-demokracja Rzeczpospolitej Polskiej), the Democratic Party, which formed the Democratic Left Alliance (Stronnictwo Demokratyczne), the populist political parties that emerged after the fall of the communist Polish United Workers' Party representing socialist economic arrangements and socially conservative values (Polska Zjednoczona Partia Robotnicza), the centre, left and religious-nationalist right-wing parties emerging from Solidarity, as well as the social movement representing the democratic opposition against the communist regime from 1980 to 1990. These studies suggest that the relationship between cognitive functioning and political opinion is different when cognitive skills are analysed than when motivation to use available cognitive ability is examined. They provide an insight into the issue but do not claim to represent a systematic and comprehensive analysis. More studies and larger samples would be needed for that purpose, thus the present studies offer a starting place from which to guide further research.

Cognitive skills for democratic debate and political opinions in Poland

Cognitive skills that are of particular importance for effective functioning in the context of democratic debate include the ability to go beyond one's own perspective, to understand others' viewpoints and to coordinate these in a comprehensive overview of a problem (Habermas, 1984). Such capacity demands understanding of the relativity of all the political positions involved. The ability to coordinate various perspectives requires the pre-existence of a multifaceted perception of political phenomena. Both of these abilities emerge in the course of individual cognitive development (Selman, 1980; Kohlberg, 1981, 1984; Rosenberg, 1989).

Individual cognitive development can be thought of as a process of increasing abstraction, in which the mental operations people are able to perform become less concerned with the concrete aspects of objects. A higher level of developmental advancement indicates a higher ability of abstraction, going beyond one perspective in perceiving problems and coordinating different aspects and viewpoints. The more advanced cognitive skills people possess the greater the chance that their thinking will be complex and flexible.

It has been suggested that the rate at which cognitive development occurs may vary from domain to domain and it may be delayed in those which are abstract and distant from immediate, daily experience (Brainerd, 1978). For example, it takes a relatively long time to develop the skills of coordinating perspectives in the domains of interpersonal relations (Selman, 1980) and morality (Kohlberg, 1984) and even longer in the domain of politics (Rosenberg, 1989). Therefore, adults may differ in terms of the range of cognitive skills they are able to employ in more abstract domains, while some individuals never develop the highest levels of understanding posited by theories of cognitive development (Kohlberg, 1984; Rosenberg, 1989). Thus, politicians may differ with regard to the range of cognitive operations they are able to perform while interpreting political problems. The first study described here examines levels of development of political thinking among Polish high- and mid-level politicians, investigating whether politicians of disparate political opinions differ in the development of the cognitive skills they possess.

The participants in study 1 were forty-six mid- to high-level Polish politicians who either played active political roles as Members of Parliament (MPs) or as non-MPs and those representing non-parliamentary opposition within political party leadership. They were not 'front-page' leaders at the time of the research, as it was assumed that the individuals selected would be those most likely to participate in the generation of political decisions without feeling overly restricted in their ability to express themselves in a research interview, i.e., by a need to represent the party to the public. Twenty-five participants were Members of Parliament (MPs) and twenty-one were party functionaries representing seven main political parties that can be classified as post-communist, centre or right-wing. The post-communist party was represented by thirteen members of Social Democracy of the Republic of Poland (Socjaldemokracja Rzeczpospolitej Polskiej); centre parties that emerged from the former Solidarity movement were represented by eight members of the Union of Liberty (Unia Wolności) and fourteen members of the Polish Peasants Party (Polskie Stronnictwo Ludowe); the political right was represented by three members of Electoral Action 'Solidarity'(Akcja Wyborcza 'Solidarność'), four members of Movement for Poland's Defence (Ruch Obrony Polski) and four members of the Confederation of Independent Poland (Konfederacja Polski Niepodległej). The participants included seven women and thirty-nine men, whose ages ranged from twenty-three to sixty-nine. Thirty-two of the politicians had received a college education and a further fourteen had attended high school.

Participants were interviewed by means of the modified Polish version of Rosenberg's Political Thinking Interview (1989; for details see Golec, 2002a) in order to assess the level of development of the cognitive operations they were able to perform when analysing problems within the domain of politics. The interview first presented participants with a short description of the problem of 'decommunisation', a topic which has been widely discussed in Poland at the time of the interview.

Decommunisation refers to the process of removing from the political scene all people who were in power during the communist period and/or who were high-level functionaries in the then hegemonic Polish United Workers' Party (Polska Zjednoczona Partia Robotnicza). Supporters of that process saw it as a moral requirement for actual and symbolic separation of the past from the newer, more just political system. They argued that decommunisation would bring social justice and necessary compensation to the victims of the communist regime. However, opponents of decommunisation argued that the process was impossible to execute without causing further social injustice. They also claimed it was impractical as political expertise acquired under the former system was also needed in a new regime. Participants were asked whether or not decommunisation should take place in Poland and afterwards to justify their point of view. In the next step, interviewees were confronted with three different arguments and asked to comment and provide their perspective. The three arguments were constructed with increasing levels of abstraction and complexity. This procedure was used in order to encourage the participants to issue arguments at the highest level of cognitive sophistication of which they were capable. The responses were tape-recorded, transcribed and coded.

The structural aspects of political argumentation prompted by an in-depth interview were analysed by two independent scorers. There was an

84 per cent rate of agreement between their assessments. The method of qualitative analysis proposed by Rosenberg (1989; see also Golec, 2002a) was used. Participants' levels of cognitive development were assessed by documenting the cognitive operations they were able to perform in dealing with the problem of decommunisation. The expert judges analysed the level of abstraction present in the statements of the interview (differentiating description of concrete events from explaining patterns, generating general rules, explaining and relating concepts). This was assessed as the ability to generalise norms and principles regulating political behaviour (differentiating an egocentric perspective governed by individual interest from understanding the role of principles regulating functioning of complex systems), the ability to see more than one perspective on a problem, to demonstrate more than one applicable norm or principle guiding its understanding, as well as the ability to coordinate differentiated aspects in the coherent understanding of the problem (differentiating simple and one-sided perceptions from complex and multifaceted ones). Participants were classified as representing two categories: simple or complex thinking. The ability to see beyond their own perspective and one aspect of a political problem was a dividing criterion.

'Simple thinkers' showed low levels of ability to generalise and derive abstract rules from their political experience. Their decisions were guided by preferences and/or one preferred principle or value and they could not see political phenomena as complex and multifaceted. At times they were able to acknowledge that differences of opinions existed but they did not show an understanding of their nature. They were not able to transcend their own perspective and analyse different points of view in developing comprehension of political problems. 'Complex thinkers' were, at least, able to see and understand arguments beyond their stance and were able to see opposite arguments not only from their own point of view, but also within the perspective that formed the arguments. They were able to see all political positions and choices as relative, with the most advanced able to build a comprehensive system of relationships between various points of view on an issue and weigh them against each other. Complex thinkers saw the relativity of each of the perspectives and created cognitive procedures for differentiating between more and less valid points, viewing political problems with reference to multiple values and contexts. A comparison of the distribution of simple and complex thinking between politicians representing post-communist, centre and right-wing political parties was conducted (see table 5.1, which contains sample statements representative of each group).

The results indicate that there were systematic differences in the development of political thinking between participating politicians. The

Table 5.1. *Sample arguments of simple and complex thinkers against decommunisation*

Simple thinking	Complex thinking
'We cannot forget the past because it is history. We cannot destroy history. I oppose changing street names and destroying monuments because that way we destroy history and my grandchildren will not know what happened then.'	'[Decommunisation] would cause deep interference in the structure of democratic mechanisms because communists as well function within the context of democratic society and according to its rules. Decommunisation is not possible without undermining and breaking the rules of a democratic country. Besides I do not think technically it is possible, because I do not see any social movement that would be able to decommunise in an effective way without it just being a liquidation of certain threatening political groups as is done in revolutions.'
'It is a clearly political act and it is motivated by a desire for revenge but everybody has a right to be innocent before proven guilty . . . people cannot be denied a right to change their opinions and adjust to new structures.'	

political thinking of twenty-four out of forty-six (52.2 per cent) politicians was classified as simple. In other words, these politicians showed low levels of abstraction when analysing political problems. They had a tendency to simplify political phenomena analysing them with reference to only one principle or perspective. Their statements did not evidence understanding of opposing viewpoints of political problems. A further twenty-two (47.8 per cent) politicians possessed more advanced cognitive skills with six (13 per cent) of them being able to perform highly complex, systemic analyses of political problems.

Importantly, there were systematic differences in the way the levels of development of political thinking were distributed across political opinions. Among representatives of the political right, cases of complex thinking (two out of eleven; 18.2 per cent) were not as common as among representatives of the centre (fourteen out of twenty-two; 64 per cent) and of the post-communist party (five out of thirteen; 39 per cent), with simple thinking and less advanced cognitive levels dominating. Among politicians representing the political centre, cases of complex thinking were found more often than those of simple thinking. Representatives of the

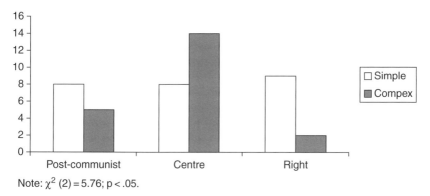

Note: χ^2 (2) = 5.76; p < .05.

Figure 5.1. Simple and complex thinking among representatives of different political opinions

political centre tended to perform systematic analyses of political problems and were able to understand different points of view and understand how the same problem may involve different norms and values.

The number of complex and simple thinkers among members of the post-communist party was more or less equal. Interestingly, among members of this and the centre parties a systematic difference was found between MPs and party representatives who did not have parliamentary experience. Almost all of the post-communist party MPs (seven out of nine) and all nine members of the centre parties were classified as possessing advanced cognitive skills, whereas party members who were not parliamentarians issued judgements classified as representative of simple thinking and less advanced cognitive skills (all four of the post-communist party members and eleven out of thirteen from the centre parties (χ^2 (2) = 94, 88; p < .001). Interestingly almost all of the post-communist parliamentarians and MPs representing the Union of Liberty centre party were involved in the Round Table talks in 1989, i.e., the negotiations that allowed for the peaceful change of political system in Poland.

The implications for democratic debate and political opinion in Poland

The results of this study indicate that the levels of development of political thinking are not equally distributed across the political spectrum. As such these results corroborate earlier findings suggesting that politicians representing different political opinions differ with respect to the cognitive operations they are able to perform when analysing and solving political problems. However, the results do not offer clear support for any of the models of the relationship between cognitive sophistication and political opinion. They confirm that in this study simple thinking and less advanced cognitive skills are found mostly among representatives of the political right and complex thinking is found predominantly among members of the political centre. However, no firm conclusions can be offered regarding the development of political thinking among representatives of the political left, i.e., the non-communist, left-wing party, as this was under-represented in the study. Although the number of results was too small for detailed consideration here, all four members of this side of the political spectrum possessed advanced cognitive skills and their interviews were classified as evidencing complex thinking and higher stages of cognitive development.

It is important to point out that politicians from the post-communist parties (there were two active at the time of the study, but only members of one participated) cannot be considered as representatives of the political left in the way it is understood within established democracies, i.e., support for greater social equality, social and cultural liberalism. The members of the post-communist party were not motivated purely by support for left-wing ideology and values of social equality. Instead for fifty years the communist regime in Poland was a hegemonic political organisation that granted power and privilege to its members. In the late 1990s members of post-communist parties represented mostly beneficiaries and supporters of the former regime and were recognised as political opportunists rather than communist or socialist ideologues (Jasiewicz, 2008). Approximately equal numbers of cases of simple and complex thinking were found among members of the post-communist party, who differed from representatives of the political right because they possessed more developmentally advanced cognitive skills and were capable of more complex political thinking. They also differed from representatives of the political centre, comprising fewer cases of complex thinking.

Interestingly, several of the representatives of the post-communist party and members of the parties representing the political centre and right participated in the Round Table talks in 1989 and importantly, those politicians (on the side of the former communist regime as well as on the side of the democratic opposition) showed higher levels of cognitive development, which suggests that political thinking develops through political experience. This interpretation is also supported by results revealing that, among centre and post-communist politicians, those who displayed complex political judgements were MPs, whereas those whose interviews were classified as demonstrating less advanced cognitive skills were party members who did not hold parliamentary positions. In other words, complex thinking, at least in this group, was related to holding a more responsible political role and therefore a more multifaceted and challenging experience.

Over half of the politicians in Study 1 were not assessed at a level of cognitive ability likely to foster constructive democratic debate and, more precisely, they had demonstrated they were incapable of going beyond their own point of view. Other analyses confirm that Polish politicians in the new regime rarely transcended their own perspective during political debates (Polkowska, 1993). They limited themselves to a presentation of their own viewpoints and arguments which supported these. The most common strategies they used in order to resolve conflict were voting and acceptance of the will of the majority. These results suggest that the cognitive preconditions for adequate participation in democratic discourse may be quite difficult to achieve, perhaps most of all in developing democracies. However, in the broader context of political changes in Poland, these results seem to suggest that in certain political conditions it may take only the cognitive sophistication of a limited number of influential politicians to peacefully change the political system, even if afterwards, this change posits a cognitive challenge for others (see Reykowski (1993) for an analysis of the context in which such a negotiated change is possible).

The first study described here examined the levels of development of cognitive operations that politicians were able to perform when analysing political problems, which amounted to an assessment of differences in the cognitive potential of representatives of different opinions in Poland ten years after the transformation of the political system. In the second study it was considered whether politicians representing different political opinions in Poland differ systematically with respect to their motivation to adequately and fully use their cognitive abilities.

Epistemic motivation among representatives of different political opinions in Poland

Epistemic motivation defines the extent to which people engage in information-processing, search for new information, look at different aspects of phenomena and examine alternative interpretations of the same data. Individual differences in this respect are determined by the need for cognitive closure (Kruglanski and Webster, 1996; Webster and Kruglanski, 1994), which in turn is defined as the degree to which one is motivated to seek out and rely on knowledge that is clear, unambiguous and stable. It describes the way in which individuals approach and reduce cognitive uncertainty, consisting of a desire to quickly formulate and firmly hold onto a clear opinion on an issue, rather than accepting confusion and ambiguity. It manifests itself as a preference for order, stability and predictability in one's surroundings, as well as decisiveness and a closed orientation to new experiences. Research suggests that the need for cognitive closure has important effects on information processing when opinions about a new issue are being formulated and also on the subsequent rigidity of these opinions (Kruglanski and Webster, 1996; Webster and Kruglanski, 1994). People characterised by a high need for closure are motivated to reduce the discomfort associated with uncertainty as fast as possible, usually by seizing on whatever cognitive cues are easily available in their social environment in order to achieve clarity. When an opinion has already been crystallised, they are motivated to protect the closure provided by this opinion. As a result, their thinking becomes rigid and their opinions are resistant to change even in the presence of contradictory information. People with a high need for closure are less likely to develop advanced cognitive skills in analysing abstract and complex phenomena and even when in possession of such skills they are not likely to use them (Kruglanski and Webster, 1996).

The second study described here compared mean levels of the need for cognitive closure between representatives of the political left, centre and right as well as among members of the post-communist party, in order to answer the question whether representatives of some political standpoints who are more open than others to new information and alternative perspectives are motivated to use the cognitive skills they possess. In this study, the broad political spectrum was covered and distinctions were drawn between the left-wing party that emerged after the systemic change in Poland in 1989 and the post-communist party.

There were ninety-two participants from the membership of eight political parties surveyed during the party congresses: a left-wing party that emerged after the collapse of the Communist system, the Union of Labour (Unia Parcy; n = 23); the two post-communist parties, Social Democracy of the Republic of Poland (Socjal-demokracja Rzeczpospolitej Polskiej) and the Democratic Party (Stronnictwo Demokratyczne), which held power during the time of the study and were united as the Democratic Left Alliance (Sojusz Lewicy Demokratycznej; n = 21); the political centre represented by the Union of Liberty (Unia Wolności) and Civic Platform (Platforma Obywatelska; n = 23); right-wing parties were represented by the League of Polish Families (Liga Polskich Rodzin), the Union of Real Politics (Unia Polityki Realnej) and Law and Justice (Prawo i Sprawiedliwość; n = 25). Participating politicians were aged eighteen to thirty-seven years old (mean age of twenty-four) and the age distribution across each political opinion was mainly uniform, although members of the Union of Real Politics were a little older (mean age of twenty-nine). There were thirty-three women and fifty-eight men among the participants (one person failed to indicate their gender). Participants had different levels of education (with no systematic differences between parties): ten persons had received vocational education and thirty-five had had a high-school education. There were twenty-four students and twenty graduates (three participants failed to provide information about their level of education).

Participants were asked to fill out a questionnaire containing the Polish version of the Need for Cognitive Closure Scale (α = .75; Webster and Kruglanski, 1994; Golec, 2001, 2002b). This consists of forty-two items assessing the five aspects of the construct: desire for predictability (e.g., 'When dining out, I like to go to places where I have been before so that I know what to expect'), preference for order and structure (e.g., 'I think that having clear rules and order at work is essential for success'), discomfort with ambiguity (e.g., 'I feel uncomfortable when I don't understand the reason why an event occurred in my life'), decisiveness (e.g., 'When faced with a problem I usually see the one best solution very quickly'), and closed-mindedness (e.g., 'I dislike questions which could be answered in many different ways'). Participants provided their answers on a scale from 1 ('totally disagree') to 6 ('totally agree'). The higher the score the higher level of the need for closure it indicated. Differences were analysed comparing mean scores on the Need for Cognitive Closure Scale of the left-wing, post-communist, centre and right-wing political parties in Poland in 2001.

In the first stage of analysis the mean levels of need for cognitive closure were compared between members of political parties representing the same aspect of the political spectrum. This did not show any systematic differences between the parties representing the political centre (the Union of Liberty and Civic Platform), nor were there any significant differences between members of the three right-wing parties or post-communist parties. However, there were significant differences in mean levels of need for closure between members of different political opinions. The highest level of need to avoid cognitive uncertainty as well as intolerance of ambiguity was found among members of the post-communist parties (mean = 4.20), followed very closely by members of right-wing parties (mean = 4.16). The levels of need for cognitive closure in these two parties were significantly higher than the levels of need for closure found among members of the left-wing Union of Labour (mean = 3.01) and those representing the political centre (mean = 3.33) (see figure 5.2).

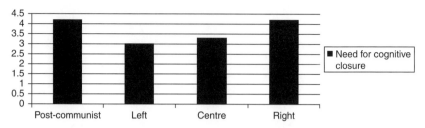

Note: F(2, 90) = 3.71; p < 0,02; post hoc Bonferonni tests revealed differences between the following groups of politicians: post-communist and left (p < .04); right and left (p < .04); post-communist and centre (p < .05); right and centre (p < .06).

Figure 5.2. Need for cognitive closure among representatives of different political opinions

Implications of epistemic motivation among representatives of different political opinions in Poland

The second study followed the line of numerous studies exploring the differences in epistemic motivations between representatives of different political opinions. A large body of work, thoroughly examined in a seminal review by Jost *et al.* (2003a), suggests that the need for cognitive closure (and other associated variables, such as intolerance of ambiguity, uncertainty avoidance, low cognitive complexity and closed-mindedness) is reliably associated with conservative political beliefs. In the context of Western democracies this usually means that motivated cognitive simplicity is associated with support for the political right (see also Chirumbolo, 2002; Golec, 2001, 2002a, 2002b; Jost, Kruglanski and Simon, 1999; Kemmelmeier, 1997; Kossowska and van Hiel, 2003). The question why motivated closed-mindedness and cognitive simplicity are associated with political conservatism is not easy to answer; however, some insights are provided by studies conducted in political contexts that differ from established Western democracies.

There are at least two ways in which political conservatism can be understood. One of the possible explanations emphasises the content of conservative ideology. From this perspective political conservatism can be seen as a coherent ideology cherishing three types of principles: civic and economic freedom, traditional, national and religious values in state policy as well as law and order in social life. Jost *et al.* (2003a) define political conservatism more broadly as an ideology that resists change and emphasises the importance of hierarchical social order. An alternative understanding of political conservatism emphasises its social and psychological functions. Within this perspective, political conservatism can be seen as support for the known, traditional status quo whatever the social and economic arrangements that constitute it. Thus, at a given time in a given society, a conservative outlook may emphasise the merits of the status quo and endorse the prevailing distribution of power, wealth and social standing. According to this definition any set of political beliefs may be conservative provided that it fulfils the function of protecting the familiar and secure status quo (Golec, 2002b).

Results from the second study described here and others in the Polish political context (Golec, 2002b; Kossowska and van Hiel, 2003) offer opportunities to gain an insight into the nature of the relationship between the need for cognitive closure and political conservatism. In the context of Western democracies, political beliefs supporting conservative ideology and arguing for the value of a stable and hierarchical social order are at the same time supporting the status quo. However, in Poland, for historical reasons, the particular content of beliefs protecting traditions is somewhat different. At the time when this study was conducted, conservatives defending the status quo were represented by members of post-communist parties, whereas the ideological conservatives promoting nationalism and supporting social hierarchy and the market economy were represented by the right-wing parties that emerged after communism collapsed (Golec, 2002b; see also Fleishman, 1988). High levels of need for cognitive closure were found among members of both of these parties but not among representatives of centre parties nor members of the new Union of Labour socialist party that emerged after systemic change in 1989. Thus, cognitive conservatives expressed political opinions that differed substantially from the particular values and vision of social order they would be expected to endorse. They chose these options either because of sentiment for the old social arrangements and opposition to the new ones or because of support for an ideology promoting social hierarchy and social order. As a consequence, and somewhat paradoxically, people of similar cognitive characteristics ended up on opposite sides of the political spectrum.

According to Jost et al. (2003b), relationships between the need for closure and political beliefs other than conservative ones are rare and constitute exceptions that prove the more general rule that the need for closure should be associated with whatever beliefs support a hierarchical social order combined with minimal potential for change. In response to Jost et al. (2003a), Greenberg and Jonas (2003) argued that different political beliefs might be driven by the same cognitive motivation. Our results suggest that the positions offered by Jost et al. (2003a) and Greenberg and Jonas (2003) are not mutually exclusive. Social beliefs that are quite different in content may attract cognitive conservatives because they share similar formal characteristics. For example, people high in need for closure were found to be attracted to worldviews in which values are understood as absolute rather than relative even if the particular content of the values they supported was strikingly different (e.g., Christian morality vs scientific rationality) (Golec de Zavala and van Bergh, 2007). The results presented here suggest that cognitive conservatism is related to preference for what is cognitively easier to comprehend either because it is already known (as in the case of post-communist party politicians) or because it proposes a simpler social structure and unquestioned social norms (as in the case of right-wing politicians).

Cognitive skills in a political context

The systemic change in Poland provided an opportunity to study how political representatives deal with novelty, cognitive uncertainty and the workings of a democratic political system that sets high requirements for cognitive functioning. The studies described here found that representatives of different political opinions differed with respect to their cognitive predispositions to adequately function within this system and in their motivation to adjust to a new political reality. Importantly, the results from members of political parties representing the whole political spectrum (including left-wing, post-communist, centre and right-wing parties) also suggest that the relationship between cognitive functioning and political preference may look quite different when the cognitive skills which politicians possess are examined, than when one looks at differences in their epistemic motivation. Thus, the differences between the models of this relationship (e.g., Altemeyer, 1996; Rokeach, 1960; Sidanius, 1988) may be due, at least in part, to the fact that cognitive ability and epistemic motivation are usually not differentiated when cognitive functioning is analysed. In order to deal adequately with the requirements of a democratic political system, both advanced cognitive skills and a motivation to use them are needed. They are, however, not equally distributed across the political continuum.

Politicians differ with respect to the range and advancement of cognitive operations they are able to perform when dealing with abstract problems. The results of the first study described in this chapter indicate that politicians representing the political right, whether they are MPs or not, possess less advanced cognitive skills. The majority are not able to see beyond their own perspective on political problems or beyond one value or norm that the problems involve. In addition, representatives of this political opinion are not motivated to engage in comprehensive knowledge gathering as indicated by results from the second study. They tend to avoid cognitive uncertainty and simplify ambiguous, complex problems.

On the other hand politicians representing the political centre and left, as well as post-communist politicians (MPs rather than non-parliamentarians) possess advanced cognitive skills. They are able to see and appreciate alternative ways of understanding the same political problem and some of them are able to coordinate different perspectives on that problem into a comprehensive understanding. In other words, cognitive skills important for effective political communication are found mostly among the politicians representing the political centre, left and post-communist parties. In addition, those from the centre and left are motivated to analyse political problems thoroughly and do not avoid ambiguities and cognitive uncertainty. Interestingly, members of the post-communist party are characterised by a large cognitive potential but low motivation to use it. They exhibit the highest need for closure which manifests itself through low motivation to engage in detailed information processing, low levels of openness to new experience, a high need for order and structure and a high intolerance of unpredictability and cognitive uncertainty.

Thus, the results of the studies presented here suggest that there are two types of cognitive conservatism and simple cognitive style associated with different political opinions. One is related to a limited range of cognitive skills and additionally the motivation to stop cognitive processing as soon as possible by seizing on the first solution to a problem regardless of its quality. This is the cognitive conservatism of the political right in Poland. Another type of conservatism is encountered among beneficiaries of the former communist system. They possess quite advanced cognitive skills but they are motivated to hold on to their perspective and oppose alternative points of view which embrace change and innovation.

The cognitive simplicity of the political right

The data presented here confirm that simple political thinking is mostly characteristic of politicians representing the political right wing in Poland. These politicians have less advanced cognitive skills and less motivation to see political problems as complex. They seem both unable and unwilling to consider opposite points of view when issuing political judgements. Similar results are reported by studies of the integrative complexity of political reasoning in different political contexts. Integrative complexity is a formal characteristic of the knowledge structures people use to make sense of the world, which takes into account 'differentiation' and 'integration'. Differentiation refers to the degree to which individuals are able to simultaneously analyse many independent dimensions or aspects of a problem, while integration refers to the degree to which individuals perceive conceptual connections among these dimensions. Integrative complexity of political judgement is likely to be shaped by available cognitive skills and motivation to use them (but it does not differentiate between the two). Empirical results indicate low integrative complexity of political thinking among supporters of the political right in the United States of America and in the United Kingdom (Gruenfeld, 1995, Tetlock, 1983, 1984).

Studies of epistemic motivation and political preference confirm that supporters of the political right are motivated to avoid cognitive uncertainty and complex information-processing. They prefer clear, simple and unambiguous situations, a familiar and predictable environment, avoiding change and tending to hold on to their opinions despite contradictory information. These tendencies were found among supporters of conservative parties in established Western democracies, e.g., Germany (Kemmelmeier, 1997) and the USA (Jost *et al.*, 1999), as well as among politicians representing right-wing parties in post-communist countries (Golec, 2002b).

Why do right-wing parties appeal to people who possess less advanced cognitive abilities and who are motivated by a high need for cognitive closure? Perhaps the vision of political reality these parties propose is adequately uncomplicated for people whose cognitive abilities are limited and it is sufficiently unambiguous and clear to attract people who are motivated to avoid cognitive uncertainty. The political programmes of parties representing the right wing of the political spectrum in Poland advocate a stable and hierarchical state, able to protect the social order and execute severe laws against insubordination and misconduct. They suggest that legal rules and political choices should be grounded in absolute authority, a source of unquestionable guidance (e.g., God, tradition, custom). In the presence of such guidance, independent 'bottom up' information-processing in problematic situations seems unnecessary, as prescriptions for desirable opinions and behaviour are given in a 'top down' mode, despite the particular features of each situation. The world proposed by the vision of the political right is simple, predictable and promises that uncertainty and chaos will be reduced to a minimum. In addition, Polish political parties define their identities through opposition to something: e.g., communism, European integration, cultural liberalism, etc. Thus, they propose a reality defined by dualistic divisions which are easy to understand, clear-cut and definite. This sort of environment provides easy closure, does not require advanced cognitive skills or thorough information-processing, yet at the same time limits cognitive challenge and development.

The motivated closed-mindedness of post-communist politicians

Our results show that members of the post-communist parties, although proposing a very different social order from members of right-wing parties and despite their larger cognitive potential, were motivated by a high need for cognitive closure. In their political rhetoric and political programme, the post-communist parties were closer to the political centre than to the left, arguing for a market economy and European integration. More importantly, their most prominent members were functionaries and beneficiaries of the communist regime in Poland before 1989. They were likely to be drawn to represent this party not by its ideological appeal (which it lost in the late 1970s) but by political opportunism (e.g., see Jasiewicz, 2008; Reykowski, 1993).

Why did the post-communist party in a new political system gather politicians with a high need for cognitive closure? One of the defining features of the need for closure is opposition to cognitive uncertainty and novelty. The post-communist parties alliance gave a sense of continuity to people who found accepting systemic change difficult. Perhaps the structure of this organisation also bore characteristics reminiscent of the former system, e.g., high levels of group cohesion, unanimity and hierarchy and in this way the post-communist parties might have represented a connection to the familiar status quo of social organisation before the systemic change. Such an organisation might have also offered a similar unequivocal sense of authority that is found in parties representing the political right. The possible explanations outlined here require further exploration and analyses that the data presented here do not allow.

Methodological limitations

There are several methodological shortcomings in the present studies that need to be acknowledged. These suggest that these analyses should be treated as a proposition and a starting point for a future systematic research programme rather than the results of a programme based on unequivocal evidence. Firstly, cognitive skills and individual levels of need for cognitive closure were analysed among different participants; thus, it cannot be concluded that the same post-communist politicians who possess advanced cognitive skills also have low levels of motivation to use them. Conclusions are made about average tendencies among representatives of different political opinions, but it is worth noting that different parties were classified as representing the political centre and right in both studies, mostly as a result of political changes and fluctuations at the time the research was conducted and reflecting rapid changes on the Polish political scene in the late 1990s.

In addition, two of the three right-wing parties in the first study comprised non-parliamentarians and members of the political opposition at the time the study was conducted. This might have influenced the results as significant differences between parliamentarians and non-parliamentarians were found. Results of earlier studies also indicate that the political judgement of representatives from the political opposition shows less integrative complexity than the political thinking of representatives of governing parties (Tetlock, 1981). However, in the first study the difference in cognitive skill levels between members of governing and opposition parties was not significant (see also Golec, 2002a).

In summary, the present results obtained in two samples of Polish politicians suggest that lower cognitive sophistication and higher cognitive conservatism can be found among members of the political right wing, whilst among post-communist politicians – who represent a 'catch-all' populist and opportunist approach towards politics – higher levels of cognitive conservatism are also evident. The cognitive functioning of these politicians is related to a narrow perspective on political problems, a tendency to hold on to an opinion despite changing conditions and information and a competitive attitude towards political adversaries. Such cognitive functioning impairs effective democratic discourse.

References

Adorno, T., Frenkel-Brunswik, H., Levinson, D. and Sanford, N. (1950). *The Authoritarian Personality*. New York: Harper and Row Publishers.

Altemeyer, R. (1996). *The Authoritarian Specter*. Cambridge, Mass.: Harvard University Press.

Brainerd, C. J. (1978) *Piaget's Theory of Intelligence*. Englewood Cliffs, N.J.: Prentice Hall.

Chirumbolo, A. (2002). The relationship between need for closure and political orientation: the mediating role of authoritarianism. *Personality and Individual Differences*, 32, 603–10.

Durrheim, K. (1997). Theoretical conundrum: the politics and science of theorizing authoritarian cognition. *Political Psychology*, 8, 625–47.

Eysenck, H. J. (1954). *The Psychology of Politics*. London: Routledge and Kegan Paul.

Fleishman, J. A. (1988). Attitude organization in the general public: evidence for a bidimensional structure. *Social Forces*, 67, 159–84.

Golec, A. (2001). Konserwatyzm polityczny a potrzeba poznawczego domknięcia w badaniach polskich. *Studia Psychologiczne*, 1, 423–58.

(2002a). Cognitive skills as predictor of attitudes toward political conflict: a study of Polish politicians. *Political Psychology*, 4, 731–59.

(2002b). Need for cognitive closure and political conservatism: studies on the nature of the relationship. *Polish Psychological Bulletin*, 4, 5–13.

Golec de Zavala, A. and van Bergh, A. (2007). Need for cognitive closure and conservative political beliefs: differential mediation by personal worldviews. *Political Psychology*, 28, 587–609.

Greenberg, J. and Jonas, E. (2003). Psychological motives and political orientation – the Left, the Right, and the Rigid: comments on Jost et al. (2003). *Psychological Bulletin*, 129, 376–82.

Gruenfeld, D. H. (1995). Status ideology, and integrative ideology on the US Supreme Court: rethinking the politics of political decision making. *Journal of Personality and Social Psychology*, 68, 5–20.

Habermas, J. (1984). *The Theory of Communicative Action*, vol. I: *Reason and the Rationalization of Society*. London: Heinemann.

Jasiewicz, K. (2008). The (not always sweet) uses of opportunism: post-communist political parties in Poland. *Communist and Post Communist Studies*, 41, 421–42.

Jost, J. T., Glaser, J., Kruglanski, A. W. and Sulloway, F. (2003a). Political conservatism as motivated social cognition. *Psychological Bulletin*, 129, 339–75.

(2003b). Exceptions that prove the rule: using a theory of motivated social cognition to account for ideological incongruities and political anomalies. *Psychological Bulletin*, 129, 383–93.

Jost, J., Kruglanski A. and Simon L. (1999). Effects of epistemic motivation on conservatism, intolerance, and other system justifying attitudes. In L. Thompson, D. Messick and M. Levine (eds.), *Shared Cognition in Organizations: The Management of Knowledge* (pp. 91–116). Mahwah, N.J.: Erlbaum.

Kemmelmeier, M. (1997). Need for closure and political orientation among German university students. *Journal of Social Psychology*, 137, 787–9.

Kohlberg, L. (1981). *Essays on Moral Development*, vol. I: *The Philosophy of Moral Development*. San Francisco: Harper and Row Publishers.

(1984) *Essays on Moral Development*, vol. II: *The Psychology of Moral Development*. San Francisco: Harper and Row Publishers.

Kossowska, M. and van Hiel, A. (2003). The relationship between need for closure and conservatism in Western and Eastern Europe. *Political Psychology*, 24, 501–18.

Kruglanski, A. W. and Webster, D. (1996). Motivated closing of the mind: 'seizing' and 'freezing'. *Psychological Review*, 103, 263–83.

Lipset, S. (1960). *Political Man: The Social Bases of Politics*. Garden City, N.Y.: Doubleday.

McCrae, R. (1996). Social consequences of experiential openness. *Psychological Bulletin*, 120, 323–37.

McFarland, S. G., Ageyev, V. S. and Abalakina-Paap, M. A. (1992). Authoritarianism in the former Soviet Union. *Journal of Personality and Social Psychology*, 63, 1004–10.

Neuberg, S. L., and Newsom J. T. (1993). Personal need for structure: individual differences in the desire for simple structure. *Journal of Personality and Social Psychology*, 65, 113–31.

Polkowska, A. (1993). The process of coordinating viewpoints in a debate of the Sejm commission. *Polish Psychological Bulletin*, 24, 135–50.

Pruitt, D. G. and Carnevale, P. (1982). The development of integrative agreements. In P. Derlega and J. Grzelak (eds.), *Cooperative and Helping Behavior: Theories and Research* (pp. 151–81). New York: Academic Press.

Reykowski, J. (1993). Resolving large-scale political conflict: The case of the round table negotiations in Poland. In S. Worchel and J. Simpson (eds.), *Conflict Between People and Groups: Causes, Processes, and Resolutions* (pp. 214–32). Chicago: Nelson-Hall.

Riemann, R., Grubich, C., Hempel, S., Mergl S. and Richter, M. (1993). Personality and attitudes towards current political topics. *Personality and Individual Differences*, 15, 313–21.

Rokeach, M. (1960). *The Open and the Closed Mind*. New York: Basic Books.

Rosenberg, S. W. (1989). *Reason, Ideology and Politics*. Princeton University Press.

Selman, R. (1980). The growth of interpersonal understanding. *Developmental and Clinical Analyses*. New York: Academic Press.

Sidanius, J. (1988). Political sophistication and political deviance: a structural equation examination of context theory. *Journal of Personality and Social Psychology*, 55, 37–51.

Sidanius, J. and Lau, R. R. (1989). Political sophistication and political deviance: a matter of context. *Political Psychology*, 10, 85–109.

Stone, W. F. (1980). The myth of left-wing authoritarianism. *Political Psychology*, 2, 3–19.

Tetlock, P. E. (1981) Pre- to post-election shifts in presidential rhetoric: impression management or cognitive adjustment? *Journal of Personality and Social Psychology*, 41, 207–13.

   (1983). Cognitive style and political ideology. *Journal of Personality and Social Psychology*, 45, 118–26.

   (1984). Cognitive style and political ideology in the British House of Commons. *Journal of Personality and Social Psychology*, 46, 365–75.

   (1986a). Integrative complexity of policy reasoning. In S. Perloff and S. Kraus (eds.), *Mass Media and Politics* (pp. 267–89). Beverly Hills: Sage.

   (1986b). A value pluralism model of ideological reasoning. *Journal of Personality and Social Psychology*, 50, 819–27.

Van Hiel, A. and Mervielde, I. (1996). Personality and current political beliefs. *Psychologica Belgica*, 36, 221–26.

Webster, D. M. and Kruglanski, A. W. (1994). Individual differences in need for cognitive closure. *Journal of Personality and Social Psychology*, 67, 1049–62.

6 Political leadership and its development

Jean Hartley

Introduction: are politicians leaders?

The literature about political leadership is relatively sparse, and somewhat disparate, across psychology, sociology and political science, with relatively few studies taking an integrative approach (Hartley and Benington, 2011; Morrell and Hartley, 2006). In that sense, not much has changed since the comment by one of the founders of the leadership field, Stogdill, who noted: 'Leadership in various segments of the population (students, military personnel and businessmen) [has] been heavily researched while others (politicians, labour leaders, and criminal leaders) have been relatively neglected' (quoted in Blondel, 1987, p. 1). In the generic leadership literature, charismatic and highly visible leaders, such as J. F. Kennedy, Thatcher or Mandela, are widely quoted as examples of leadership, but only rarely is the political, policy and public context of their work acknowledged (though see Burns, 1978; Heifetz, 1994; Tucker, 1995). Instead, they are often treated as examples of typical – if somewhat heroic – leadership and the distinctiveness of their political leadership occluded. On the other hand, the disciplines concerned with politicians, such as political science and public administration, have neglected political leadership in part with their greater focus on institutions and regimes, and also because the traditional view was that politicians (national and local) make policy while public servants executed that policy, leaving little room for leadership (Hartley, 2010a; Behn, 1998). For politicians, leadership, other than by very senior figures such as prime ministers and presidents, was not countenanced because their work was mandated by their political party, their manifesto and the electorate. Leadership development was also irrelevant because performance would be judged at the ballot box, and in the interim, at the despatch box.

That situation has changed quite substantially, at least in the UK, from the early 1990s. The worldwide interest in public sector reform (Pollitt and Bouckaert, 2004) has been accompanied by a language more receptive to the idea of leadership. This is partly because there is now a

97

recognition that public policy and public management needs to go beyond traditional hierarchical administration and beyond 'new public management', with the more recent paradigm shift to 'networked governance' (Benington, 2000; Stoker, 2006b; Newman, 2001). Within networked governance, it is widely recognised that public sector renewal has resulted in a weakening of the hierarchically organised state in favour of more differentiated partnership arrangements that cut across the boundaries of the public, private and voluntary sectors. Additionally, governance is polycentric in that governance operates simultaneously across different tiers or levels of government (Benington and Hartley, 2009). Managing the tensions and paradoxes of these governance regimes has become the order of the day for politicians and public managers, strengthening the need for leadership (Pedersen and Hartley, 2008). Political leadership is increasingly important to deal with the complex cross-cutting problems of society (Benington and Hartley, 2009) and to work within such polycentric, networked governance arrangements.

So, if leadership is important, what is meant by that term? Grint (2000) and Hartley and Benington (2010) note that this is an essentially contested concept, with many and varied interpretations of its significance and meaning. At least three conceptualisations are relevant to considering political leadership. Hartley and Allison (2000) characterise these as approaches based on the person, the position and the process. These may coexist in practice but it is helpful to distinguish them conceptually.

Research on the person, based on the personal characteristics of leaders, is popular (see Yukl, 2006, for a review) and tends to focus on the skills and abilities, the personality, the styles of engagement and the behaviours of individual leaders. The journal *Political Psychology* includes many such analyses of presidents and other prominent political leaders. Such analyses can be insightful, but can be problematic if divorced from a contextual analysis of leadership (Hartley and Benington, 2010). Increasingly, the interest in leadership focuses on the interaction between person and context (e.g., Bryman, 1992; Grint, 2000; Hartley and Allison, 2000; Porter and McLaughlin, 2006).

Leadership sometimes refers to a formal position in an organisation or institution. For political leaders, the most senior of these roles are familiar – prime minister, or secretary of state; leader of the council, or elected mayor; president or senator. A formal role is specified in terms of constitutional arrangements and powers and/or in standing orders and rules. On this basis, certain political leaders are empowered to take decisions (to call an election; to go to war; to sign legislation) while others are not. Being in government as opposed to being in opposition provides different formal roles as well as different tasks to achieve. 'Twin-hatted' politicians may have one role in one institution and a different one at another (e.g., a French mayor who is also in parliament; a UK local politician serving on both district and county councils). Some will experience political control at local level but be in opposition on the national political stage (or vice versa). Roles matter in political leadership, though research shows that roles are also shaped by informal rules, cultures and practices (Leach, Hartley, Lowndes, Wilson and Downe, 2005).

In a democracy, the source of legitimacy for elected politicians comes from the process of free and fair elections (Stoker, 2006a), but the legitimacy to take decisions and to act on behalf of society has to be won and rewon, often on a daily basis, because the withdrawal of support (by political party colleagues or activists, by the media, by the public or by various stakeholders) can lead to the loss of power, sometimes overnight. One can think of the fall from power of Margaret Thatcher as an example of this. Thus, leadership seen as a role or formal position may appear secure and static, but in fact is underpinned by dynamic processes of legitimacy, and so this takes us into the third approach to leadership which is about the processes of influence between groups of people. Leadership requires more than simply holding a particular office, though the role itself provides authority and legitimacy to take particular actions and decisions (but these may be contested by various groups in society). Heifetz (1994) makes the point well:

I define authority as conferred power to perform a service. This definition will be useful to the practitioner of leadership as a reminder of two facts: First, authority is given and can be taken away. Second, authority is conferred as part of an exchange. Failure to meet the terms of the exchange means the risk of losing one's authority: it can be taken back or given to another who promises to fulfil the bargain. (Heifetz, 1994, p. 57)

In this approach leadership is a set of processes or dynamics occurring among and between individuals, groups and organisations, between 'leaders' and 'followers'. It is also a set of activities or processes concerned with motivating and influencing people, and shaping and achieving outcomes. Political leadership is given the task of shaping, articulating and making choices on behalf of society and the mandate comes from the population. As Wren (2007, p. 1) notes:

If concentration shifts from 'leaders' to 'leadership' ... new possibilities begin to unfold. Leadership should be understood as an influence relation among leaders and followers that facilitates the accomplishment of group or societal objectives. This shifts the focus from leaders to all members of the polity, and suggests an ongoing process of mutual influence.

Or as Burns (1978, p. 19), the seminal writer on political leadership, puts it: 'The genius of leadership lies in the manner in which leaders see and act on their own and their followers' values and motivations. Leadership, unlike naked power-wielding, is thus inseparable from followers' needs and goals.' From these three concepts or approaches to leadership, there are different insights into who exercises elected political leadership. The focus on role or position tends to emphasise senior politicians, e.g., prime ministers and secretaries of state, or at the local level as leaders of councils, cabinet members or elected mayors. However, the emphasis on leadership as an influence process means that every politician is to a greater or lesser extent a leader by virtue of their role in articulating and representing the needs and aspirations of the public and their constituency (regardless of who voted for them, they are expected to represent the whole constituency, and indeed to take account of future generations not just the current electorate). In this sense, each elected politician is a civic or community leader (Hartley, 2004). They are leaders in their electoral unit, and they contribute, as members of a ruling administration or an opposition, to the overall leadership of the government (national, devolved or local). Political leadership is inevitably not solely about individual leadership but about creating, negotiating and being part of a coalition of political support which enables parties and groups to govern.

In summary, all politicians can be regarded as leaders in that they all exercise influence and aim to mobilise support for action and decisions, while some have a larger, wider, more visible and more senior leadership role than others. This suggests that we need to turn our attention to considering the varied challenges and the associated roles of political leadership.

The arenas and contexts of political leadership

At the heart of political leadership is contest (Hartley and Benington, 2011). This is not only because different parties and politicians offer different policies and programmes to tackle societal issues and this is played out in debates and arguments in political arenas such as parliament or congress and in the media. It is also because public goals are inevitably ambiguous, contested and subject to competing values and interests between different groups within the population (Hoggett, 2006; Stoker, 2006a; Leftwich, 2004; Crick, 2000). What constitutes public value has to be subjected to continuous debate in a range of forums and in varied media (Benington and Moore, 2011).

Leadership is increasingly exercised not only inside the organisation, but also outside it, with other groups and organisations. This is somewhat

Figure 6.1. The five arenas of political leadership for local elected politicians

different at local compared to national levels. Research with local elected politicians in local government and with informed commentators (Hartley and Morgan-Thomas, 2003), draws on the framework of arenas of civic leadership, developed by Taylor (1993) and subsequently tested in research (Hartley, 2002) and in leadership development support activities (Hartley and Pinder, 2010). We added a fifth arena for most political leaders which is that of the arena of the political party. These arenas are shown in figure 6.1.

Figure 6.1 shows the arenas involving work by local politicians:
1. Shaping and supporting the development of grassroots communities;
2. Negotiating and mobilising effective partnerships with other public, private and voluntary agencies, i.e., lateral inter-organisational leadership;
3. Voicing the needs and interests of the local community in regional/ devolved, national, European and international arenas, i.e., vertical inter-organisational leadership;
4. Managing the local authority organisation and giving its services clear strategic direction;
5. Working within the political party group, both inside and outside the council, and developing political coalitions as appropriate.

The mapping of arenas for ministers in UK government is even more complex. A minister of state has a role in leading a government department in terms of developing and shaping government policy and mobilising support for policies and for relevant legislative intentions. They also have a role in parliament, in being a frontbench spokesperson, speaking at the despatch box, appearing before select committees, ensuring a base of support in the parliamentary party and so on. In addition, they have a role

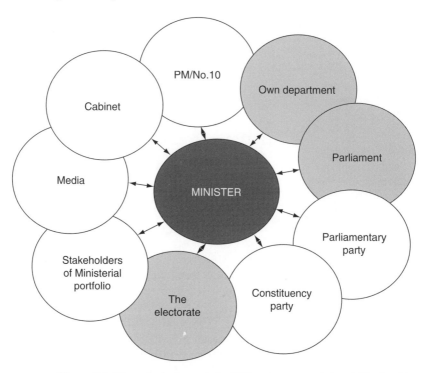

Figure 6.2. The principal arenas for UK government ministerial leadership
Note: PM/No.10 refers to the prime minister, who in the UK lives at 10
Downing Street.

in their constituency in articulating the needs of the locality and responding to problems and pressures experienced by individuals, groups and
organisations. To ignore the electoral base of their leadership would be to
imperil their future as a politician – and many ministers also comment that
being able to bridge between the worlds of Westminster and Whitehall,
with the worlds of citizens and groups in their constituency, is central to
being an effective minister. Such varied and sometimes contrasting arenas
enable the politician to think through the practical implications of policies
for democracy and public services. Unlike many other forms of leadership, political leadership at the national level involves leadership in at least
three distinct geographical locations – though in practice there are many
others too, and these are shown in figure 6.2.

Arenas are not only about physical spaces, though some (but not all)
may be geographically identifiable, such as parliament. Arenas can be
conceptualised as social processes of mutual influence between a variety

of stakeholders and the political leadership (Hartley and Benington, 2011). Arenas can be thought of as spaces and flows of people, ideas, problems, legitimacy and resources. This requires thinking about political leadership as dynamic not static, and as contested between different groups in a dialectical space of values, interests, ideas and actions. Contestation, mobilisation of support, legitimacy and consent are critical to political leadership, yet are perhaps imperfectly theorised in the orderly and somewhat rational accounts of some aspects of the workings of the 'political machine'. Simpson (2008) draws attention to these processes in his proposal that politicians are thinkers, fixers and communicators. Morrell and Hartley (2006) suggest that figurational sociology is a useful framework for thinking about individuals and networks in dynamic inter-actions involving individuals, interests and power, focusing as it does on both the individuals and the networks in which they are embedded.

As political leadership takes place in a range of different arenas, it is difficult to think of another leadership role subject to trying to exert influ-ence in so many varied and disparate settings, each with many stakeholders and topics of concern to society. Generic leadership theory, located as it often is on the shopfloor or in the boardroom, is sometimes more static in its depiction of 'followers' and locations. Senior leaders are involved to a greater extent in a wider range of arenas (compare a minister, a chair of a select committee and a backbench MP). The arenas framework is also important because it illustrates how political leadership is as much to do with informal influence with a range of stakeholders as it is with formal authority to take particular decisions. Leach *et al.* (2005) showed that effective local political leaders exercise influence through culture and infor-mal practices not just through constitutions and formal terms of reference.

The challenges of political leadership

There is little point in analysing leadership unless thought is also given to what leadership is for. The work of Heifetz (1994) is valuable for its emphasis on leadership as an active process of work to achieve outcomes. Leadership involves working with individuals, groups, communities and organisations to 'tackle tough problems'. Heifetz (1994) makes the dis-tinction between technical and adaptive leadership, based on the type of problem or challenge that the leader is attempting to address. Technical leadership may occur where the problem is fairly well understood and where there is a broadly agreed course of action. Here, leadership can be based on bringing together and energising resources and people to achieve agreed goals. However, adaptive leadership is needed where the challenge is complex and where different individuals or groups may not agree either on what the problem is or how it can be tackled. Many of the complex cross-cutting problems of contemporary society are of this type (e.g. community safety, alcohol-fuelled violence, public transport). Political leadership is particularly concerned with adaptive leadership, i.e. influencing individuals and groups to engage in difficult problem-solving, where the best way to tackle a problem may not yet be known or where views and values are contested. This requires the management of influence beyond the organisation, with a range of stakeholders and groups, in a range of different arenas and in the context, noted earlier, of polycentric governance (Hartley, 2010).

Fundamental to political leadership is developing, negotiating and sustaining a critical mass of support. Given that political leadership has the ultimate purpose to achieve outcomes in spite of diverse and pluralist interests, views, opinions and values in society, which are continually contested, then gaining and maintaining support are sine qua non. Unlike managerial leaders who are appointed to represent a particular section of society, political leaders achieve their leadership role through election not selection and their authority derives from 'the people'. Naturally, political parties are involved in selection but this is for candidates not for leaders. In addition, political leaders require the consent of the governed more overtly than managers, given that theirs is a representative role, with explicit forms of accountability and scrutiny. The initial mandate to lead comes from the ballot box but we have already noted that this is temporary and contingent because trust and the mandate to act as a representative can be withdrawn at any stage. The 2009 expenses scandal in the UK amongst national politicians has led to a dramatic loss of trust not only in individual politicians but also politicians as a class, and this has made the work of political leadership at the national level so much harder. A key job for politicians therefore is to be continually seeking to garner, mobilise and shape support, and they do this in the arenas analysed above. Coalitions are inherently unstable, and need to be maintained on a regular basis.

Beyond the need to create a mandate for action, there are a number of other tasks, outlined by Leach and Wilson (2000) and Leach et al. (2005), including developing and articulating strategic direction, pursuing leadership priorities outside the organisation; and ensuring task accomplishment. Hartley and Benington (2011), drawing on Dewey (1927), Ruscio (2004) and Wren (2007), add the task of creating and sustaining public debate so that democracy is enacted.

Strategic thinking and action has always been a crucial part of military, political, organisational and social movement leadership. It is particularly important for political leadership given the complexity of the problems facing society. Those who are in formal political leadership positions leading a government department or a local council report having to spend considerable time and energy ensuring that they stay focused on the big picture, rather than getting caught up in micro-management and the immediate concerns of a range of stakeholders.

It can be tempting to become focused on activities inside the political institution (e.g., the government department, parliament, the town hall) but seeking to further leadership priorities outside the organisation is increasingly important in the context of polycentric 'networked governance' (Benington, 2000; Stoker, 2006b). This has led political leaders to place a greater emphasis on partnerships between the private, public and voluntary sectors as a means to plan, design and deliver services and achieve societal outcomes. The implications for political leadership are considerable – to work through influence as well as through formal authority and to work with a range of partners and stakeholders in a variety of arenas (as noted above). A further aim is to ensure policy delivery (e.g., legislation, service delivery). This is the work to be done, with and through appointed officials, to ensure that the political party manifesto is carried out, that strategic aims are accomplished, that promises are kept (or explained away) and that innovative ways of tackling complex problems are sought. Research with local political leaders (Leach *et al.*, 2005) using Version 1 of the Warwick Political Leadership Questionnaire (WPLQ) found that frontbench political leaders, compared with backbenchers, are more likely to report that the tasks of creating coalition and support within the political party and also working in partnerships were more of a challenge.

Capabilities of political leadership

This consideration of the arenas of political leadership and the challenges of political leadership suggest extraordinary complexity in roles, purposes and processes of leadership. Therefore in relation to leadership capabilities (skills, knowledge and understanding, mind-sets, competencies), the degree of 'fit' between the individual and the context may vary.

Kanungo and Sasi (1992) argue that competencies, also called capabilities, represent a wider set of abilities that enable the non-specific, non-routine, discretionary and unstructured parts of the job or role to be achieved. Boyatzis (1994) argues that competencies need to be set in the context both of role demands and the environment. This reinforces the conceptual approach presented here, which is that capabilities cannot be seen in isolation, but must be set in the context of the environment (context) and of the role demands (challenges).

Leadership development for elected politicians[1]

As noted, a number of social sciences have neglected political leadership. Until recently, this has also been mirrored in the approach to leadership development, where politicians were sceptical about what they saw as 'training' or even 'brainwashing', believing that it undermined the sovereign rights of the electorate to support a candidate of their choice (see Hartley and Pinder, 2010 for more about this background). However, over the last ten years in local government and over the last five years in central government, there has been a sea-change in approach. In local government, the argument that professional development is very valuable for such a complex role has been accepted. In central government, there is greater awareness that more can be done than thrusting a red box[2] into a minister's hands and expecting them to appear on national television the following day. Junior ministers have been receptive to and engaged in leadership development, and there has been support at higher levels as well. At both local and national levels, there is considerable interest in how political leadership can be developed more rapidly and more systematically. There is a range of leadership development activities, events and experiences to support ministers and ministerial teams, run by the National School of Government (the leadership development body for the civil service and the government of the day), by the Institute for Government and by Warwick Business School.

This section describes the development of 360-degree feedback instruments to help political leaders become more aware of their leadership qualities, and to gain feedback from others about their abilities and performance as political leaders. It focuses on the development of a 360 feedback instrument for local government political leaders, though recently a 360 development instrument for ministers has also been developed by Warwick in conjunction with the National School of Government.

360-degree feedback describes the process whereby an individual rates themselves on key capabilities or competencies and is also rated on the same capabilities by others. This process enables the individual to see themselves as others see them and to explore differences in assessments of leadership skills. It is widely seen as an effective approach to leadership

---

[1] There are a small number of ministers in the UK who are not elected, either because they have been appointed by the prime minister from the House of Lords or because of particular expertise (e.g., the 'government of all the talents' under former Prime Minister Gordon Brown). However, the numbers of such ministers is a tiny minority compared with elected politicians.

[2] A red box is the briefcase in which ministerial papers for decision and information are put by civil servants. It is a key symbol of being a UK government minister.

development (Day, 2001; Fletcher, 2007). 360-degree feedback origi-
nated in leadership development for managers, and reflects the assessments made from all around the role-holder; technically, this should be
called multi-source, multi-rater feedback (Fletcher and Baldry, 1999).
The feedback for elected members is derived from a range of sources not
only inside the organisation that they govern, but also from across the key
arenas.

360-degree feedback is only one of a number of development tools, and
its use depends on the person and the context. The organisational climate
and personal conditions must be conducive for it to be appropriate,
suitable and effective (Fletcher, 2007; Thach, 2002) and here can be
added the institutional and political climate (i.e., it would not be suitable
in periods of intense political rivalry such as during an election campaign).
Creating and using appropriate 360 feedback instruments for political
leaders – for local government and separately for ministerial roles – is a
considerable challenge. Political leaders work in the full glare of scrutiny
of their decisions (by local people, other politicians, other organisations
and the media) and also have to make decisions which are sometimes
unpopular and often contested about the allocation of resources to
achieve public value (Moore, 1995). Although political leaders do receive
a considerable amount of feedback about their behaviour and performance, much of this can be described either as hostile (since they address
difficult problems) or sycophantic (since they are in positions of power).
This can leave political leaders either feeling defensive about their competencies, or with a false sense of security, or sometimes feeling only as
good as their last achievement (Hartley and Pinder, 2010).

Development of the Warwick Political Leadership Questionnaire (WPLQ): a 360-degree instrument for local politicians

The 360-degree feedback instrument for local political leaders is based on
extensive and systematic research, and is distinctive in a number of ways,
because it focuses on political not generic leadership, it uses raters from
outside the organisation across a range of arenas and is not limited to
internal organisational ratings and because the 360 is about performance
across that set of arenas.

Elected members who agreed to participate (focal persons) are asked to
provide contact details for several feedback givers (raters) each. These are
selected, following guidance from the researchers, to cover, where appropriate, the five arenas of local political leadership. Raters are therefore
selected from: other political leaders from within the council (also called

elected members); council managers and other council staff; community representatives and constituents; partners in the public, private or voluntary sectors; representatives of other tiers of government (e.g., regional or devolved government, national government, European Union government). To try to encourage feedback from a number of different sources, and in line with the logic underpinning a 360-degree instrument, focal persons are advised to choose no more than five raters from each arena. However, some may be advised to only select some rather than all arenas depending on the range of their work as local politicians. Once raters complete the questionnaire, they return it directly back to the researchers. This is to preserve confidentiality and to encourage open and honest responses. Once the returns are analysed, a personalised report is produced for each politician, covering their own assessment of their leadership skills, contexts and challenges and those same dimensions as rated by their anonymised raters, and including some open-ended comments. Areas of strength and areas of development need are indicated, a discussion is offered on the results, and the elected member is also provided with a booklet with ideas about further leadership development (Pinder and Hartley, 2005), which is used in conjunction with coaching.

Development of the 360 instrument for local government politicians

The instrument was created from three related strands of research. Its use in leadership coaching with politicians is analysed in Hartley and Pinder (2010) but here we focus on the WPLQ's construction and properties. The 360 development is based on a bedrock of literature reviews on leadership, on political leadership, and on community and civic leadership (reported in Hartley and Allison, 2000; Hartley, 2002, 2004, 2010; Hartley and Benington, 2011). In addition, a number of semi-structured interviews (including using critical incident technique to examine both effective and less effective leadership) were carried out with political leaders, through dedicated sessions in the National Leadership Academy for councillors (a national programme for the personal, political and community leadership development of locally elected politicians). A total of 110 political leaders from sixty-five councils, across all political parties, and in both political control and opposition, participated in interviews and in group discussions about what constitutes effective and ineffective political leadership, across different arenas and with varied challenges. In addition, twenty-one informed commentators working closely with political leaders were interviewed about the skills which contribute to effective or ineffective performance. Commentators included chief executives of local government, police and health service senior managers, business leaders and community representatives.

The interviews were used to identify themes in political leadership, based on the conceptual framework of contexts, challenges and capabilities described earlier. The interviews were also used to identify and isolate items of behaviour relevant to political leadership and to form an item pool for the construction of the 360 instrument (Rust and Golombok, 1999). These were linked in a grid to the themes of context, challenges and capabilities and within capabilities to the dimensions which started to be identified from the behaviours. The item pool was narrowed down, based on duplication, ambiguity or inconsistency, using three domain-relevant experts.

An initial pilot was trialled with seventy senior political leaders in England and Wales, drawn from across political parties, all forms of political control and roles (i.e., leader/mayor; cabinet; scrutiny; regulatory committees; 'backbench' politicians). A second pilot version was trialled in four authorities, with locally elected politicians from all parties completing the questionnaire in the presence of a researcher, and providing a running commentary on any ambiguous or poor questions, which were later rephrased or removed. In total, 201 elected members, again across all parties and in varied roles, then took the self-assessment (Version 1) of the WPLQ instrument over a period of eighteen months. A series of statistical tests, including factor and reliability analyses helped to identify items from the pilot version of the instrument that were suitable for translation into 360-degree format. The item base was reduced substantially from 185 to sixty-five questions, as is usual procedure following statistical item analysis. A workshop with academics from organisational psychology, political science and from local government studies helped to probe the structure and presentation of the instrument. Version 1 of the WPLQ was also used in detailed research in five case studies of local political leadership in England and Wales and triangulated with interview data (Leach *et al.*, 2005).

The same structure of ten capabilities, five contexts and five challenges was then used to refine the instrument for use in 360-degree feedback. The final instrument drew on the psychometric analysis of the original version of the self-assessment instrument, as well as feedback from local politicians, in accordance with accepted practices (Kline, 2000; Rust and Golombok, 1999; Fletcher and Baldry, 1999). The researchers improved a number of items on this basis, leading to a revised instrument which consists of fifty-five items on ten dimensions of capability (competency), each completed on a six-point scale and with the option of 'can't say or don't know' as a response to each item. The ten capabilities, in the order

Table 6.1. *Ten capability dimensions of effective political leadership*

---

1. Public Service Values (the extent to which you make clear the public service values which underpin your work).
2. Questioning Thinking (the extent to which you challenge yourself and others in ideas and suggestions).
3. Decision Making (your effectiveness at making decisions).
4. Personal Effectiveness (your skills at dealing with others and in your own self-awareness and self-control).
5. Strategic Thinking and Action (the extent to which you think and act strategically in your work).
6. Advocacy and Representation (your skills at representing others).
7. Political Intelligence (the degree to which you show astuteness and political awareness).
8. Communication (your skills in listening and talking).
9. Organisational Mobilisation (your ability to bring about major changes in your authority).
10. Systems and Tasks (the degree to which you are able to ensure the implementation of policies and practices).

© Hartley and Fletcher

they appear on the questionnaire, are as follows: Public Service Values, Questioning Thinking, Decision Making, Personal Effectiveness, Strategic Thinking and Action, Advocacy and Representation, Political Intelligence, Communication, Organisational Mobilisation; and Systems and Task. These are shown in more detail in table 6.1.

The questionnaire also incorporates five items about the context in which political leadership takes place, and five items on the challenges or purposes of leadership. Raters are invited to add anonymous open-ended comments on three behaviours that the focal person could do more frequently and three behaviours they could exhibit less often. These are collated and presented in the feedback report, along with the results about context, challenges and capabilities.

The final pilot research for the 360 instrument was undertaken with nineteen political leaders and 241 raters. The political leaders came from all political parties and all types of council (i.e., metropolitan, unitary, London borough, county and district). There were leaders in political control and in joint administration as well as in opposition. In total, they provided 281 raters, who were contacted by the research team and provided with the raters' version of the WPLQ. The very high response rate of 86 per cent indicated that politicians had selected commentators who were committed to giving feedback. Raters found the questionnaire interesting to complete and found the questions and categories clear and understandable. The mean number of raters per politician was thirteen.

This is a high number of raters compared with many 360 instruments, indicative of the complexity of the leadership role, and the number of arenas in which political leadership operates.

The effectiveness of the WPLQ 360-degree feedback instrument

In order for the instrument to be effective in analysing and developing local political leadership, research is needed to check, firstly, that the instrument measures what it sets out to measure (i.e. that it is reliable and valid); secondly, that these dimensions are related to effective political leadership; and thirdly, that the instrument is useful to politicians in strengthening their skills in political leadership.

To check reliability and validity, the data were analysed on the basis of the ten capability dimensions, in line with the theoretical framework outlined above. Reliability checks the degree to which the instrument contains measurement error. Statistical tests were undertaken to produce a Cronbach's alpha for each capability dimension. Each was high, with the exception of one, which is fairly high (alpha values ranged from 0.86 to 0.68) and all are acceptable (Rust and Golombok, 1999). These are shown in table 6.2.

To examine construct validity (i.e., does each dimension/scale measure what it claims to measure), the researchers undertook a principal

Table 6.2. *Alpha ratings, and factor loadings (eigenvalues) for each of the ten scales of the Warwick Political Leadership 360-degree instrument*

Scale	Number of items	Cronbach's alpha	Eigenvalue for first component	Eigenvalue for second component
Public service values	7	0.825	3.452	0.931
Questioning thinking	6	0.729	2.560	0.883
Decision making	5	0.797	2.766	0.878
Personal effectiveness	6	0.815	3.126	0.998
Strategic thinking and action	4	0.832	2.673	0.695
Advocacy and representation	5	0.855	3.188	0.682
Political intelligence	5	0.814	2.805	0.854
Communication	5	0.687	2.095	0.725
Organisational mobilisation	6	0.841	3.057	0.795
Systems and tasks	6	0.824	3.210	0.887

components analysis, using orthogonal rotation (varimax). Both the statistics and the visual inspection of the scree plot indicated that each scale is based on a single factor structure (see also table 6.2 for eigenvalues). We therefore have evidence of construct validity (and further evidence of reliability) of the instrument. The next check was to see how well the data supported the idea that the instrument as a whole measures ten separate dimensions of political capability. To do this, a ten-factor solution was generated using varimax rotation, and the overall factor structure of the instrument was explored via the loadings of each item onto the expected dimensions. The evidence supports a ten-dimensional account of political leadership capability, since for seven of the ten scales (values, questioning thinking, decision making, strategic thinking, advocacy, organisation mobilisation and systems and tasks) the majority of items loaded onto the expected factor.

Items from the remaining three scales (personal effectiveness, political intelligence and communication) largely loaded onto the same factor, which suggests some overlap of capability in these dimensions. All ten dimensions are being retained in the WPLQ for several reasons. This is consistent with the theoretical approach, and also consistent with some emerging research on the difference between political and social skills in other settings (e.g., Douglas and Ammeter, 2004; Hartley and Fletcher, 2008). In addition, politicians have found the ten dimensions helpful for their leadership development (Hartley and Pinder, 2010). In personal development terms, it is valuable to differentiate between behaviours that may be quite closely related. For example, personal effectiveness, and communication skills can be understood as overlapping areas of skill, and these also relate quite closely to the notion of political intelligence, which involves exercising judgement in when to intervene, awareness of power and group dynamics and skill in organising coalitions. Although local political leaders responded to items tapping these concepts in a similar way, in a developmental setting it is appropriate to invoke these as separate dimensions of capability, since this furnishes learners with a conceptual framework that they can apply to their personal development.

Evidence on the links between WPLQ scores and effective political leadership is derived from Version 1 and consists of two data sets. First, the research by Leach *et al.* (2005) analysed the WPLQ profile of the senior leadership teams (cabinets) in five local authorities and found that the WPLQ data identified strengths and weaknesses of the cabinet similar to those obtained from interview and other case material collected by other research team members. Second, senior frontbench leaders as individuals self-reported higher levels of capability compared with backbench leaders on four dimensions of political leadership: personal effectiveness, strategic thinking and action; political intelligence and organisational mobilisation. Some capabilities seem to be sharpened through experience and practice, and this is particularly true for strategic thinking and action, as well as political intelligence (Leach *et al.*, 2005).

With senior political leaders, over and above the empirical basis for the survey, acceptability of the instrument is a pertinent consideration. Political leaders were interviewed in person or by phone about their experience of being the focal person. All political leaders reported that they found undertaking the WPLQ degree assessment to be valuable and thought-provoking, as well as providing them with ideas for further leadership development activities. Interestingly, elected members overall were more self-critical about their skills than those who rated them. This is contrary to what has been recorded in a number of situations where 360-degree feedback has been used in managerial leadership development (Fletcher and Baldry, 1999) and where the focal person is subject to a so-called 'leniency effect'. However, in contrast this research indicates that, despite their reputation for arrogance, local political leaders are more self-critical about their skills than those who know them well through working with them. This suggests that development and training may help political leaders to identify and capitalise on the skills that they possess or can strengthen. Further detailed research is needed to replicate and explore these findings.

Case study from the WPLQ 360 (by Kate Pinder and Jean Hartley)

A case study example of a political leader using the WPLQ 360 to clarify their contribution as a politician is given in Hartley and Pinder (2010) and a further example case is given here.

Carole completed the WPLQ 360 version at the end of a series of four coaching sessions, with the 360 feedback forming a fifth session. The presenting issue was one of self-perceived low performance. As the minority party leader in opposition, she was 'punching above her weight' according to local authority managers, but she personally felt that she was not operating to full capacity. It quickly became apparent that most of this was due to a family bereavement. Politicians obviously have the same human issues in life as everyone, and may find it more difficult to share such information, despite assurances of confidentiality. This is particularly the case if there is a local connection, because the politician is a local representative and may feel 'on show' even when off duty, or vulnerable to press interest if any details become public. Alternatively, it may be part of the denial of the depth of how the bereavement had affected Carole or the rapport built with the coach at the first meeting, but they agreed to continue, even though the coach noted that she felt she was operating at times at the limits of her professional capability. The coach used professional supervision and her counselling background to set goals which were steps along the way to finding some acceptance, some celebration of the person's life and some ways through the loneliness and misery that bereavement brings. There had also been loss in the politician's previous professional life, which had been cut short through a redundancy and this also formed part of working through the specific bereavement looking for positives. In addition, the politician addressed issues of making an impact as a minority senior politician, even when emotionally drained, dealing with anger and going through bereavement. Such stages are never clear and often circular, and having a coach was helpful to reinforce the normality of what often felt abnormal and extreme to the coachee, whilst retaining the public performance necessary for the political role. The 360 feedback reinforced the respect and high regard with which the coachee was viewed and ended the coaching series on an additionally high note. Having felt low in mood, she may have underestimated the regard in which people held her and rated her abilities and this may have contributed to her renewed sense of worth.

Discussion

Overall, these results provide strong and systematic empirical evidence for an instrument that measures capabilities, and sets these in the light of contexts (or arenas), and challenges for local political leaders. The initial development of the WPLQ was carried out so as to enhance acceptability to political leaders, by involving them and informed commentators in the design and piloting of the self-assessment version. This in turn contributed to the development of a 360-degree instrument, in a process that captures the different arenas within which members act. Based on these survey data, each dimension shows evidence of high reliability, and unifactorial structure, suggesting that we can be confident in the measure and the results it has produced. There is also evidence to suggest that a ten-factor solution is sensible.

The research on local political leadership has been extended to examine and develop UK national political leadership in a programme of Warwick research. The first research project, based on interviews with ministers and using informed commentators, has resulted in the Warwick Ministerial 360. This draws on the conceptual framework of contexts, challenges and capabilities, with the arenas being rather different (see figure 6.2) and with some overlap of dimensions, though some new dimensions reflect the particular contexts and challenges of ministerial leadership and the need to work closely with the civil service. This work has not yet been reported scientifically.

There is scope to extend research and application of the 360-degree feedback instruments for elected political leaders in a number of ways. First, there is the potential to examine the relationship between scores on the 360 instrument and the presumed outcomes of political leadership, such as democratic performance, organisational performance and the perceived effectiveness of political leaders by a range of stakeholders. In such a complex and multi-causal setting as democratic political leadership, there are likely to be many variables which have an impact on outcomes but some mapping through research would be helpful in teasing out key strands related to performance. Consistent with the basis for development of the instrument, higher ratings on these capability dimensions ought to be associated with improved leader effectiveness, and this might in turn enhance organisational performance. There is an urgent need to conduct further research of this type, given the assumptions about the relationship between effective local political leadership and organisational performance which underlies much of the current central government assessment of local authorities (e.g., audit and inspections). Some recent failures of local authorities have been attributed to ineffective political and managerial leadership, and the interface between them (e.g., Doncaster Council as reported by the Audit Commission, 2010).

At the national level, research which examines political leadership effectiveness could help to rebuild or reconfigure public trust in politicians through a greater appreciation of the skill and the challenges of political leadership. Trust is at a historic low, but the current trends to 'do-it-yourself' government may be misleading: 'Many recent scholars and practitioners have sought to avoid the perceived evils of leaders by championing a participationist approach to the workings of democracy, but many thoughtful observers remain unconvinced that merely gathering stakeholders together yields wise policy'(Wren, 2007, p. 1). In future research, it would be interesting to explore in more detail the perceptions of the rater sub-groups, which represent the different arenas within which political leadership is enacted. For example, do council managers who work directly with elected members have different perceptions of the leadership capabilities, contexts and challenges of local political leaders than those in other sub-groups, for example those working in partnerships? While it is reasonable to expect a relationship between overall assessment of leadership capability and organisational performance, different stakeholder group ratings may help policy-makers, practitioners and researchers to develop a more refined and detailed understanding of the links between capabilities and performance. This would be consistent with other research indicating that the absence of convergence between different raters may not be due to experimental error, or variance, but instead reflect salient differences arising from diversity in the roles of raters (Salam, Cox and Sims, 1997). It is likely that different stakeholder groups will have different perceptions of leaders' effectiveness across particular dimensions of the ten capability framework. For example, when reflecting on communication, or personal effectiveness, those groups in more frequent contact with members may have different perceptions to those groups who only meet members infrequently, or in different contexts.

There is reason to believe that some of the scales in the Warwick Political Leadership Questionnaire can be adapted or transferred into other contexts. Civic leadership and community leadership both have some degree of overlap, although important differences in terms of arena, challenge and therefore capability. Leadership through the governance of public bodies, such as non-executive members of health trusts, or of the members of police authorities, or of regeneration boards, could be examined using this conceptual framework. They are responsible for the governance of public services, with a responsibility to engage with the broader public and a range of stakeholders. Consequently they will need to share some of the values underpinning public service work, as well as be able to represent the needs of different parts of the public realm. Finally, there is also potential for learning for generic leadership theory in thinking about how to lead in the context of diverse and sometimes competing interests (Hartley and Fletcher, 2008).

Conclusions

Some observers (Wren, 2007; Ruscio, 2004; Benington and Hartley, 2009) have suggested that societies around the world face unprecedented challenges to cope with environmental, social, economic and political change and sustainability. At times of turbulence and change, ideas and practices about political leadership, and the relationship of political leadership to the electorate tends also to shift (Wren, 2007). There is an urgent need to understand political leadership, both in itself, and in relation to its role in addressing the adaptive challenges (Heifetz, 1994) society faces.

The research reported here, based both on literature reviews and on empirical research, has recognised that political leadership is both very complex and also under-theorised and under-researched. The conceptual framework offered here is based on the need to take account of the contexts (arenas), the challenges and the capabilities of political leadership. While psychology has traditionally focused on the personal qualities of leadership, this chapter argues for a multi-disciplinary approach which takes account not only of the personal qualities of individual leaders but also the situations in which political leadership aims to exert influence, and the inevitably contested and disputed nature of political leadership, due to its embedment in democratic society.

Acknowledgements

A number of researchers contributed to the conceptual framework and empirical development of the Warwick Political Leadership Questionnaire. I would like to thank John Benington, Clive Fletcher, Anita Gulati, Anna Morgan-Thomas, Kevin Morrell and Kate Pinder for ideas, research, statistical analysis and leadership development applications, which contributed to the instrument.

References

Behn, R. (1998). What right do public managers have to lead? *Public Administration Review*, 58 (3), 209–24.

Benington, J. (2000). The modernization and improvement of government and public services. *Public Money and Management* (April–June), 3–8.

Benington, J. and Hartley, J. (2009). *Whole Systems Go! Leadership across the Whole Public Service System*. London: National School of Government.

Benington, J. and Moore, J. (2011). *Public Value: Theory and Practice*. Basingstoke: Palgrave Macmillan.

Blondel, J. (1987). *Political Leadership: Towards a General Analysis*. London: Sage.

Boyatzis, R. E. (1994). Beyond competence: The choice to be a leader. *Human Resource Management Review*, 3 (1), 1–14.

(2006). Leadership competencies. In R. Burke and C. L. Cooper (eds.). *Inspiring Leaders* (pp. 119–31). London: Routledge.

Bryman, A. (1992). *Charisma and Leadership in Organizations*. London: Sage.

Burns, J. (1978). *Leadership*. New York: Harper and Row.

Crick, B. (2000). *In Defence of Politics*. 5th edn. London: Continuum.

Day, D. (2001). Leadership development: a review in context. *Leadership Quarterly*, 11, 581–613.

Dewey, J. (1927). *The Public and Its Problems*. New York: H. Holt and Co.

Douglas, C. and Ammeter, A. (2004). An examination of leader political skill and its effect on ratings of leader effectiveness. *Leadership Quarterly*, 15, 537–50.

Fletcher, C. (2007). *Appraisal, Feedback and Development: Making Performance Review Work*. 4th edn. Abingdon: Routledge.

Fletcher, C. and Baldry, C. (1999). Multi-source feedback systems: a research perspective. In C. L. Cooper and I. T. Robertson (eds.), *International Review of Industrial and Organizational Psychology*, (vol. XIV, pp. 149–93). London: John Wiley.

Grint, K. (2000). *The Arts of Leadership*. Oxford University Press.

(2005). Problems, problems, problems: the social construction of 'leadership'. *Human Relations*, 58, 1467–94.

Hartley, J. (2002). Leading communities: capabilities and cultures. *Leadership and Organizational Development Journal*, 23, 419–29. Special issue on public sector leadership.

(2004). *Civic Leadership. Briefing Paper for the Review of Public Administration in Northern Ireland*. Belfast: Northern Ireland Office.

(2010). Public sector leadership and management development. In J. Gold, R. Thorpe and A. Mumford (eds.), *Gower Handbook of Leadership and Management Development* (pp. 531–46). Farnham: Gower.

(2010). Political leadership. In S. Brookes and K. Grint (eds.), *The Public Leadership Challenge*. London: Palgrave.

Hartley, J. and Allison, M. (2000). The role of leadership in modernisation and improvement of public service. *Public Money and Management*, 20 (2), 35–40.

Hartley, J. and Benington, J. (2010). *Leadership for Healthcare*. Bristol: Policy Press.

(2011). Political leadership. In A. Bryman, B. Jackson, K. Grint and M. Uhl-Bien (eds.), *Sage Handbook of Leadership*. London: Sage.

Hartley, J. and Fletcher, C. (2008). Leadership with political awareness: leadership across diverse interests inside and outside the organization. In K. James and J. Collins (eds.), *Leadership Perspectives: Knowledge into Action* (pp. 157–70). London: Palgrave.

Hartley, J. and Morgan-Thomas, A. (2003). The development of the Warwick Political Leadership Questionnaire: conceptual framework and measurement properties. International Leadership Conference. Lancaster. December.

Hartley, J. and Pinder, K. (2010). Coaching political leaders. In J. Passmore (ed.), *Leadership in Coaching* (pp. 159–75). London: Kogan Page.

Heifetz, R. (1994). *Leadership Without Easy Answers*. Cambridge, Mass.: Harvard University Press.

Hoggett, P. (2006). Conflict, ambivalence and the contested purpose of public organizations. *Human Relations*, 59 (2), 175–94.

Kanungo, R. and Sasi, M. (1992). Managerial resourcefulness: a reconceptualisation of management skills. *Human Relations*, 45, 1311–32.

Kline, P. (2000). *Handbook of Psychological Testing*. 2nd edn. London: Routledge.

Leach, S., Hartley, J., Lowndes, V., Wilson, D. and Downe, J. (2005). *Local Political Leadership in England and Wales*. York: Joseph Rowntree Foundation.

Leach, S. and Wilson, D. (2000). *Local Political Leadership*. Bristol: Policy Press.

Leftwich, A. (2004). *What Is Politics?* Cambridge: Polity Press.

Moore, M. (1995). *Creating Public Value*. Cambridge, Mass.: Harvard University Press.

Morrell, K. and Hartley, J. (2006a). Ethics in leadership: the case of local politicians. *Local Government Studies*, 32 (1), 55–70.

(2006b). A model of political leadership. *Human Relations*, 59 (4), 483–504.

Newman, J. (2001). *Modernising Governance: New Labour, Policy and Society*. London: Sage.

Pedersen, D. and Hartley, J. (2008). The changing context of public leadership and management: implications for roles and dynamics. *International Journal of Public Sector Management*, 21 (4), 327–39.

Pinder, K. and Hartley, J. (2005). *Political Leadership Development Booklet: a Resource for Elected Members*. Coventry: Institute of Governance and Public Management.

Pollitt, C. and Bouckaert, G. (2004). *Public Management Reform: a Comparative Analysis*. Oxford University Press.

Porter, L. and McLaughlin, G. (2006). Leadership and the organizational context: like the weather? *Leadership Quarterly*, 17, 559–76.

Ruscio, K. (2004). *The Leadership Dilemma in Modern Democracy*. Cheltenham: Edward Elgar.

Rust, J. and Golombok, S. (1999). *Modern Psychometrics: the Science of Psychological Assessment*. 2nd edn. London: Routledge.

Salam, S., Cox, J. and Sims, H. (1997). In the eye of the beholder: how leadership relates to 360 degree performance ratings. *Group and Organization Management*, 22 (2), 185–209.

Simpson, J. (2008). *The Politics of Leadership*. London: Leading Edge Publications.

Stoker, G. (2006a). *Why Politics Matters: Making Democracy Work*. London: Palgrave Macmillan.

(2006b). Public value management: a new narrative for networked governance? *American Review of Public Administration*, 36 (1), 41–57.

Taylor, M. (1993). *The Four Axes of Civic Leadership*. Research paper. Local Government Centre, University of Warwick.

Thach, E. (2002). The impact of executive coaching and 360 feedback on leadership effectiveness. *Leadership and Organization Development Journal*, 23 (4), 205–14.

Tucker, R. (1995). *Politics as Leadership*. Columbia: University of Missouri Press.

Wren, T. (2007). *Inventing Leadership: The Challenge of Democracy*. Cheltenham: Edward Elgar.

Yukl, G. (2006). *Leadership in Organizations*. 6th edn. Upper Saddle River, N.J.: Pearson Prentice Hall.

Part III

Coping with pressure?

7   Should the job of national politician carry a government health warning? The impact of psychological strain on politicians

Ashley Weinberg

Psychological health remains a fascinating area for research, not least because it integrates so many expressions of the natural human state: emotions, thoughts, actions and well-being. On the side of the equation which is ill-health, these states are laced with the potential for unpredictable and undesirable outcomes which have come to be labelled and categorised, although not always with clarity or helpful results. In this chapter, psychological strain will refer to the experience of symptoms of poor psychological health and its impact on serving national politicians. Chronicled here are a number of quantitative studies conducted by the author mainly in the UK between 1992 and 2010.

It is thought that one in five people will experience some form of psychological disorder during their working life and that similar difficulties are likely to affect one in three of us at some stage (Weinberg, Sutherland and Cooper, 2010). Naturally this includes elected representatives, who are relied upon to take key decisions which affect the functioning of the nation. In the case of a doctor who makes important choices at the level of the individual, one would not normally consider asking about his or her health, as this is often taken for granted; additionally if they went on sick leave, a replacement is usually available. However, in the case of a national politician, constituents are equally unlikely to be preoccupied with their representative's health, yet there is little prospect of an immediate substitute in the event of their becoming ill. Furthermore, a politician is less willing to admit to that aspect of ill-health characterised by psychological strain where it might be considered likely to jeopardise their position, especially given the existence of high levels of ambition within this occupational group (Weinberg, Cooper and Weinberg, 1999). In this circumstance, the politician is apt to carry on in the job for fear of signalling weaknesses to their colleagues and rivals – the results of this scenario for the individual job-holder or the democratic process are hard to estimate, but the financial cost of presenteeism (working while ill) is thought to be considerably more than that of absenteeism (Sainsbury Centre for Mental Health, 2007). The Member of Parliament's (MP) role is both cognitively and socially demanding and routinely requires assimilation of large quantities of information, considerable analytical ability, finely tuned judgements as well as effective communication skills for dealing with political allies and opponents, party members, constituents and the media. Notwithstanding the politician's likely personal resilience and track record of motivation and conviction, the potential for overload is clear. For a politician experiencing symptoms of strain, the threat to their health posed by further exacerbating their symptoms in such a challenging role may be significant.

Psychological strain incorporates both mental and physical outcomes, whereby the former can include low self-worth, lacking confidence, feeling unhappy, anxiety, difficulties in facing challenges such as problem-solving, and the latter may feature poor sleep, loss of appetite, psychosomatic pains, unaccountable tiredness and a decrease in sexual interest, aside from maladaptive coping strategies such as increased use of alcohol and drugs. In distinguishing strain from a recognised psychological disorder, it is important to take note of the frequency, duration and severity of such negative symptoms, as well as the degree of impairment an individual may suffer in their daily functioning. In this case, the phenomenon popularly known as 'stress' tends to refer to more short-lived experiences, possibly linked to particular problems in an individual's life and the symptoms of which may dissipate or instead progress into a more profound episode of ill-health.

The need for politicians, like doctors and others enacting weighty public duties, to identify appropriate coping mechanisms is of obvious importance, not simply for their well-being and job performance, but also for withstanding the public and media focus and the impact this can have on their careers. The alleged finding by a bogus TV crew in 2008 of widespread cocaine use among a sample of Italian politicians, as evidenced from swabs taken during the application of film make-up, showed both the lengths to which the media will go to entrap public figures and the potential for maladaptive strategies for coping to be relatively commonplace (*Guardian*, 2006). The confirmation of cocaine use by junior doctors in a bona fide research study (Birch, Aston and Kamali, 1998) suggests that this is one strategy used by some carrying out well-paid and highly pressurised jobs, but it also undermines confidence in the ability of the job-holders to carry out their work effectively or safely.

For extremely negative political outcomes, examples from international politics and history abound, ranging from ill-conceived declarations of war to widespread neglect leading to countrywide famine and disease. It is not uncommon for such instances to have occurred when the psychological strain on key politicians involved has been considerable. British Prime Minister Anthony Eden and United States President John F. Kennedy initiated infamous and ill-fated military adventures, in Egypt (Suez Canal crisis) and Cuba (Bay of Pigs invasion) respectively while relying on quantities of mind-altering drugs prescribed to alleviate physical health disorders, which are thought to have substantially affected their powers of political judgement (Freeman, 1991). Similarly former Russian President Boris Yeltsin attracted media attention for his unpredictability, poor health and enjoyment of alcohol, making headlines in 1998 for dismissing his entire government on two occasions, as well as remaining asleep on his plane and keeping the Irish prime minister waiting for some hours.

Aside from the influence of substances as described above, psychological strain has manifested itself in many other ways which may be attributed to sources of pressure ranging from major life events to ongoing work-related stressors. The incidence of depression is widespread in the general population and unsurprisingly affects politicians too, whether those experiencing distress following bereavement or simply struggling to cope with the everyday rigours of national political office. The Norwegian prime minister, Kjell Magne Bondevik, broke new ground in admitting to his depressive illness, standing aside for a few weeks in order to receive treatment in 1998. His openness ran counter to the attitude of many politicians, but was rewarded with a show of public support at the time of his re-election in 2000. Such frankness is unusual and there are many other instances in which one can only wonder at the role of psychological pressures in the thoughts and actions of national politicians, for example, the combination of marital relationship difficulties and intense job demands faced by former US President Bill Clinton during one week in August, 1998. Within twenty-four hours of courtroom testimony from Monica Lewinsky which could have led to his impeachment for perjury, he was awoken at 5.30 a.m. to be told of embassy bombings in East Africa which had killed 263 people – within two weeks he had authorised American planes to attack targets in Afghanistan and the Sudan. The implications of these personal and public events for the psychological health of the US leader are likely to have been considerable, as indeed they proved on the ground.

Such examples clearly feature those in leadership positions which, it should be noted most national politicians do not attain. One might imagine that medical and psychological advice is 'on tap' for such figures, but for representatives who do not aspire or succeed to higher office, help is less consistently available. For UK MPs there is occupational health provision on-site at the long-established Houses of Parliament, but such a service had not even been considered for the opening of the new Scottish Parliament in 1999. Given the consistent finding that one-fifth or more of

UK politicians report mental health difficulties, and that one-third fear stigma and discrimination resulting from public disclosure of such an illness (Royal College of Psychiatrists, 2008), greater consideration is needed to help politicians at all levels with such challenges. Indeed the UK law bars an individual from standing for national political office if they have previously been sectioned under the mental health legislation for more than six months – no such preclusion faces those with a history of severe physical illness.

As for the potential impact of political errors and their relationship with psychological health, there are two factors which should be considered. Firstly, it is anticipated that the process of consensus politics which pertains in many democratic systems generally prevents the taking of extreme decisions by an individual leader suffering poor health, notwithstanding the examples already presented. Secondly, if such a step were taken by an elected representative outside of high office, what would the consequences be, given their relative lack of power? A potentially lesser impact is logical to deduce, but the issue of a politician struggling to fulfil the duties for which they were elected remains. As head of a government department or as a backbench MP representing a locality, the impact of poor psychological health is likely to be seen in terms of poor communication, increased strain on working relationships, potentially erratic or destructive behaviours as well as low team morale and a suboptimal working climate. Such negative outcomes are not confined to the individual politician, but permeate the local political organisation and possibly the electorate too. Whether one is concerned about politicians as role models for workplace behaviour or not, the efficacy of a political system could be damaged. As stated in the introductory chapter of this book, this should not be taken as a reason to be intolerant of politicians experiencing strain, but a reason instead to be aware and prepared to provide support as appropriate. In other words, the mental health of politicians, is of concern to the electorate in a way which need not compromise confidentiality, but instead ensures that safeguards for this group of public employees are in place and also effective. The contrasting examples reported above from the UK and Norway are testament to both what is feared and what can be achieved.

The 'House of Stress'?

In the early 1990s, the UK parliament established a select committee chaired by Sir Michael Jopling to gather evidence about the functioning of the elected House of Commons. The focus was primarily on the timing of debates, called 'sitting hours', the spread of MPs' workload throughout a seven-day working week and the concentration of parliamentary activity at certain times of the year. Interestingly the existing pattern of work had been agreed in the nineteenth century during an era when there were no phones, cars or planes and when all MPs were men and tended to have other jobs in the financial centre of London, to which they would attend first, before coming to the House of Commons for afternoon debates. In other words, the modern working hours of the UK parliament towards the end of the twentieth century were rooted in the traditions of Victorian England! It is fair to say that the United Kingdom is proud of many of its traditions, including its parliament, which at Westminster dates back to 1264, but there are times when some of these have become a handicap to progress. The impetus for scrutiny of working practices came from recognition of numerous extra demands placed on the elected representatives in the ten to fifteen years preceding 1990. These amounted to an increased volume of legislation – particularly in relation to the European Union – the introduction of select committees to gather evidence on wide-ranging topics from the railways to abortion, and from nuclear power to overseas development, as well as a dramatic rise in work related to politicians' constituencies. The concentration of parliamentary debates between Monday and Friday left only the weekend for MPs to see their constituents, unless they were within travelling distance of London. Naturally for MPs who returned to their constituencies this clashed with time for their families and friends, unless they too had relocated to the capital, thus creating an unavoidable conflict of personal and professional roles. As the Jopling Committee gathered evidence, it became abundantly clear that the UK's elected politicians were struggling to a greater or lesser extent to cope with the pressures of the job, particularly the long working hours, as these spilled over into non-work life, meaning reduced time for their partners and children. One MP summed up the all-consuming nature of the job:

The unceasing delivery of boxes packed with papers that have to be read; the endless meetings and committees in Whitehall [civil service offices] and Westminster [parliament]; a long list of unadvertised engagements, lunches and dinners, the very dubious joys of official travel; seeing off, sometimes daily, the hostile opinions of opponents (not only to be found on the official opposition benches) and the press; the entirely false respite of the weekend, when angry constituents need to be mollified; the calls for television and radio interviews at ridiculous hours, and the chief whip [political party organiser within parliament] commanding presence for some obstreperous backbench party committee and crucial votes at the end of a long, long day. (*The Times*, 23 December 1992)

Prominent cabinet-level politicians spoke of a 'trail of broken marriages, ruined health and exhausted irrationality' (Jopling Committee Report, 1992) which resulted in a situation where 'outside bodies usually know far more about impending legislation' than those who were supposed to debate it. It was at this time that the author began investigating the psychological strain experienced by MPs.

The decision to televise UK parliamentary proceedings served to further sharpen MPs' awareness of their image and behaviour as conveyed to the watching public. After the initial investigations into the workload demands on the UK's national politicians and a change of government in 1997, the Modernisation Committee of the elected House of Commons took responsibility for improving the functioning of the elected chamber. A number of reforms were trialled, ranging from the more obvious, such as proper induction processes, to the less certain task of scheduling what constitutes the best arrangements of politicians' working hours. Giving advance notice of debates to permit MPs to organise their work was agreed early on, as was the freeing up of a limited number of Fridays for MPs to return to their constituencies and have more time to spend with their family and friends at the weekend. However the start times for parliamentary debates at 2 p.m., a tradition dating back over 100 years, often led to late-night sittings which frequently saw important issues being discussed at unsocial times, often after midnight. This presented a challenge not only for the individuals striving to concentrate or even stay awake, but for the quality of the outcomes.

Evidence of psychological strain among MPs

The first survey of the psychological health of UK MPs took place in 1992 prior to the introduction of the first reforms to parliamentary debating hours. 124 (20 per cent) of the elected members of the House of Commons completed measures which included workload (Weinberg, 1992), mental and physical strain (from the Occupational Stress Indicator (OSI); Cooper, Sloan and Williams, 1988), Type A behaviour and locus of control (both OSI) as well as pressure at the home–work interface (Weinberg, 1992). Physical symptoms of strain were found to be higher among this sample than the OSI norms for UK senior managers whose level of job responsibility was comparable (Weinberg *et al.*, 1999); however, for one-third of the MPs their scores exceeded the OSI norm range (Weinberg, 1992). The most frequently reported signs of strain were 'eating, drinking and smoking more than usual' (35.5 per cent), lack of sleep (30.6 per cent) and a decline in sexual interest (29.0 per cent). Additionally there was a minority of politicians who experienced psychosomatic symptoms, representing physical signs of potential underlying psychological strain. These included between 9–17 per cent of the sample experiencing headaches, shortness of breath or dizziness, heart-pounding, indigestion or sickness, muscle trembling (e.g., eye twitching) and sweating.

Scrutiny of the personality variables highlighted a range of results. Type A behaviour has been a popular area for study given its emphasis upon time urgency, abruptness of manner and competitiveness, which together may be taken to 'portray the stereotype of the dynamic executive' (Cooper, Sloan and Williams, 1988, p. 13). Politicians' overall levels of Type A behaviour were higher than comparable norms and included raised ratings of ambition. The significance of this finding relates more to physical rather than emotional well-being as a number of studies have found a link between increased Type A behaviour and coronary heart disease (e.g., Friedman and Rosenman, 1974). For some observers this might explain sudden deaths among prominent politicians, not to mention the raised levels of physical strain reported by this sample, but it is also known that lifestyle behaviours, such as alcohol use and smoking, play a more significant role in cardiovascular problems than Type A traits (Sanderman, 1998). From a psychological standpoint, the surprising finding was that MPs' overall perceived control was much lower than for workers outside of politics, including a lack of autonomy in relation to the functioning of the organisation and how much say they had over their careers and daily work events. This pattern of reduced control was emphasised among those not in the party of government and those whose constituencies were over 200 miles from parliament. Politicians' working hours helped to shed some light on these findings as 41 per cent reported working on average more than 70 hours each week and a further 40 per cent estimated that their working week lasted 55–70 hours. Such high working hours are likely to take a toll on all-round health (Michie and Cockcroft, 1996), but the combination of high workload and low levels of control is one highlighted as potentially toxic for well-being (Karasek and Theorell, 1990; Wood, 2008).

As expected from the evidence to the Jopling Committee, the clashing of boundaries at the home–work interface constituted a major source of pressure for the politicians. Over 75 per cent agreed that they did not spend enough time with their partner and 80 per cent felt similarly about the contact with their own children. 75 per cent recognised that work-related pressures caused or exacerbated arguments at home, with over 80 per cent reporting that they found it difficult to switch off from the job. More than one-fifth admitted that they had not done the best job either at work or at home. When it came to time for themselves, 60 per cent claimed they had insufficient time for hobbies (Weinberg et al., 1999).

In addition to the highly statistically significant relationships identified between both measures of psychological strain and Type A behaviour as well as perceived control, strong links between well-being and aspects of the job were also evident. MPs' physical symptoms of strain were significantly lowered if they had spent the week in Westminster rather than in the constituency, which was consistent with the reduced need to juggle conflicting work and home lives, whereas the association between greater quantities of postal mail and poorer mental health suggested the negative impact of increased work demands. The need for the introduction of new technology to the ancient UK parliament building was underlined by the positive correlation between computer access and MPs' improved experiences at the home–work interface. Consistent with these findings, psychological well-being was significantly predicted by politicians' levels of perceived control, which in turn appeared to be in greater abundance for those who had served longest in the job. This suggested a survivor effect among politicians, although it was not possible to deduce whether staying in the job predicted feelings of control, or vice-versa.

The impact on MPs of their working conditions

The reforms to UK parliamentary debating hours inspired by the Jopling Committee Report came after the study described above and they presented an opportunity to assess the psychological impact of the changes on politicians. The findings from this follow-up study highlighted an increase in the levels of both physical and emotional symptoms of strain (although not statistically significant). 79 per cent of the sample reported that the reforms had made their working lives either a little or a lot easier, but results from the measure of home–work pressure revealed an actual increase in dissatisfaction with work–life balance (Weinberg *et al.*, 1999). The timing of this follow-up survey within eighteen months of an approaching general election as well as the continuing demands of MPs' workloads may have contributed to these results; however, this examination of politicians' working conditions had for the first time shed light on the limited support provided by parliament as an organisation for politicians as its 'employees', and also revealed less than optimal working conditions for the UK's lawmakers. On the positive side, there was an occupational physician on site who offered healthcare checks and medical interventions to MPs as necessary.

Staffing resources for MPs to run offices both in parliament and in the constituency varied considerably, with funding for an average of one person for four days per week in each office, with a sizeable minority having less than this level of support (Weinberg *et al.*, 1999). MPs' resource allocation has since increased greatly, but at the time belied the challenges facing the politician in representing the interests of around

70,000 constituents. Access to computing facilities has also since radically improved with the building of new offices neighbouring the Houses of Parliament, but prior to this a startling example of inadequate working space was provided by the politician who attested to sharing what amounted to a corridor with fourteen other MPs! From the perspective of work psychology, it was also mildly astounding to discover that the Houses of Parliament were exempt from the Health and Safety legislation by which all other UK workplaces are bound. The undermining effect of this culture of complacency was illustrated by one politician who on starting their job after election, was shown a desk and phone and told to 'get on with it'. Another experienced MP put it more bluntly: 'The House is a backward institution which needs to be dragged into the twentieth century!' Perhaps it should have come as no surprise that reform to debating hours alone did not result in a reduction of symptoms of psychological strain.

The experience of newly elected politicians

The landslide victory of the Labour Party at the 1997 general election presented a rare opportunity to assess the impact on the psychological health of large numbers of national politicians of doing the job for the first time. 236 new MPs were elected to a role they had never previously carried out and 40 per cent of this cohort completed measures in the pre- or post-election phases of this study (Weinberg and Cooper, 2003). Analysis compared twenty-nine candidates before the general election (who went on to win their seats in parliament), with a matched sample of sixty-five successful colleagues three months later. 34 per cent of the participating MPs were women, reflecting the increase in the number of women MPs after the 1997 UK election. The qualitative responses from individuals who had never before worked in parliament illuminated their experiences to outsiders and conveyed a stark and confounding reality.

Certainly there was delight at being elected to parliament and an accompanying sense of honour, with 39 per cent of respondents reporting they were glad to be in a position to make a positive difference to the lives of others both locally and nationally. In addition, 20 per cent of those questioned were positive about the friendliness of the support staff already working in Westminster, as well as the historical nature of their surroundings. However, over half of the new study cohort were appalled by the 'archaic', 'unwritten' and 'opaque' procedures under which the elected assembly operated, which often resulted in clear frustration. The voting system provides a clear example. This began (and still does at the time of writing) with the announcement of a 'division' of the House, whereby all those wishing to vote walk out of the debating chamber to the 'division lobby', where they are counted by the tellers before returning to their seats. This process is repeated for every vote which takes place in the UK parliament, in both the elected House of Commons and the upper chamber, the House of Lords. It is perhaps not surprising that new MPs described it as a 'bizarre', 'time-wasting' and 'unpredictable' process enacted in a 'hot, sweaty lobby'! Some objected to the adversarial and often 'aggressive' nature of the debates, which frequently involved politicians shouting, gesticulating and interrupting. All of this, often accompanied by much noise, is presided over by the Speaker, whose role is to maintain order in an impartial manner. Away from the chamber and echoing the discontent of longer-standing politicians, 39 per cent of this sample of MPs criticised a lack of resources or even an office, while 41 per cent believed that the induction procedures for new MPs had been unhelpful, too little or even non-existent – only 25 per cent of the respondents felt that they had received sufficient guidance or training. The situation was tersely summarised by one new MP: 'This is bloody chaos'!

Reminiscent of the earlier findings with longer-serving politicians, one-fifth of new MPs similarly reported difficulties at the home–work interface. The adjustment process for MPs and their families meant that, having won the election, they were not able to see each other for most of the week. Given the tumultuous nature of the change in the UK's political landscape in 1997, swinging from the political right to the left, it is conceivable that there were a number of candidates who stood at the general election without initially having realistic hopes of winning, who then found themselves unexpectedly catapulted into a new job fraught with both professional and personal challenges. The quantitative results showed that strain – in terms of high scores on both the General Health Questionnaire (GHQ; psychological symptoms) and OSI (physical symptoms) – had increased in the period from pre-election to three months post-election. The percentage of high scores (above the 3/4 threshold and therefore indicative of psychological strain) on the GHQ-12 went from 24 to 30 per cent, with statistically significantly higher levels for MPs with school age children (up from 19 to 34 per cent). Interestingly there was an additional increase in reported psychological strain for women politicians but not in their physical symptoms of strain, whereas the reverse pattern was observed among men. An emotional adjustment reaction could be expected after taking on a new job (Schonfeld, 1999) and for those experiencing the worst symptoms of psychological strain, 'taking work home', 'very long hours' and an 'absence of emotional support' were significantly greater sources of pressure. Indeed 'taking work home' featured as the largest predictor of both emotional and physical symptoms of strain, followed by family problems in adapting to the new situation of having a national politician in it. Travel between Westminster and the MP's constituency, where their families were often based, as well as insufficient material and staffing resources, were reported as key sources of pressure for the newly installed politicians.

At follow-up one year later, the symptoms of psychological strain had subsided to pre-election levels; however physical symptoms of strain remained elevated with government MPs recording significantly higher levels than their opposition counterparts. The key problems reported at this stage were related to sleeping, a tendency to eat, drink and smoke more than usual, as well as headaches and indigestion. The long and often unsociable debating hours, the negative toll on family life, the accessibility of numerous bars and restaurants in the parliamentary buildings and changes in established patterns of eating and exercise were likely contributors to the long-term raised levels of physical symptoms of strain. Such findings are consistent with those from other samples of UK public servants, where a combination of work and non-work factors has been found to predict psychological health and disorder (Weinberg and Creed, 2000). In 1997, the key issue for the UK House of Commons was how a modernisation programme might change working practices in order to alleviate pressure on MPs and thereby facilitate a more robust democratic system.

New wine in old bottles?

At the turn of the millennium, devolution laws in the UK established a new parliament in Scotland, housed in the capital, Edinburgh, as well as a National Assembly for Wales, based in Cardiff. Both exercise policy and decision-making capacities on national issues in Scotland and Wales, with overall UK foreign policy still decided by parliament in London. The shift in power across the countries which make up the UK also signalled the opportunity to design a parliamentary workplace better suited to the needs of those engaged in modern political work, i.e., without the constraints of age old traditions. Thus the Scottish and Welsh institutions incorporated new technology into their infrastructure and business processes – including electronic voting – as well as encouraging collaborative working conditions in the spirit of national rather than party political considerations. This was illustrated by the circular design of the new debating chambers in contrast to the adversarial seating layout of the Houses of Parliament. In addition, a family-friendly approach to the job of national politician in the new legislatures was hailed as the prevailing philosophy – another major departure from how political work had been conducted for so long in London.

Members of the Scottish Parliament (MSPs) and the Assembly of Wales (AMs) were surveyed at the time of their election, prior to the opening of the new institutions and again after six and twelve months. At baseline 105 out of a potential 189 responded and almost half of these responded to follow-up questionnaires (Weinberg and Cooper, 2001). After six months, one-third of the combined sample of MSPs and AMs admitted working over seventy hours each week, with a further half working 55–70 hours per week, consistent with previous findings about politicians' workloads. An increase in reported psychological strain (measured by the GHQ-12) was noted, from a baseline of 25 per cent of politicians to 39 per cent half a year later. Although the numbers of respondents were smaller at follow-up, the raised symptom levels among parents of school-age children and those whose constituencies were over 100 miles from the capital city confirmed the pattern previously detected among new MPs at Westminster. The finding that 76 per cent of the Scottish and Welsh politicians acknowledged the negative impact of their job on family life suggested that the much heralded emphasis on a family-friendly approach in the new parliamentary institutions had failed. Similar to results obtained from new Westminster MPs, 22 per cent of MSPs and AMs recorded that their families had experienced difficulties in adjusting to the job.

As expected and in contrast to the old Houses of Parliament, 80 per cent of MSPs and AMs were satisfied with the new technology available to them, but it seemed that this had only repackaged their workloads rather than rationalised them. 61 per cent of the sample rated the perceived impact of the long hours on their health as 'moderate' or 'severe', while 69 per cent attested to a similar outcome in terms of their job performance. In relation to organisational procedures no difference was found from the outdated approach complained about by Westminster MPs: only 20 per cent rated induction procedures as 'sufficient', but the new institutions had made an even more staggering omission – there were no occupational health facilities for the elected politicians! Scrutiny of the sources of pressure reported by the MSPs and AMs showed that high workloads, long hours, travel and a lack of resources were common to all, whether they reported high or low psychological strain. However, for those suffering with the highest symptom levels, the issues of long working hours and a lack of emotional support from family and friends were significantly linked to psychological strain. Viewed in the context of raised symptom levels after taking on the job of politician, even in modern institutions, it had become clear that there were grounds for including a government health warning with any induction pack for new politicians. For a proportion of UK elected representatives, the job is linked with poorer psychological health.

Job redesign in parliament

It was not until 2003, that the UK parliament trialled further reforms to MPs' working hours by introducing time-limited speeches in the House of Commons, morning start times for debates (to avoid the prospect of all-night sittings), more debate-free days to allow MPs to carry out constituency work, as well as the scheduling of parliamentary recesses to coincide with the school holidays. Immediately prior to these being implemented, 132 MPs (20 per cent of the total of 659) completed measures of strain (i.e., GHQ-12 and OSI) and of home–work pressure, along with a bespoke assessment of feedback from colleagues on their own decision making. Sixty-three MPs responded in the follow-up phase six months after the introduction of the reforms (Weinberg, 2004).

At the start of the study, one quarter of the sample recorded that long working hours had negatively affected their work performance to a moderate or extreme degree, with a third claiming a negative impact on their health and two-thirds a similar toll on family relationships. Following introduction of the latest reforms to working hours, changes in these perceptions were slight, with only pressure at the home–work interface showing a small decline. At follow-up, responses revealed a mixed reception to the new arrangements, with 46.7 per cent actually perceiving less time for constituency duties and 45.9 per cent reporting a negative impact of the new debating hours on their work performance. In contrast another 49.2 per cent felt they now had more time to spend at home with their families. Meanwhile, within the job itself, a significant relationship was found between higher levels of psychological strain and poorer feedback from colleagues on their own decision making (Weinberg, 2004). This resonates with the question posed earlier in this chapter about the potential consequences for decision making of impaired psychological health among national politicians. It particularly highlights the need for further research into how MPs perceive their own performance in this key aspect of the job.

Overall the responses to the changes in working hours appeared to be split between MPs whose constituencies were near to the capital and those based further afield. Roughly equal proportions claimed either the new arrangements made their working lives harder or produced no difference. Either way, higher levels of satisfaction with the reformed working hours were negatively correlated with psychological strain and with increased distance of MPs' constituencies from parliament. The opportunities for nearby MPs to go home at the end of the parliamentary day were far greater, meaning that a more usual family life could be maintained, an option which distance had denied those of their colleagues who were obliged to remain in the capital for the duration of the parliamentary working week. To make matters worse for those who relied on the social networks established around work for company in the evenings, a sizeable proportion of their friends were now at home. This meant that those with constituencies far from London faced a week without family and now without like-minded colleagues too. This raised the possibility that for a number of MPs, the reforms had unwittingly eroded their social support network. Given the large number of MPs (659 at the time) and the inevitable variation in individual politicians' working patterns, it was no great surprise when, in 2005, the House of Commons duly approved a partial reversion of the reforms. This represented a compromise between those who favoured modernisation and those who considered themselves survivors of the long-standing rigours of UK parliamentary procedure. The strength of feeling in evidence at the 2005 debate served to remind any student of the workplace that politicians experience as strong emotions about their job as any other occupational group.

The impact of leaving the job of national politician in the UK

What happens after the 'party is over' and the politician moves on from the job they have held at the 'centre of things'? Given the findings detailed so far in this chapter, it would seem logical to expect that politicians would be less likely to experience symptoms of strain after they are relieved of the pressures which come with the job. An opportunity to test this hypothesis was presented by the reform in 1999 of the UK parliament's non-elected upper house, the House of Lords, which performs a scrutinising role in the legislative process. The changes obliged all those holding seats – as a result of the centuries-old practice of inheriting titles from their ancestors – to stand for election by their colleagues. From this process a reduced number of hereditary members of the House of Lords (peers) resulted. However, it is important to realise that peers are likely to work fewer hours than MPs and many have additional work roles outside political life; they are not paid a wage but are entitled to claim expenses. Despite these differences in working practices, a survey of 40 per cent of all hereditary peers who had stood for election, conducted one year after the reforms came into effect, showed that twenty-eight peers who were successfully elected reported significantly higher levels of physical symptoms of strain than twenty-eight who had left parliament (Weinberg, 2001). This measure of strain was correlated with weekly working hours, the demands of the job on family relationships and the inability to 'switch off' from work when at home.

The 'winners' also recorded higher scores on the GHQ-12, which in turn were significantly linked to an absence of emotional support, their partner's attitude to the job and the demands of their non-parliamentary work roles. 42.3 per cent of those losing their political role did not rate its impact as negative and 26.9 per cent were actively positive about the new opportunities which had opened up instead. Once again the findings suggested that political work in the UK is inherently likely to promote psychological strain.

What the House of Lords study does not illustrate is the impact of losing one's political job where this is the individual's primary occupation as well as their predominant source of income. Furthermore the study described above was limited by its post-hoc design. In order to assess the impact of job loss more rigorously, a follow-up of the longitudinal cohort recruited for the working hours reforms study was conducted. Data was obtained from sixty-two individuals who fought for their seat in the UK 2003 general election. This yielded pre- and post-election data on forty-seven individuals who successfully retained their parliamentary seat and fifteen who left Parliament (including five MPs who lost and an additional ten who had taken the decision to stand down and not fight for their seat) (Weinberg, 2007). Bearing in mind the smaller numbers of ex-MPs, pre- versus post-election analyses revealed that those taking the decision to stand down reported a statistically significant drop in their levels of emotional strain and a non-significant decrease in physical symptoms. No significant change on either measure was observed in the symptom levels of politicians who successfully defended their seat in the general election. It is not known whether those who decided to end their political careers were relieved at no longer dealing with the stressors of the job or whether the element of control in choosing to stand down was beneficial to their well-being, however those leaving parliament had rated a significantly more negative impact of their former working hours on health than their colleagues who continued in the job. Such findings lend support to the 'survivor' hypothesis whereby those who adapt to the job and cope with the stressors and strain are more likely to remain in it.

Further longitudinal research into the differential impact of either losing or deliberately leaving one's political job is required as the numbers in the study described here were too small to compare. However, there were calls for redundancy counselling for UK MPs from those who were obliged to leave parliament at the 2003 general election after years in the job. Continuing debate about the 'career' politician who is ill-prepared for any other kind of occupation suggests that the type of support offered by many modern organisations to employees who are being made redundant is also needed by ex-MPs. The issue was given tragic impetus by the death in

2007 of a former MP who had lost the support of both the political party and the electorate and subsequently died from a alcohol-related illness. The issue of having control over the potential end of one's career is clearly absent from political work, where most unusually for employment situations, a public vote decides the fate of individuals. This echoes the low levels of perceived control which MPs describe and highlights the gap in the employment relationship experienced by national politicians in the UK.

The political party sponsors an individual and has a major role in selecting, promoting and disciplining its politicians; however, after the election, the House of Commons and the electorate assume a greater significance in the politicians' employment situation. The revelations about UK MPs' expenses in 2009 clearly showed that many MPs felt misled by the House of Commons procedures for claiming financial remuneration and struggled to find a satisfactory method for resolving the issues. The lack of clarity allowed conflicts of interest to persist and led to a breakdown in trust between the electorate and many of its representatives across the political spectrum. Large numbers of MPs announced their intention to stand down in advance of the 2010 UK general election, although relatively few publicly attributed their decision to the expenses row.

UK parliamentary crisis

The expenses crisis provided a potential watershed in UK parliamentary politics as it was revealed that the process by which MPs claimed expenses had been exploited and in some cases abused. This was due in part to the actions of individual politicians, but also to the insufficient safeguards operated by the House of Commons in monitoring the distribution of significant amounts of public money to elected politicians. In acknowledgement of part blame for the scandal, the Speaker (effectively the chair of the House of Commons) was the first to be obliged to resign for 300 years. Many MPs apologised to their constituents and repaid sums they had claimed, which although legitimate according to the rules of the organisation, were viewed dimly by an electorate unable to claim for mortgages on second homes, for the cleaning of their homes, or for the dredging of a moat around a stately home! Given the timing of the crisis – during the worst economic recession for decades – there was little that MPs could do to cover their embarrassment.

Whatever the rights or wrongs of the whole debacle, the impact on the UK's national politicians, heightened by the daily campaigning of a national newspaper, was palpable. A survey of the previously described longitudinal cohort of serving MPs was conducted after the expenses scandal and drew responses from forty-five out of 101 MPs. This showed that levels of psychological strain, as assessed using the GHQ-12, had significantly increased since the previous survey earlier in the same parliamentary term. In fact, the proportion of MPs reporting high levels of strain had almost doubled from 19.6 to 38.6 per cent (Weinberg, 2010). MPs' psychological strain was significantly correlated with their having negative views of the House of Commons as an organisation and of the job itself in the wake of the expenses crisis. Furthermore poor psychological health was highly significantly correlated with MPs' ability to carry out their job role.

This phase of the research had been designed to collect the first data on the Big Five personality traits among UK MPs. This revealed strong associations between neuroticism and psychological health (both physical and emotional symptoms), in the wake of the expenses crisis, while increased levels of agreeableness were linked with retaining a positive view of the job (Weinberg, 2010). Consistent with the findings of Caprara *et al.* from Italy (see chapter 9), the UK MPs scored higher than population samples on both extraversion and agreeableness scales, as well as lower in relation to neuroticism (Weinberg, 2010).

In attempting to justify MPs' behaviour in relation to expenses, one politician claimed that they should be considered differently from the rest of the population. It is unlikely the data on personality traits supports such an assertion, however in relation to their psychological health, UK politicians cannot claim to be any different from their public sector colleagues as they are just as likely as other occupational groups to respond negatively to crises within their organisation. If nothing else, the expenses crisis had identified the need for parliament to play the role of an accountable employer, not only in monitoring organisational procedures, but also in exercising a duty of care to the unusual occupational group which is made up of politicians.

International comparisons of job strain in politicians

Clearly, from a job-holder viewpoint, the ideal parliament has yet to be established in the UK and it is interesting to see that similar issues of symptoms of strain have arisen in Austria, where the parliamentary system is different (Olbrich, 2004). However, a study conducted with forty-eight (32 per cent) Members of the Australian Federal Parliament, has shown that high levels of symptoms of psychological strain are not inevitable for those carrying out a political job. Nevertheless the main stressors found in UK studies before the 2003 reforms to working hours were also common to Australian politicians (UK figures quoted first): high workloads (81 vs 78.3 per cent), difficulties at the home-work interface (76.2 vs 54.3 per cent) and travel (49.2 vs 50.0 per cent) (Weinberg, 2002). Differences between national systems can play a part and it was noticeable that, unlike the UK, Australian parliamentary sessions were spread more evenly throughout the year, making it possible for MPs to have more regular contact with family, despite substantially greater travelling distances. With these types of work pattern, length of tenure is likely to self-select those individuals who are able to cope with the conflicting demands of heavy workloads and family life and it was noted that the average length of service of these comparable groups of UK and Australian politicians was eight years.

The main difference between the two samples was in terms of the levels of psychological strain. Only 8.3 per cent of Australian MPs recorded high scores in excess of the commonly used threshold of 3/4 (Goldberg and Williams, 1988), compared to 15.9 per cent of UK MPs, i.e., almost double the rate of poor psychological health. Interestingly the physical signs of strain were just as high as for both Australian and UK politicians (Weinberg, 2002). These results raise the possibility that strain among politicians is widespread but there may be cultural differences which influence whether or how symptoms are experienced or expressed. This underlines the need for use of a range of measures in future cross-cultural and inter-parliamentary comparisons.

In summary

The question posed in the first chapter of this book is if mental health does affect political job performance, could the nightmare scenario of unbridled irrationality in key decisions really come true? Interviews for this chapter carried out with cabinet-level politicians in the UK suggest that this is unlikely to be the case here. Indeed attempts to sensationalise the existence of uncharacteristic behaviour among the UK's top politicians, such as a government minister banging his head on the table at a cabinet meeting, are attributed to media hype. According to one government minister, the reality of such high-level meetings amounts to polite expressions of difference over the wording of documents under consideration. One wonders how much this reflects long-established bureaucratic traditions within a democratic system. However, the decorum which pervades these situations is not always as evident behind the scenes, where emotions inevitably run high in relation to issues of importance. Indeed those who rise to high office admit to being 'survivors', accustomed to withstanding the pressures of conflicting demands and high workloads and with the ability to carry effectively the 'scary' prospect of ultimate responsibility. This does not mean that the issue of psychological ill health is absent from government, but that conventions in behaviour can create a generally productive atmosphere, seemingly tolerant of political manoeuvres for power.

The pressure on ordinary backbench MPs is more straightforward in one sense and is likely to be geared towards achieving higher office or surviving the identified rigours of the job. As promotion is only likely to be available to a successful minority, there are bound to be casualties along the way, either precipitated by a lack of success or faltering psychological resources which render the individual vulnerable to illness or unhealthy coping strategies. However, the lack of objective governance over parliamentary procedures, such as that evidenced by the 2009 furore over many MPs' expense claims, demonstrated the need for a much more clearly defined and transparent relationship between national politicians and their employer(s). In many ways the circumstances of the job differ from other occupations, but there are clearly work factors – such as job change, long hours, work-to-home conflict and negative events – that are not unique to politicians and do impact on their psychological health. Therefore the contribution of occupational psychology could be a necessity for the working group identified as national politicians, requiring relevant and non-politicised professionals to be consulted in the design of the parliamentary workplace. What is missing so far is the safety net within the political institution to rescue those for whom the job is becoming a health hazard, as well as organisational effectiveness in reforming challenges to good job performance. As research in this area evolves, it would seem prudent to advise all would-be politicians of the potential risks as well as the benefits of electoral office.

References

Birch, D., Ashton, H. and Kamali, F. (1998). Alcohol, drinking, illicit drug use and stress in junior house officers in north-east England. *The Lancet*, 352, 785–6.

Cooper, C. L., Sloan, S. and Williams, S. (1988). *Occupational Stress Indicator*. Windsor: NFER-Nelson.

Freeman, H. (1991). The human brain and political behaviour. *British Journal of Psychiatry*, 159, 19–32.

Friedman, M. and Rosenman, R. H. (1974). *Type A behaviour and Your Heart*. New York: Knopf.

Guardian (2006). Italian TV show on drug-taking politicians pulled from schedules. 11 October.

Goldberg, D. and Williams, P. (1988). *A User's Guide to the General Health Questionnaire*. Windsor: NFER-Nelson.

Jopling Committee Report (1992). *Report from the Select Committee on Sittings of the House*. Vol. I. London: HMSO.

Karasek, R. A. and Theorell, T. (1990). *Healthy Work*. New York: Basic Books.

Michie, S. and Cockcroft, A. (1996). Overwork can kill? *British Medical Journal*, 312, 921–2.

Olbrich, A., Zandonella, M., Leitenbauer, M. and Prudil, G. (2004). *Illness and Healthcare of Austrian Members of Parliament*. International Society of Political Psychology Annual Conference, Barcelona.

Royal College of Psychiatrists (2008). Survey reveals MPs forced to hide mental health problems. Accessed on 16 April 2010 at www.rcpsych.ac.uk/press/pressreleases2008/bank2008/prparliament.aspx.

Sainsbury Centre for Mental Health (2007). *Mental Health at Work: Developing the Business Case*. Policy paper 8. London: Sainsbury Centre for Mental Health.

Sanderman, R. (1998). *New Insights into the Onset of Heart Disease and Cancer*. 22nd European Conference on Psychosomatic Research, University of Manchester.

Schonfeld, I. S. (1999). An updated look at depressive symptoms and job satisfaction in first-year women teachers. *Journal of Occupational and Organizational Psychology*, 72, 363.

Weinberg, A. (1992). Workload, stress and family life in MPs. University of Sheffield. Unpublished M.Sc. thesis.

(2001). Stress among elected and former members of the House of Lords. BPS Centenary Conference, Glasgow. *Proceedings of the BPS*, 9 (2).

(2002). A comparison of symptoms and sources of stress between national politicians in the United Kingdom and Australia. *World Congress on Stress, Edinburgh. Stress: The International Journal on the Biology of Stress*, 5, supplement, 47.

(2004). Stress and decision making and new working hours among MPs. BPS Annual Conference, London. *Proceedings of the BPS*, 12 (2).

(2005). The efficacy and psychological functioning of MPs. BPS Annual Conference, Manchester. *Proceedings of the BPS*, 13 (2).

(2007). Your destiny in their hands: job loss and success in Members of Parliament. BPS Annual Conference, York. *Proceedings of the BPS*, 15 (2).

(2010). Too hot to handle? MPs' personalities and their experiences of stress and controversy. BPS Annual Conference, Stratford upon Avon. *Proceedings of the BPS*, 18 (2).

Weinberg, A. and Cooper, C. L. (2001). *The Lasting Stress of Entering Politics*. 7th European Congress of Psychology, London. Book of Abstracts, p. 236.

(2003). Stress among national politicians elected to parliament for the first time. *Stress and Health*, 19, 111–17.

Weinberg, A., Cooper, C. L. and Weinberg, A. (1999). Workload, stress and family life in British Members of Parliament and the psychological impact of reforms to their working hours. *Stress Medicine*, 15, 79–87.

Weinberg, A. and Creed, F. (2000). Sources of stress in the NHS workforce. *The Lancet*, 355, 533–7.

Weinberg, A., Sutherland, V. J. and Cooper, C. L. (2010). *Organizational Stress Management: a Strategic Approach*. Basingstoke: Palgrave Macmillan.

Wood, S. (2008). Job characteristics, employee voice and well-being in Britain. *Industrial Relations Journal*, 39, 153–68.

8 When cognitions reach boiling point: the impact of denial and avoidance by policy-makers during a foreign policy crisis

Max V. Metselaar

Introduction

This chapter examines when, how and why politicians in key positions employ strategies of denial and avoidance which can lead to serious short-comings in their government's preparedness when danger threatens. A theory of political coping is proposed and applied to a case study of a well-known foreign policy crisis. This focuses on how US President Lyndon Johnson and Defence Secretary Robert McNamara responded to the gradually increasing stream of intelligence reports and threat assessments that warned them of the 'Tet Offensive' during the Vietnam War and the impact of their denial and avoidance on their state of preparedness on 30 January 1968, when Viet Cong insurgents and the North Vietnamese Army (NVA) began the offensive.

This chapter puts forward four claims. Firstly, denial and avoidance form an essential part of the coping responses of politicians when faced with threat-related information and impending danger during domestic or foreign policy crises (see also Golec in chapter 5). Secondly, irrespective of the type of political system in which the politician operates, where responding to the danger may tax or exceed available resources and/or lead to political and moral dilemmas and psychological strain, the more likely s/he is to deny and avoid aspects of threat-related information (TRI). Thirdly, the degree to which some political systems permit and in some ways even encourage denial and avoidance by politicians during crises varies from one type of system to another. For example, multi-party-based coalitions and democratic governments may be less tolerant of denial and avoidance by their key policy-makers than governments characterised by authoritarian or one-party-dominated presidential systems. Fourthly, this chapter claims that denial and avoidance by individual politicians during 'pre-encounter' phases in advance of a crisis can have a profound impact on a government's state of preparedness when dangers actually strike.[1] Politicians in key executive positions in a governmental warning-response process, such as president, prime minister, minister of defence or minister of interior affairs, often have the institutionalised task and political responsibility of playing key roles in domestic and foreign policy crises. Given the significance of policy-makers in the collation and utilisation of TRI and in translating these signals into political decisions and timely counter-measures, it is plausible to expect that the way they cope with TRI can have a profound impact on governmental preparedness. In other words, the longer and more intense the politicians' denial and avoidance, the more marked the impact on the government's preparedness. In a global context which demands both awareness of, and responses to, impending threats to security, an insight into politicians' ability to cope with TRI and conflicting political demands is essential.

A Political Coping Theory of denial and avoidance by policy-makers

Repeated exposure to warnings of a serious threat to national interests and values in policy areas for which he or she may be held politically accountable, tends to form a major pressure for almost any politician. Conditions such as these activate various forms of coping, including denial and avoidance (Lazarus and Folkman, 1984; Monat, Averill and Lazarus, 1972; Janis and Mann, 1977; Janis, 1989; Breznitz, 1983; Edelstein, Nathanson and Stone, 1989; Krohne, 1986, 1993, 1996; Holsti and George, 1975; Hermann, 1979). Of course, it is not expected that politicians, even with the best possible system of intelligence production, can predict events in advance and attempts to command all such information could easily result in overload. Therefore avoidance and denial can be seen as a necessary part of an individual's information processing. Denial is defined here as a person's set of cognitive attempts to refuse acknowledgement of danger-related information by negating, distorting, minimising and/or repudiating potential disturbing information and its implications.[2] Similarly avoidance is defined as, a person's set of cognitive

---

[1] Systematic academic studies on 'unpreparedness-despite-warning' scenarios started during the early 1960s. Research since then has attributed serious shortcomings in the state of preparedness of policy-makers and their governments to a wide variety of causes (Levite 1987; Kam, 1988; Metselaar, 1999). Despite the wealth of publications over five decades on potential causes, the impact of denial and avoidance on individual policy-makers has received scant attention.

[2] The full meaning of denial cannot be grasped without considering its opposite: acceptance or acknowledgement, which may be defined as the act of receiving incoming signals and confirming them as true.

and behavioural attempts to ignore, neglect and/or turn attention away from disturbing danger-related information, although the person may acknowledge the existence of potential problems or challenges related to this information.

Factors which may lead to increasing denial and avoidance among politicians

The intensity, frequency and duration of a politician's avoidance and denial of TRI and its impact on a politician's level of preparedness are usually governed by a complex interplay of person- and context-related-factors (Lazarus, 1968, 1986; Monat *et al.*, 1972; Folkman and Lazarus, 1985; Mechanic, 1978; Janis and Mann, 1977; Breznitz, 1983; Krohne, 1986, 1993, 1996). Five such factors are included in the Political Coping Theory outlined in this chapter.

Politicians' primary and secondary appraisals of threat   Primary appraisals consist of a politician's ongoing judgements of whether or not, and to what extent, external developments may form a serious challenge to political interests, values and objectives or to the activities and well-being of citizens and armed forces at home or abroad. Secondary appraisal refers to a politician's awareness and evaluations of available resources, abilities, opportunities and constraints for meeting the impending danger and its probable implications (Lazarus and Folkman, 1984; Lazarus, 1986).

Political warning-response dilemmas   A dilemma can be regarded as a cognitive, emotional and often stressful inner conflict in which a politician experiences simultaneous pressures requiring a choice between alternative courses of action and their potential consequences.

Strain on the politician   Strain will be defined here as a dynamic state of emotional, physical, cognitive and behavioural tension experienced by a policy-maker during potentially challenging situations in which the demands of responding to a scenario (like a predicted danger) are appraised as taxing or exceeding available resources. Additionally failing to cope carries serious risks of endangering important assets and interests (Lazarus and Folkman, 1984; Lazarus, 1986; Hermann, 1979; Holsti and George, 1975; see also chapter 7).

The domestic political and institutional context   Depending on the type of domestic political setting in which the policy-maker operates, his/her tendencies to deny or avoid threat-related signals will be moderated to

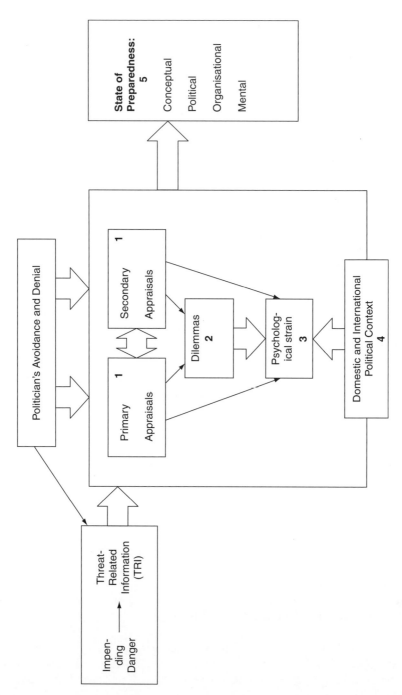

Figure 8.1. A model of Political Coping Theory

some degree (Verbeek, 2003; Farnham, 1997; 't Hart, Stern and Sundelius, 1997). On the other hand, depending on the type of political system and any history of previous threats or struggle for survival, some domestic political systems may also trigger or stimulate denial and avoidance of its key policy-makers.

State of preparedness Governmental preparedness can be regarded as the degree to which policy-makers are conceptually, organisationally, politically and mentally ready to respond when a danger strikes. This refers especially to those areas for which individual or collective policy-makers are responsible and for which they can be held politically accountable.

Data collection for this case study

In order to assess Johnson's and McNamara's state of preparedness on 30–31 January 1968, as well as the components of the model highlighted in figure 8.1 (i.e., primary and secondary appraisals, dilemmas, etc.), archival documents gathered mainly in the holdings of the Lyndon B. Johnson Presidential Library in Austin, Texas were consulted. In addition, the author reviewed declassified CIA reports and a wide range of government documents including notes, memos and transcriptions of phone calls. Approximately 700 archival documents were collected and analysed from relevant websites and the *Pentagon Papers*. As far as possible, primary sources were combined with memoirs, oral history interviews and a number of secondary sources.

The Political Coping Theory applied to an historical case study – the Tet Offensive

The Tet Offensive became a turning point in the war and in US Vietnam strategy, not so much because of its military significance as because of its deep psychological impact on the American public and media. It became the decisive trigger for one of the most serious political, military and psychological blows to foreign policy a US government had ever experienced. 'Tet' completely overturned the notion which President Johnson and his administration had tried to sell, that the United States had seen 'the light at the end of the tunnel' in terms of the military and state-building process in Vietnam (Schandler, 1977; Braestrup, 1983). Johnson later described his own disturbed state of mind during this period in quite revealing terms: 'I felt that I was being chased on all sides by a giant stampede coming at me from all directions ... The whole situation was unbearable for me' (Kearns 1976, p. 343). It started a completely new 'ball game'.

How foreseeable was the Tet Offensive?

Most features of the Tet Offensive and its impact were more or less foreseeable. During the thirteen months between 1 January 1967 and the early-morning hours of 30 January 1968, an impressive stream of at least 112 strands of TRI reached the offices of both policy-makers (see also table 8.1). Although available intelligence did not provide a complete and unambiguous picture until mid-December 1967, both President Johnson and Secretary of State McNamara were capable and experienced enough to derive the most likely threat scenarios. The timing, locations, types of attack and most objectives of the Tet Offensive were predicted relatively well in intelligence reports at least six weeks before it started (Brewin and Shaw, 1987; Wirtz, 1991; Ford, 1995; Ford, 1998; Prados and Stubbe, 1991). For example, both politicians were confronted with reports which pointed out that there was a significant increase in troop reinforcements and it was also correctly predicted that the willingness of South Vietnamese citizens to support Hanoi's calls for a massive public uprising to coincide with the Tet Offensive would be low. While intelligence reports correctly assessed that the communist leaders in Hanoi overestimated the public support they would receive in South Vietnam, their willingness to take the substantial risk of an all-out offensive was largely overlooked (Wirtz, 1991; Ford, 1995). Both American politicians were well aware that whatever they did or did not do, almost every action involved more political risks than usual because 1968 was a presidential election year.

Serious shortcomings in governmental preparedness at the eve of 'Tet'

Despite several excellent forewarnings both politicians were caught largely unprepared in several respects. They were *conceptually* surprised by the actual scale of targets, the level of coordination and the nature and timing of the Tet attacks. Both politicians were also surprised by the risks the communist leaders and the Viet Cong were willing to take (Ford, 1998; Wirtz, 1991; Ford, 1995; Shapley, 1993; Allen, 2001).

Johnson's and McNamara's *political preparedness* on the eve of 'Tet' revealed many serious shortcomings as well. Both politicians largely failed to prepare political institutions like the Senate and the Congress, as well as the press and the public, for a wave of attacks by an enemy who had been repeatedly presented as the losing side. Consequently, during the weeks before 'Tet' both politicians failed to create sufficient political credibility and support at home for rapid counter-measures in order to exploit

Table 8.1. *An overview of the evolution of the 'threat-related information' (TRI) available to President Johnson and Secretary of State McNamara between 1 January, 1967 and the start of the Tet Offensive on 30 January, 1968*

Phase number	Start and end of each phase	Quantity (n)	Characterisation of the TRIs for each 'pre-encounter' phase
Phase 1	January–June 1967	(n = 5)	First deductions that communist leaders in Hanoi would change their strategy to force a breakthrough.
Phase 2	July–13 September 1967	(n = 7)	More concrete indications that Hanoi was considering a radical deviation from its strategy in the Vietnam War.
Phase 3	14 September–30 November 1967	(n = 18)	This phase starts with repeated statements on Radio Hanoi and widespread publicity by North Vietnamese Defence Minister, General Vo Nguyen Giap of: (a) Hanoi's view on the vulnerabilities of the US and the South Vietnamese regime, (b) Hanoi's change of strategy, (c) several features of the planned Tet Offensive and the Public Uprising, (d) a call-up for Viet Cong irregulars and sleeping cells in South Vietnam. This phase includes the capture of a three-page memo in which the phrase 'Winter–Spring Offensive' was broadly described. TRIs based on observations and captured enemy documents became more specific. During the last two weeks of this phase, an authoritative assessment by the US National Intelligence Community on the Vietnam War was disseminated, including estimations of the enemy's Order of Battle.
Phase 4	1 December 1967–20 January 1968	(n = 38)	This phase starts with several quite specific and well-founded TRIs. Between 10 and 17 December, Johnson and McNamara were exposed to two detailed threat reports from the CIA's Saigon Station Team and from General Westmoreland and his military analysts in Saigon, as well as alarming remarks from two key military commanders. Starting from late December TRIs emphasised repeatedly that the enemy probably intended to launch a serious offensive in the north, including the US marine bases in Khe Sanh, and the border areas. Other target areas including Saigon were regularly mentioned too.
Phase 5	21 January–30 January 1968	Late warnings (n = 24)	This phase begins with reports that North Vietnamese divisions had started a siege of the US Marines' base at Khe Sanh. There is a significant increase in specific, accurate, and consistent TRIs during this phase, ending with a last-minute warning shortly before the Tet Offensive commenced.

the situation in the battlefield, for example by sending between 10,000 and 22,000 additional troops as immediate reinforcements to the area, by calling up 245,000 reserves and lengthening the tours of duty by US soldiers already in Vietnam (Barrett, 1993; Oberdorfer, 1971; Braestrup, 1983). Johnson and McNamara were also largely unprepared for the psychological and political consequences of the near-live television coverage of the Viet Cong suicide bombing of the US embassy in Saigon and the fighting across the capital. Archival evidence reveals that it took at least three to six weeks before both politicians started to realise and acknowledge that the Tet offensive had triggered a complex chain of events that represented a decisive turning point in the Vietnam War (Johnson, 1971; Oberdorfer, 1971; Braestrup, 1983).

In various respects, Johnson and McNamara were also *organisationally* poorly prepared. For example, they had not ordered their staff members at the White House and Pentagon to take additional measures in order to ensure effective crisis management of simultaneous crises, i.e., an unusually large enemy offensive in Vietnam and as a result, potential spill-over effects on the domestic front. They had also failed to request their subordinates to produce, discuss and test adequate contingency plans for different scenarios. This meant a lack of possible counter-measures and emergency procedures for dealing with Congress, the press and the public, as well as guiding and coordinating public statements and 'media management' in the wake of an attack.

Moreover, Johnson's and McNamara's *mental preparedness* on the eve of 'Tet' was less than optimal. They were certainly not in the best psychological condition to maintain all of their political roles in initiating interventions as part of the defensive measures against the waves of Tet attacks and the counter-attacks on the battlefield in South Vietnam. The same limitations applied to their ability to recover from the blows of managing 'crisis after the crisis', which began to escalate at the domestic front. For example, both Johnson and his wife suffered recurring nightmares in the early weeks of the offensive, whereby the president repeatedly dreamed that he was paralysed.

Applying the Political Coping Theory: testing two hypotheses

The impact of the politicians' appraisals, dilemmas and strain on their denial and avoidance

Hypothesis 1 is focused on the status of President Johnson's and Defence Secretary McNamara's cognitive appraisals, dilemmas and strain during the five pre-encounter phases (January 1967–30 January 1968) on their denial and avoidance (see table 8.1).

The more a policy-maker appraises that s/he is confronted with TRI related to a serious danger and that the demands of altering or controlling the danger and minimising its damage may exceed available resources, the more likely s/he will experience dilemmas and strain leading to increased use of denial and avoidance.

Primary appraisals It was no earlier than phase 4 (1 December 1967–20 January 1968) that several 'Tet-related' parts of the threat assessments and intelligence reports started to become prominent in President Johnson's primary appraisals. Triggered by these reports, he began to appraise that something 'unusual' was brewing in the Vietnam battlefield which could be regarded as a serious threat with implications for the situation on the domestic front. However, he also hoped that it could provide a long-awaited opportunity to enforce an acceptable way out of the 'endless' nightmare of the Vietnam War (Schandler, 1977; Johnson, 1971). Near the end of December President Johnson's primary appraisals became increasingly dominated by the much narrower, but also more straightforward, threat of North Vietnamese divisions against US marines in Khe Sanh (Prados and Stubbe, 1991). Johnson feared that a future North Vietnamese attack against Khe Sanh might turn into a political fiasco similar to the French defeat at Dien Bien Phu in 1954, which had decisive strategic implications for the power position and military involvement of the French in Indochina and ended French colonial rule there. In particular Johnson feared repercussions from a North Vietnamese military success at Khe Sanh for the administration's political credibility at home (Prados and Stubbe, 1991). In comparison to the prominent threat against Khe Sanh and the northern and border zones of South Vietnam the TRI, which pointed at NVA and Viet Cong preparations for attacks against cities and hamlets elsewhere in South Vietnam, including the capital city Saigon, hardly figured in Johnson's or McNamara's appraisals.

Secondary appraisals Throughout the five pre-encounter phases neither Johnson or McNamara were never specifically focused on how to control or mitigate negative consequences in the battlefield and on the domestic front if a 'Tet-like' offensive took place. In different ways, both politicians continued to have strong doubts whether they would be able gain sufficient control over the Vietnam War and especially about the possibilities of continuing the war of attrition, breaking the enemy's determination and pushing them into negotiations. The president's remark in Phase 3 was illustrative when he complained that, 'I am like the steering wheel of a car without any control.'[3] Both politicians struggled to find a balance between alienating either the 'hawks' or 'doves' inside and outside the administration[4] (McNamara, 1999; Johnson, 1971; Shapley, 1993; Hendrickson, 1997). Throughout phases 1–4, Johnson's assessments of all the military efforts – for example the ongoing 'Rolling Thunder' air campaign on the Ho Chi Minh line, search-and-destroy missions and the implementation of an electronic barrier (the so-called McNamara line), changed from relative optimism to scepticism and even pessimism. Johnson was especially aware that the time to increase control and change the situation on various fronts was 'running out', not least because 1968 was a presidential election year. McNamara was much more pessimistic and cynical; his 'dark' assessments were often reinforced by his reliance on CIA intelligence, pessimistic visions from his own advisors and scientific reports from Pentagon think-tanks (Shapley, 1993; Hendrickson, 1997).

Dilemmas   Johnson and McNamara experienced various dilemmas. Some of these were structural and started between 1964 and 1965, long before the first confrontation with Tet-related TRI. Throughout the five phases Johnson and McNamara experienced unremitting pressure from 'hawks' inside and outside the administration and the US armed forces to increase the number of armed forces in Vietnam and to expand areas and targets for air strikes in order to 'win' the protracted war. On the other hand, during 1967 there was a significant increase in the proportion of 'doves' inside and outside of the administration (more or less privately McNamara had become one of them) wanting to stop the Vietnam War or at least end or significantly limit American involvement in it. Both politicians were reluctant to take the risk of becoming more entrapped in a seemingly endless conflict with which many Americans were becoming increasingly impatient. The mounting budgetary problems, the implications for other policy programmes, especially the president's 'Great Society' (which formed Johnson's domestic policy priority) and concerns over political feasibility in the Congress and the Senate of a call-up of military reserves, played significant roles in Johnson's and McNamara's reluctance for further reinforcements and expansion of operations (Kearns, 1976; Johnson, 1971; McNamara, 1995).

---

[3] Meeting with foreign policy advisors, Thursday, 2 November 1967; National Security Files, Country Files: Vietnam; LBJ Library.

[4] The term 'hawks' refers to those in favour of maintaining conflict, while 'doves' are those preferring peace.

Moreover, sending more troops might suggest to the domestic press and the public that almost half a million soldiers were still not enough to keep the conflict under control or indeed to win it. Yet, the more it was perceived that tangible progress in the Vietnam War could not be demonstrated, or that despite all the American efforts communist influence in Indochina and East Asia was increasing, the greater the pressures on both politicians to send more troops. Johnson was concerned that sooner or later he would be blamed and held accountable for not doing enough to protect US soldiers and US interests, regularly experiencing an inner fear that he did not want to be the first president to lose a war (Kearns, 1976).

Other dilemmas were caused by a combination of chronic and conflicting Tet-related constraints and needs. For example, McNamara faced the dilemma of how to react to the ongoing enemy troop reinforcements without offering the joint chiefs of staff (JCoS) and Field Commander General Westmoreland a pretext for new requests and pressures which could lead to politically uncontrollable escalation of the ongoing bombings and military activity. On the one hand, McNamara persistently hoped to create the best possible atmosphere for fruitful negotiations with Hanoi and was eager to offer some concessions, as he appraised this as the best of available, yet less desirable options. On the other hand, he was fully aware that he needed to be careful not to lose the support and trust of the president any more than he already had (McNamara, 1995; Shapley, 1993; Hendrickson, 1997).

A specific Tet-related dilemma during December 1967 and January 1968 was whether or not to propose another one-sided ceasefire. On the one hand both politicians realised that refusing to initiate or accept ceasefires would further undermine their image and credibility on the domestic and international front as a government intent on a peaceful solution. On the other hand, both politicians were quite certain that every ceasefire or cessation of bombing was exploited by the communists in order to reinforce Viet Cong insurgencies and prepare future terrorist attacks. Moreover, McNamara and especially Johnson feared that the initiation of one-sided ceasefires could be perceived by communist leaders in Hanoi, Moscow and Beijing as a sign of weakness.

During the second half of phase 4 (1–21 January 1968) Johnson experienced a major dilemma: whether or not the president as commander-in-chief should inform and warn parties inside and outside the government about indications that the North Vietnamese and Viet Cong were preparing an unusually large offensive around the time of the Tet celebrations. On the one hand, the risk remained that the TRI was not accurate, that these could turn out to be false alarms, or that a public warning would alert the enemy and therefore waste the chance to punish the enemy's frontal attack – an opportunity long awaited by his military commander General Westmoreland. Such a public warning might also raise serious public doubts about the administration's carefully orchestrated public relations campaign, begun in the summer of 1967, that everything was under control and that the enemy was actually losing the war (Braestrup, 1983; Barrett, 1993). Furthermore, there was a considerable risk that 'hawks' in the administration, Republican Party members in the Senate (e.g., Richard Nixon) and in Congress, the Joint Chiefs of Staff or even field commander General Westmoreland might exploit the president's public acknowledgement of a predicted enemy offensive by exerting public and political pressure to send more troops, call-up the reserves and escalate military actions in Vietnam. Johnson's public acknowledgement could also undermine economic investments as well as political acceptability and support for Johnson's key priority in domestic politics, i.e., the 'Great Society'. In summary, the penalties for taking the warnings seriously and publicly acknowledging the threat could have been profound and were difficult if not impossible to control. On the other hand, Johnson was well aware that waiting too long or being too cautious in warning the public of impending enemy attacks could backfire too.

Strain   There is a lot of evidence, based on direct observations by close witnesses and remarks from Johnson and McNamara, that both politicians regularly experienced moderate to high physiological and emotional strain during the five pre-encounter phases. Johnson's level of strain peaked during phases 3, 4 and 5. There is relatively strong evidence that the increased strain Johnson experienced in the last half of phase 4 and also in phase 5 was also related to the incoming warnings and the emerging threat against Khe Sanh.

During phases 4 and 5 Johnson suffered chronic lack of sleep and recurring nightmares which were dominated by Vietnam-related thoughts and feelings of guilt and helplessness towards dead military soldiers and their parents. Johnson regularly dreamed that everyone shouted at him that he was a murderer and blamed him for the death of American soldiers in Vietnam. Johnson also had periods of unstable moods of anger, despair and impatience, for example, when he heard contrary advice from his senior advisors on how to respond to the increasing threat against Khe Sanh (Kearns, 1976). During these phases, Johnson regularly displayed symptoms of paranoia, fearing that everyone (including McNamara) was betraying him. Occasionally he suspected that the ongoing stream of crises (i.e., racial riots in Detroit, the North Korean 'Pueblo' crisis, the North

Vietnamese offensive and siege of Khe Sanh and finally the Tet Offensive) formed a carefully orchestrated communist plot managed by the Soviet Politburo leaders in Moscow (Kearns, 1976).

Although McNamara's levels of strain peaked differently from Johnson's, his own chronic strain ranged from moderate to severe. McNamara later admitted that he regularly felt 'as tense as hell' and that he had recurring sleep problems, feelings of anger and deep frustration mixed with symptoms of mild depression (McNamara, 1995; Hendrickson, 1997). Several observers recall meetings in McNamara's office at the Pentagon and at other locations where his face was thin and pale and he spoke in a very emotional and trembling voice. Sometimes he cried although he usually tried to hide this (Shapley, 1993; Hendrickson, 1997). The personal pressure on McNamara was compounded by a combination of other stressors, including deep frustrations and growing scepticism that an acceptable solution for the war could be found, given his own conviction that the war could not be won. In addition, McNamara struggled for months with an increasing inner conflict of loyalties between his job responsibilities as defence secretary and as a subordinate to the president (Hendrickson, 1997; Shapley, 1993). McNamara perceived that his influence and credibility as defence secretary in the Johnson administration was significantly declining.[5] McNamara also experienced distress and feelings of helplessness caused by his wife's regular hospital visits since midsummer 1967 for surgery and medical follow-up for stomach cancer and frequent quarrels with his only son, who was deeply troubled by his father's involvement in the Vietnam War, including personal attacks on McNamara and the president as cold-hearted 'murderers' and war criminals (Shapley, 1993; Hendrickson, 1997).

Evidence of avoidance and denial of Tet-related warnings As for Johnson's and McNamara's avoidance and denial throughout five phases identified prior to the Tet Offensive, a number of observations can be made. Firstly, the characteristics of the TRI rather than avoidance or

---

[5] McNamara's influence on Johnson declined especially after: (1) McNamara's memos to the president in May 1967 and October 1967, (2) a controversial statement in the Senator Stennis committee in August 1967 which made Johnson very angry, and (3) McNamara's emotional confessions during small group meetings in October and November 1967 with formal and informal advisors on Vietnam that he was worried that everything he (and Secretary of State Rusk) had done (as key architects in the Vietnam War) might have been wrong. Despite this decline of influence, the number of meetings and communications between McNamara and Johnson did not decline. McNamara remained Johnson's key advisor on all Vietnam War affairs until his resignation.

denial, seem to have formed an important reason for the fact that the slowly but steadily emerging 'Tet' threat did not play a significant role in Johnson's or McNamara's primary and secondary appraisals. It would have required a remarkable insight into the enemy's thinking – combined with strong imagination – to connect the twelve early intelligence reports as the first potential foreshadows of 'Tet'. It is all the more understandable given the fact that both politicians were preoccupied with more salient topics in other areas which carried serious threats and political risks, e.g., the Six Days War in the Middle East in June 1967 and race riots in Detroit. Given the increasing specificity and accuracy TRI (eighteen pieces) during phase 3 (14 September–30 November), it steadily became more unlikely if not impossible for both politicians to overlook them. For example, they must have become aware of the repeated public statements and aggressive intentions of North Vietnamese Defence Minister General Vo Nguyen Giap issued in September in which he referred to (a) vulnerabilities of the US and the South Vietnamese regime, (b) Hanoi's change of strategy, (c) several features of a Tet like offensive and public uprising and (d) a call-up for Viet Cong irregulars and sleeping cells. Later both politicians were confronted with a three-page document captured on 16 October which designated preparations and targets for the 'Winter-Spring Offensive' in broad terms. Yet, just like the first twelve pieces of TRI during phases 1 and 2, the eighteen signals in phase 3 largely went unheeded and hardly received attention. These signals were largely avoided by both politicians, who may have minimised and discredited the TRI as further examples of classic Vietnamese communist propaganda. There is also reason to believe that they were seen by Johnson and several of his advisors as indications that the communist leaders had started to become desperate.

Secondly, despite the rapidly increasing threat signals which consistently predicted an unusually large-scale offensive, Johnson and McNamara remained passive consumers in relation to the Tet-threat. Both politicians avoided thinking and discussing Hanoi's strategic intentions and plans in general (McNamara, 1995). As far as North Vietnam's position and determination was considered, it was usually biased by cognitive projection of American values, instead of serious attempts to understand the reasoning, cultural values and risk-taking of the communist leaders in Hanoi (Kearns, 1976; McNamara, 1995).

Thirdly, the author has found no evidence of reactive search and vigilance strategies as part of Johnson's or McNamara's coping in response to the thirty pieces of TRI in phases 1, 2 and 3. In other words, neither separate signals nor the combination and build-up of these early threats prompted Johnson or McNamara to request more information either via memo or in notes of the proceedings of thirty-four small-group meetings between key members of the policy group for the governmental warning-response process (this included what was known as the 'Tuesday Lunch Group'). There is also hardly any remark by Johnson or McNamara in the sixty-minute-long meetings, which refers to the possibility that there might be a threat of a serious and unusual offensive somewhere in the future. The vigilance and attention of both politicians were at best superficially focused on smaller-scale enemy preparations of the NVA or Viet Cong.

Fourthly, except for the emerging threat against Khe Sanh and occasional acknowledgements by Johnson of parts of the emerging Tet Offensive, both politicians continued their denial and avoidance during phases 4 and 5 despite the significant increase in quantity and quality of TRI. It can be concluded that from December 1967 it became more and more difficult for both politicians to avoid and deny the increasing indications (by then there had been sixty-two in total) that the enemy was preparing an unusually large-scale offensive and that this would include attacks on the South Vietnamese capital Saigon.

Remarkably, both politicians almost stubbornly persisted in their avoidance and denial of the TRI and its implications. Neither Johnson nor McNamara took a decision or initiated actions which can be regarded as an explicit or implicit acknowledgement of any of the TRI, despite the fact that time for counter-measures (in case the Offensive really did take place) was running out. The number of meetings of the Tuesday Lunch Group, which could be regarded as a crucial forum for governmental warning-response processes in phases 4 and 5, was minimal. There were three such meetings between 5 December and 30 January, as well as a meeting of the National Security Council on 23 January and a meeting of Johnson and McNamara with the chiefs of staff of the US armed forces; neither Johnson nor McNamara referred to the threat of a broad 'Tet-like' offensive.

With the exception of the North Vietnamese threat against the Marine base at Khe Sanh and against the border areas and the demilitarised zone, the threat against almost every other location in South Vietnam including its capital Saigon was simply not mentioned. It is all the more remarkable that both politicians avoided discussing this highly sensitive topic in regular or extra meetings of the Tuesday Lunch Group because this was the only small group setting (usually consisting of at most eight participants: senior foreign policy advisors and the president) in which Johnson felt relatively free and open discussion of all aspects of the Vietnam War was possible without any risk of leaks (Barrett, 1993). There is no evidence that Johnson or McNamara requested additional background information on the emerging Tet-like threat or began to consider or prepare for its likely implications. Consequently the issue of whether additional protective counter-measures should be taken against the predicted all-out offensive across South Vietnam, including Saigon, was not placed on the agenda of any of the meetings in phase 4 and 5. Consistent with this, the president and McNamara avoided discussing the option to inform the public, the press and the US Congress about a forthcoming enemy offensive. Moreover, the emerging threat is not mentioned in memos or in any of the phone calls which have been transcribed and declassified thus far.

The TRI and its most likely implications were denied by Johnson and especially McNamara in various ways: they were seen as propaganda, self-deceit and typical communist exaggeration rather than indications of Hanoi's risk-taking and determination. The attempts to 'connect the dots' by the CIA Station team in Saigon (mainly based on captured enemy documents and interrogations) were probably pushed aside as less reliable and less probable than reports and messages from General Westmoreland and his military intelligence staff. Both politicians tended to take the single source-based reports based on intercepted radio communications by the National Security Agency (NSA) rather seriously. Johnson was not very fond of what he viewed as pessimistic CIA reports and preferred those emanating from General Westmoreland's Military Intelligence and McNamara's own Defense Intelligence Agency (DIA), whereas McNamara preferred the assessments of the CIA above the TRI provided by his own military intelligence services including the DIA.

A remarkable exception to Johnson's tendency to avoid talking about the emerging threat of a 'Tet-like offensive' took place during his visit to Australia. On 21 December 1967, Johnson discussed the war in Southeast Asia with Prime Minister John McEwen and other senior Australian government officials. According to notes taken by the presidential aide and White House public relations officer George Christian, the president assessed the enemy's plans for the immediate future during the conversation. The president said that Hanoi was under extreme pressure to achieve some tactical victory. He emphasised that North Vietnamese forces had infiltrated the South and that he foresaw kamikaze attacks in the months ahead, hence his reason for pressing so hard for additional allied manpower. The president foresaw a sequence in which the US and their allies would maintain pressure on the North Vietnamese without widening the war. Sooner or later the communist leaders in Hanoi would than have to decide what to do in the face of high losses and the continued frustration of their objectives.[6] In the same conversation Johnson also seemed to acknowledge Westmoreland's assessment that the predicted desperate attacks by the NVA and Viet Cong would be aimed at the northern area of South Vietnam. Two days later (23 December) during a conversation with Pope Paul VI in Vatican City, Johnson again remarked that the North Vietnamese were under great pressure and that he expected them to employ 'kamikaze' tactics to gain a victory.[7] Overall, Johnson's remarks during these meetings suggest that at least in some small audiences he acknowledged instead of denying and avoiding aspects of the 'Tet' threat and some of its implications.

Another major exception to the overall pattern of cognitive avoidance by both politicians was the attention Johnson invested in those aspects of the TRI which informed him about the North Vietnamese threat against the US Marine base in Khe Sanh from late December. Johnson employed many proactive search and information-gathering activities which can be characterised as micro-management. During almost every meeting with his senior advisors between late December 1967 and 30 January 1968 Johnson asked specific threat-related questions to which he wanted answers as soon as possible, narrowing his focus to what it implied for the threat to Khe Sanh. It is remarkable that Johnson's preoccupation with Khe Sanh did not extend to other locations threatened by a 'Tet-like offensive'. This was despite increasing reports of a significant increase in infiltration by Viet Cong cells and preparations for future attacks against many locations in Saigon, including symbolic and politically sensitive targets such as the US embassy. During phases 4 and 5 Johnson acknowledged implicitly and explicitly that he was increasingly worried about the threat against Khe Sanh.

Part of the reasons for Johnson's close attention was that he feared that his military commanders in the Vietnam battlefield might try to shift the blame to him by levelling the accusation that he, as commander-in-chief, had not provided them with sufficient troops and freedom of command to keep the situation under control. It was obvious that Johnson did not deny or avoid his political responsibility for handling this specific part of the enemy's threat. At the same time, Johnson wanted reassurances from his

---

[6] Meeting of the president with the Australian cabinet, 11:13 a.m., 21 December; the full text of the notes is printed in *Foreign Relations*, 1964–1968, volume XXVII, Document 35, Foreign Relations, 1967; Vietnam/ National Security Files, Country File, Vietnam, LBJ Library.

[7] For Johnson's remarks to the pope, see 'President's Meeting with Pope' (23 December 1967) from J. Valenti's Notes, Document 39, Meeting Notes File Box 2, Folder: 23 December 1967, LBJ Library.

military commanders that they had everything they needed to respond successfully to the North Vietnamese threat against Khe Sanh.

Finally, overt acknowledgement of serious TRI by policy-makers would have automatically led to pressure to act. To Johnson and McNamara this expectation may have largely determined how they coped with their dilemmas, for both politicians seemed to have avoided mentioning or discussing them for as long as possible. For different reasons, in various ways and on several occasions, both politicians preferred to keep most aspects of the TRI and their dilemmas at a stage between knowing and not acting until such a method of coping could no longer be sustained or would not be necessary because the danger had declined. Johnson later claimed in his memoirs that he had considered and even agonised over whether or not to refer to the possibility of a winter–spring offensive in his State of the Union Address on 17 January, 1968. He claimed that he had decided not to issue such a public warning partly because he did not want to alert the enemy.

Probably at least as a consequence of Johnson's and McNamara's relatively consistent avoidance and denial in the settings and groups in which they operated, their primary appraisals of Tet-related threats were not as accurate as one might expect. As for Johnson's and McNamara's secondary appraisals there are no indications that they seriously doubted the US and allied forces' ability to defend against a Tet-like offensive. On the other hand, it is quite likely that both politicians were less confident about their options to manage the situation inside and outside the government, as well as within the Democratic Party. The combination of steadily increasing warnings related to Tet and the accumulating situational pressures from other Vietnam and non-Vietnam related quarters created a complex pattern of political dilemmas, as well as moderate to high levels of strain during the five pre-encounter phases. Consistent with the first hypothesis, several types of implicit avoidance and denial characterised the way both politicians coped with the TRI, the impending danger and its implications.

The impact of the politician's avoidance and denial on preparedness to face a crisis

Hypothesis 2 is focused on the impact of a policy-maker's denial and avoidance during pre-encounter phases on government preparedness on the eve of an actual encounter. Hypothesis 2 is formulated as follows:

The more a policy-maker employs strategies of avoidance and denial as a form of coping with TRI about impending danger, the less prepared s/he and their government will be to deal with the crisis when this danger actually strikes.

Conceptual preparedness   The case-study indicates that the persistent avoidance and denial employed by both politicians during the pre-encounter phases had a significant impact on their primary and secondary appraisals. Johnson's and McNamara's disregard of most TRI unrelated to Khe Sanh and their avoidance of discussions about most of their implications had a profound influence on both politicians' surprise at the timing, scale, level of coordination and impact of the Tet offensive on the home front. Their selective attention also resulted in conceptual unpreparedness in relation to the Viet Cong's actions in Saigon and its impact on the domestic front (Braestrup, 1983). In some ways McNamara was probably less surprised than Johnson, as he had been more focused on generally pessimistic CIA assessments, rather than on the more positive combat intelligence reports from General Westmoreland and the DIA about enemy reinforcements and likely order of battle.

Organisational preparedness   Denial and avoidance often result in distortions, under- and over-reactions, poor decision making and delays (e.g., Janis and Mann, 1977; Janis, 1962; Breznitz, 1983). Each of these can be observed in this case study. With the exception of Johnson's responses towards Khe Sanh, avoidance was at its peak during the last six weeks before the Tet Offensive, in other words beyond the point of no return for various protective measures such as sending 50,000 additional troops. However, some counter-measures could still have been initiated and executed even a few days before the offensive started, including consulting US ambassador Bunker and Field Commander Westmoreland over potential attacks against politically sensitive locations such as the US embassy, as well as preparing the public and members of Congress. The overriding implication was that procedures in the White House Situation Centre, which had begun to work on a twenty-four-hour basis, as well as intelligence requirements, were mainly focused on the situation near Khe Sanh.

Political preparedness   The impact of Johnson's and McNamara's avoidance and denial on their political preparedness at the eve of 'Tet' was considerable. Neither they nor any of their senior advisors initiated discussions to acquire an overview of the possible immediate and longer-term political implications which might be triggered by a major offensive. Not only were considerations and decisions on political counter-measures and contingency plans delayed, but a clear and well-orchestrated public-relations campaign – including well-timed public statements by President Johnson supported by McNamara, their 'spin-doctors' and the administration's

Information Group – could have moderated the enormous political fallout which the Johnson administration subsequently experienced in February and March 1968. Although President Johnson later claimed he had considered 'preparing' the public during the televised State of the Union address, neither he nor McNamara nor any other member of the government initiated measures to increase public readiness.

Mental preparedness   The impact of Johnson's and McNamara's avoidance and denial on their mental preparedness at the eve of 'Tet' was mixed. On the one hand their strong and persistent avoidance of most aspects of the TRI certainly contributed to their shock when confronted with incoming messages about the start of the Tet Offensive. On the other hand, after experiencing months of intense pressures, accompanied by moderate to severe distress caused by multiple chronic and acute pressures, their psychological readiness could have been much worse.

Overall this analysis of the key politicians' preparedness supports the assertion of the second hypothesis proposed above. The shortcomings in Johnson's and McNamara's state of preparedness can be regarded as a more or less logical consequence of the denial and avoidance of TRI by both the president and secretary of state, especially during the last two phases before the Tet Offensive.

Conclusions

Based on this case study, the following six general conclusions can be drawn: Firstly, it was no earlier than six weeks before the start of the offensive that 'Tet-related' considerations started to become more prominent in Defense Secretary McNamara's and President Johnson's primary and secondary appraisals. Their main focus on the threat against Khe Sanh – which actually formed only a small part of the Tet scenario – presented both political challenges and potential opportunity, resulting in dilemmas for both politicians.

Secondly, both politicians suffered moderate to high levels of strain throughout the five pre-encounter phases, which probably peaked for Johnson during the last two weeks of January 1968, when he was confronted with a range of domestic and foreign policy crises prior to the Tet Offensive. For McNamara the strain was probably at its peak between July and October 1967.

Thirdly, there is evidence of the use of denial and avoidance strategies by both politicians. This is consistent with both policy-makers becoming increasingly aware of the emerging danger and, despite their likely realisation that a Tet-like offensive could create serious fallout for the credibility and political acceptability of the administration's Vietnam strategy, avoidance continued to dominate other coping strategies as both politicians ignored the predicted Tet-offensive and its implications by rarely speaking about it during important small group meetings. Johnson's focus on one relatively small aspect of the operational and tactical aspects of the impending danger during the four weeks before the offensive illustrates that politicians tend to acknowledge and pay attention to those parts of the intelligence reports which suit their expectations and motives (Ford, 1998).

Fourthly, the impact of Johnson's and McNamara's avoidance (and to a lesser extent their denial) on their overall preparedness was probably high. Their avoidance influenced each of its components on the eve of 'Tet' and in addition probably resulted in significant delays in initiating protective counter-measures in the battlefield. For example, two extended US cease fires planned for late December 1967 and late January 1968, to coincide with the Tet celebrations, were initially approved by both politicians against the advice of Field Commander General Westmoreland and the joint chiefs of staff, despite available TRI showing that the enemy tended to exploit ceasefires for troop movements and reinforcements (Ford, 1995).

Fifthly, the characteristics of the domestic institutional political setting in which both politicians were operating did not provide sufficient safeguards to identify and minimise Johnson's and McNamara's persistent avoidance and denial. Partly as a consequence of the institutional context which President Johnson had created and maintained since 1964, forums for political accountability, like the Senate or Congress, had little institutional power to control and judge the TRI presented to Johnson and McNamara. They were also unable to influence how both policy-makers coped with this situation. There was no informal or formal advisor inside or outside the circle of colleagues closely involved in the governmental warning response process and who could have functioned as a 'devil's advocate', with sufficient insight, credibility and authority to trigger thinking and discussions about worst-case scenarios before it was too late. Partly as a result of this lack in the Tuesday Lunch Group meetings (and during National Security Council meetings), Johnson and McNamara were seldom, if ever, pushed to discuss TRI or to explain how they appraised the warning messages and to what extent they had considered specific protective counter-measures in order to enhance governmental preparedness.

Finally, from the perspective of the resilience of key policy-makers this case-study provides both positives and negatives. Despite the emerging danger of an all-out enemy offensive and the potential for vertical and horizontal escalation of the conflict and simultaneous domestic and foreign policy crises, there are no indications that Johnson or McNamara became so overwhelmed that they were no longer capable to act in line with their responsibilities as political leaders. It is interesting to compare the findings here with those in pioneering crisis research at the time of the Vietnam War, which suggested that the capacities of leaders may drastically decline during situations of impending danger and rising stress (Hermann, 1972; Holsti, 1972; Holsti and George, 1975; see also Brecher, 1993; 2008). The negative conclusion is that even extremely skilled politicians, like Johnson and McNamara, can become trapped in situations and paralysed by dilemmas such that they deny and avoid emerging threats which fall within their portfolio and competencies as political leaders to address.

Based on the case-study in this chapter some concerns are triggered by considering the following question: if politicians reveal such a high propensity for maladaptive strategies in an ongoing situation where prior information and controllability appear to have been relatively good, what could this mean for other scenarios where predictability and controllability tend to be much lower? Making indirect reference to the conflicts in Vietnam and Afghanistan, more recent US policy announcements have admitted, 'We have learned through painful experience that the wars we fight are seldom the wars that we planned' (*Daily Telegraph*, 2010). However, the case study presented in this chapter demonstrates that it is not only a question of learning that wars seldom, if ever, develop the way policy-makers and senior military commanders had planned or intended. It is also a matter of playing simultaneously on a variety of chessboards each with different and sometimes deeply institutionalised rules. Politicians have to cope, while constantly finding a 'balance' between the demands and constraints of each chessboard, yet even relatively good predictions and controllability of impending danger can still lead to tremendous dilemmas and strains. In turn, these may cause persistent denial and avoidance of disturbing and distressing threats. Depending on the 'permissiveness' of the domestic political, organisational and small group context (e.g. groupthink) in which the policy-makers operate during confrontations with impending danger, a politician's denial and avoidance may become likelier and persist for longer.

References

Allen, G. W. (2001). *None So Blind: A Personal Account of the Intelligence Failure in Vietnam*. Chicago: Ivan R. Dee.

Barrett, D. M. (1993). *Uncertain Warriors: Lyndon Johnson and his Vietnam Advisers*. University of Kansas Press.

Braestrup, P. (1983). *Big Story: How the American Press and Television Reported and Interpreted the Crisis of Tet 1968 in Vietnam and Washington*. New Haven: Yale University Press.

Brecher, M. (1993). *Crises in World Politics: Theory and Reality*. Oxford: Pergamon Press.

(2008). *International Political Earthquakes*. Ann Arbor: University of Michigan Press.

Brewin, B. and Shaw, S. (1987). *Vietnam on Trial: Westmoreland vs. CBS*. New York: Atheneum.

Breznitz, S. (1972). The effect of frequency and pacing of warnings upon the fear reaction to threatening event. Research Report to the Ford Foundation.

(ed.) (1983). *Denial of Stress*. New York: International Universities Press.

Carver, C. S. and Scheier, M. F. (1993). Vigilant and avoidant coping in two patient samples. In H. W. Krohne (ed.), *Attention and Avoidance: Strategies in Coping with Aversiveness* (pp. 295–320). Seattle: Hogrefe and Huber Publishers.

Daily Telegraph (2010). We must plan for new kinds of war, says Pentagon. 3 February.

Edelstein, E. L., Nathanson, D. L. and Stone, A. M. (1989). *Denial: a Clarification of Concepts and Research*. New York/London: Plenum Press.

Farnham, B. (1997). *Roosevelt and the Munich Crisis: A Study of Political Decision-Making*. New Jersey: Princeton University Press.

Folkman, S. and Lazarus, R. S. (1985). If it changes it must be a process: study of emotion and coping during three stages of a collective examination. *Journal of Personality and Social Psychology*, 48, 150–70.

Ford, H. P. (1998). *CIA and the Vietnam Policymakers: Three Episodes*. Washington: Central Intelligence Agency.

Ford, R. E. (1995). *Tet 1968: Understanding the Surprise*. London: Frank Cass.

George, A. L. (1980). *Presidential Decision Making in Foreign Policy*. Boulder: Westview Press.

't Hart, P., Stern, E. K. and Sundelius, B. (eds.) (1997). *Beyond Groupthink: Political Group Dynamics and Foreign Policy-Making*. Ann Arbor: University of Michigan Press.

Hendrickson, P. (1997). *The Living and the Dead: Robert McNamara and Five Lives of a Lost War*. Basingstoke: Papermac.

Hermann, C. F. (ed.) (1972). *International Crises*. New York: Free Press.

Hermann, M. G. (1979). Indications of stress in policymakers during foreign policy crises. *Political Psychology*, 1, 27–46.

Hermann, M. G. and Hermann, C. F. (1989). Who makes foreign policy decisions and how: an empirical enquiry. *International Studies Quarterly*, 33, 361–87.

Holsti, O. R. (1972). *Crisis, Escalation, War*. Montreal: McGill-Queen's University Press.

Holsti, O. R. and George, A. L. (1975). The effects of stress on the performance of foreign policy makers. In C. P. Cotter (ed.), *Political Science Annual: Individual Decision Making*, 6 (pp. 225–319). Indianapolis: Bobbs-Merrill.

Janis, I. L. (1962). Psychological effects of warnings. In G. W. Baker and D. W. Chapman (eds.), *Man and Society in Disaster* (pp. 55 –92). New York: Basic Books.

—— (1989). *Crucial Decisions: Leadership in Policymaking and Crisis Management.* New York/London: Free Press.

Janis, I. L. and Mann, L. (1977). *Decision Making: a Psychological Analysis of Conflict, Choice and Commitment.* New York: Free Press.

Johnson, L. B. (1971). *The Vantage Point: Perspectives on the Presidency, 1963–1969.* New York: Holt, Rinehart and Winston.

Kam, E. (1988). *Surprise Attack: The Victim's Perspective.* Cambridge, Mass.: Harvard University Press.

Kearns, D. (1976). *Lyndon Johnson and the American Dream.* New York: Harper and Row.

Krohne, H. W. (1986). Coping with stress: disposition, strategies, and the problem of measurement. In M. H. Appley and R. Trumbull (eds.), *Dynamics of Stress: Physiological, Psychological, and Social Perspectives* (pp. 209–34). New York: Plenum.

—— (ed.) (1993). *Attention and Avoidance: Strategies in Coping with Aversiveness.* Seattle: Hogrefe and Huber Publishers.

—— (1996). Individual differences in coping. In M. Zeider and N. S. Endler (eds.), *Handbook of Coping: Theory, Research, Applications* (pp. 381–409). New York: Wiley.

Lazarus, R. S. (1986). *Psychological Stress and the Coping Process.* New York: McGraw-Hill.

—— (1993). Coping theory and research: Past, present, and future. *Psychosomatic Medicine,* 55, 234–47.

Lazarus, R. S. and Folkman, S. (1984). *Stress, Appraisal, and Coping.* New York: Springer.

Levite, A. (1987). *Intelligence and Strategic Surprises.* New York: Colombia University Press.

Mechanic, D. (1978). *Students under Stress: a Study in the Social Psychology of Adaptation* Madison: University of Winconsin Press.

McNamara, R. S. (1995). *In Retrospect: The Tragedy and Lessons of Vietnam.* New York: Times Brooks.

—— (1999). *Argument Without End: In Search of Answers to the Vietnam Tragedy.* New York: Public Affairs.

Metselaar, M. V. (1999). Is more information necessarily better? Advantages and disadvantages of the explosion of information technologies for political and military preparedness. *NL Arms,* 3, 259–76.

Monat, A., Averill, J. R. and Lazarus, R. S. (1972). Anticipatory stress and coping reactions under various conditions of uncertainty. *Journal of Personality and Social Psychology,* 24, 237–53.

Oberdorfer, D. (1971). *Tet. New York: Doubleday.* Reprinted, Baltimore: Johns Hopkins University Press, 2001.

Prados, J. and Stubbe, R. W. (1991). *Valley of Decision: the Siege of Khe Sanh.* Boston: Houghton Mifflin.

Rosenthal, U., Charles, M. T. and 't Hart, P. (eds.) (1989). *Coping with Crises: the Management of Disasters, Riots and Terrorism*. Springfield: Charles C. Thomas Publishers.

Schandler, H. Y. (1977). *The Unmaking of a President: Lyndon Johnson and Vietnam*. Princeton University Press.

Shapley, D. (1993). *Promise and Power: The Life and Times of Robert McNamara*. Boston: Little, Brown.

Tetlock, P. E. (1983). Accountability and complexity of thought. *Journal of Personality and Social Psychology*, 45, 1, 74–83.

Verbeek, B. (2003). *Decision-making in Great Britain during the Suez Crisis: Small Groups and a Persistent Leader*. Aldershot/Burlington: Ashgate.

Vertzberger, Y. (1990). *The World in Their Minds: Information Processing, Cognition, and Perception in Foreign Policy Decisionmaking*. Stanford University Press.

Wirtz, J. J. (1990). Deception and the Tet Offensive. *Journal of Strategic Studies*, 13 (June), 82–98.

(1991). *The Tet Offensive: Intelligence Failure in War*. Ithaca: Cornell University Press.

Part IV

People as politicians

9 The political side of personality

Gianvittorio Caprara, Michele Vecchione and Claudio Barbaranelli

Personality and politics

Politics involves institutions, systems of norms and principles of power management, ideally designed and set in motion for the common good. Personality involves intra-individual systems and self-regulatory mechanisms that guide people towards achieving individual and collective goals, while providing coherence and continuity in behavioural patterns and a sense of personal identity across different settings (Bandura, 2001; Caprara and Cervone, 2000; Mischel and Shoda, 1998). Just how such societal and individual systems might be related has long been a source of speculation and serious concern for philosophers, political scientists, psychologists, and laypeople. In the past, these entities were conceptualised as functioning at different levels and with different operational structures, but current views tend to emphasise communalities rather than diversities and point to reciprocal interactions between politics and personality. Governmental institutions have been created and designed to set and preserve conditions that allow society to function in harmony and individuals to experience satisfaction in their lives. Political discourse shapes basic perspectives on options, goals, attitudes, and values, but as citizens bring to the political arena needs and aspirations for personal and social well-being, they in turn influence the agenda of politics no less than the behaviour of politicians. Politics in modern democracies aims to be the realm within which citizens can operate through institutions and endorse obligations aimed to pursue optimal conditions for personal, social and communal growth. Such ambitious goals cannot be fully appreciated without clarification of the psychological processes underlying political choices, consent formation, concerted political action and effective governance. That quest invigorates investigation of the synergistic influence of affect and cognitive reasoning that leads to political preferences, decisions and actions. It also encourages new understandings of the role of leaders' and followers' personalities.

Two concepts of personality

Personality is a concept as difficult and as familiar as many others in psychology. In reality, one cannot elude such a concept in everyday discourse. A theoretical framework is needed to organise knowledge, to understand how people process information, impressions and conjectures from their own and others' personalities, and therefore to maintain a continuous dialogue with themselves and deal with others. The fact that a theory is often implicit or tacit does not limit its influence. Popular knowledge may operate as a double-edged sword rather than as a secure advantage when personal intuitions and common sense are at odds with scientific findings. In reality, personality is complex as it includes behavioural tendencies, structures and mechanisms that regulate affective, cognitive and motivational processes. It involves internal systems and processes that guide people towards the attainment of individual and collective goals, it accounts for coherence and behavioural continuity across contexts, and ultimately, it explains one's personal identity (Caprara and Cervone, 2000). Contemporary scholars have addressed personality under two distinct perspectives. The first views personality as an architecture of traits or, in other words, a system of behavioural tendencies that allows for distinguishing between one person and another and making conjectures and predictions regarding individual conduct. The second perspective views personality as a self-regulatory agentic system that is capable of reflecting on its own experiences and that interacts with the environment whilst conforming with personal criteria and goals. These two perspectives produce diverse questions and pave the way to distinct research programmes. Some programmes focus on the individual variables that are most likely to influence the impressions and evaluations drawn from the way individuals present themselves and behave. Others focus on the organisation of affect and cognitions conducive to beliefs and goals that guide individuals' behaviour from within. Both perspectives complement each other in making sense of the influence that the personalities of leaders and voters may exert on political decisions.

Two aspects of the personalisation of politics

Discussion regarding the personalisation of politics is long-standing, although ubiquitous due to the different meanings assigned to the term. By personalisation one may refer to the influential role of voters' and politicians' personalities in making sense of their own political preferences. Others, instead, may refer to how voters perceive politicians' personalities, and to the substantial investments made by political campaigns aimed at crafting and delivering personal images of political candidates that are most attractive to voters (Campus and Pasquino, 2004; King, 2002). Thus, the same concept encompasses diverse phenomena that are traceable to the above distinction between the two concepts of personality, namely personality as functioning and as perception. The first is mainly interested in the unique organisation of dispositions, values, beliefs and expectations that underlie politicians' and voters' behaviours in contemporary politics. The second is mainly interested in the individual variables most likely to influence the impressions and evaluations voters draw from politicians.

Among the elements that contribute to assigning particular importance to voters' and politicians' personalities as a self-regulating system are the declining influence of social class and party identification, electorates' higher education and citizens' increased awareness of their political rights and duties. The more people are reasoning agents who pursue the best match between their beliefs and values, and political offers and opportunities, the more the unique organisation of affect, cognitions and habits of both voters and politicians are in making sense of their political choices and engagement. Among the elements that contribute to assigning particular importance to the personality characteristics of politicians as perceived or resulting in surface behavioural tendencies are:

• the electoral system, which often leads to the formation of coalitions that converge on a single leadership or restrict voters' choices at the ballot box between two single candidates;
• the unclear ideological identity of new parties that have taken the place of traditional movements reflecting the material conditions of lives among diverse social groups;
• the shifting of opposing political coalitions towards more pragmatic platforms aimed at attracting a larger share of the electorate;
• the influence of the media and the vanishing distinctiveness of electoral programmes;
• television above all, generally seen as a potent vehicle of personalisation capable of highlighting personal features and significantly contributing to the fortunes of political actors.

Obviously, the influence of each of these elements may vary across political contexts, at different times as well as in relation to their various combinations. In the following we will address firstly the self-reported personality of voters and politicians and then the personalities of politicians as perceived by voters, focusing on political preference rather than on participation or other aspects of political choice. In particular, we will focus on how traits and values may affect political preference and orientation. Then, we will report preliminary findings attesting to the heuristics people may use to navigate through politics.

Traits and values as determinants of political preference

Personality may assume a critical role in orienting the political behaviour of both voters and politicians, in concert with a host of other political and socio-economic factors. We view personality as the whole system including traits, motives, values, attitudes, self beliefs and cognitive styles, i.e., habits that distinguish one from another and that reveal the uniqueness of each person. Thus, we believe that personality is crucial in making sense of the political behaviour of both voters and politicians, although to a different extent and through different factors due to the range of mechanisms involved in political preference, engagement and achievement in various contexts.

Early studies on the authoritarian personality (Adorno, Frenkel-Brunswik, Levinson and Sanford, 1950; Frenkel-Brunswik, 1948, 1949) started a tradition of research aimed at examining the relationship between political orientation and a variety of individual differences in the area of personality. Over the course of time studies included traits (Elms, 1976; Eysenck, 1954; Jost, 2006; McCrae, 1996), cognitive styles (Tetlock, 1983, 1984), social attitudes (Altemeyer, 1981, 1996, 1998; Sidanius, 1985, 1978; Tetlock, 1984), moral reasoning (Emler, Renwick and Malone, 1983), moral preferences (Ricolfi, 2002), and personal values (Feldman, 2003; Rokeach, 1973; Schwartz, 1992; Thorisdottir, Jost, Liviatan and Shrout, 2007). For a comprehensive review, see Jost, Glaser, Kruglanski and Sulloway (2003).

Most of the above studies have addressed the personality of voters by relying on direct methods of assessment, such as self-reports (Greenstein, 1975; Simonton, 1990). Most of the approaches addressing the personality of politicians, instead, have relied on indirect means for assessing personality through content analysis of public records, biographies or primary source material, such as speeches or interviews, or by asking experts to complete standard personality rating scales. One strand of research has focused on traits (Etheredge, 1978; Rubenzer, Faschingbauer and Ones, 2000; Simonton, 1986, 1990), cognitive abilities (Simonton, 2006), and social motives (Winter, 1987, 1992). Another has focused on politicians' worldviews, cognitive styles, competence in political tasks, modes of interpersonal interaction and orientation in conflicts (Barber, 1977; George and George, 1998; Prost, 2003; Thoemmes and Conway, 2007). Winter considered the role of broad classes of goals and goal-directed actions, including power, achievement and affiliation motives, as components of personality that are especially relevant for presidential performance and appeal (Winter and Stewart, 1977; Winter, 1987). Tetlock (1983, 1984) examined the link between the political affiliation of UK and US politicians and the complexity of political leaders' thinking, namely the degree to which thinking and reasoning involve the recognition and integration of multiple perspectives, an issue which is discussed by Golec de Zavala (see chapter 5). Etheredge (1978) examined the role of personality traits like dominance, extraversion-introversion, interpersonal trust and self-esteem in shaping the foreign policy of several US presidents, while Barber (1977) recognised character, style and worldview as the critical components in evaluating presidential personality. Simonton (1988, 1990) identified five clusters of traits especially relevant to the leadership styles of US leaders, distinguishing between interpersonal, charismatic, deliberative, creative and neurotic presidents. Rubenzer *et al.* (2000) asked a sample of experts to rate the personality profiles of US presidents through the use of structured questionnaires and adjective lists measuring the Big Five personality traits. Subsequently Simonton (1986, 2006) has provided a detailed evaluation of the intellectual abilities of the first forty-two US chief executives, from George Washington to George W. Bush.

Whereas most research continues to rely on a variety of indirect means for assessing personality 'at a distance', few studies have directly addressed the personality of politicians (Costantini and Craik, 1980; Di Renzo, 1963; Putnam, 1973). Di Renzo (1963) examined the link between dogmatism and political preference in a large number of active politicians (Congressmen and Senators in the Italian parliament). The study was subsequently replicated in the United States (Di Renzo, 1977) and later in Japan (Feldman, 1996). In a comparative study, Putnam (1973) examined the beliefs, values and attitudes of Italian and British political elites through structured interviews with 176 members of the UK House of Commons and the Italian Chambers of Deputies. Costantini and Craik (1980) achieved a direct description of members of California's presidential delegation across five US presidential campaigns, from 1968 to 1976. Participants were rated on the Adjective Check List (ACL; Gough, 1960), which includes 300 descriptions of personality. Caprara and colleagues are currently addressing the study of basic traits and values of both voters and politicians as part of a comprehensive study.

Traits are crucial in setting the basic tone for the kind of person one may become, as values are crucial in giving direction to one's life. Whereas traits infuse the body with personality and attest to how given biological potentials turn into behavioural tendencies in response to the opportunities and constraints of the environment, values combine personality with society and culture and attest to how biological needs and social motives turn into principles that guide people's lives. Traits are enduring dispositions associated with consistent patterns of thought and feelings, which describe what people are like and vary in their intensity and strength. Values are cognitive representations of desirable, abstract and trans-situational goals that refer to people's priorities and vary in their relative significance as standards for judging behaviour, events, and people. Both traits and values prove crucial in understanding: (a) the extent to which self-reported traits and values account for voters' and politicians' political preferences; (b) the extent to which the traits and values of politicians as perceived by voters contribute to their political preference (Caprara, Schwartz, Vecchione and Barbaranelli, 2008).

The role of traits in determining political preference

To address personality traits most current research relies on the Five Factor Model (Digman, 1990), a common framework for organising the major individual differences in personality traits. This model represents a meeting point of diverse research traditions in the area, providing a consensual, objective and quantifiable description of the main aspects of personality: energy/extraversion (level of activity, vigour and assertiveness), agreeableness (concern for and sensitivity toward others), conscientiousness (self-regulation), emotional stability (control of affect and emotional reactions), and openness (width of cultural interest and exposure to new ideas, people, and experiences). Numerous studies from different cultures have extensively examined the impact of the Big Five traits on the political preference of voters (e.g., Jost, 2006; McCrae, 1996; Van Hiel, Kossowska and Mervielde, 2000).

In the United States, Gosling, Rentfrow and Swann (2003) found that liberals tend to score significantly higher than conservatives on openness, whereas conservatives score higher than liberals on conscientiousness. The same pattern was found in two large samples of US voters by Carney, Jost, Gosling, Niederhoffer and Potter (2008) and by Gerber, Huber, Raso and Ha (2009). Barbaranelli, Caprara, Vecchione, and Fraley (2007) identified distinct personality profiles among voters for the two US presidential candidates in 2004: intention to vote for Democratic candidate John Kerry was associated with higher scores on openness and lower scores on conscientiousness, with the opposite pattern found for voters of Republican President George W. Bush.

In Italy, findings from election campaigns attested to similar differences between voters from either side of the political spectrum, while revealing the contribution of two other traits – agreeableness and

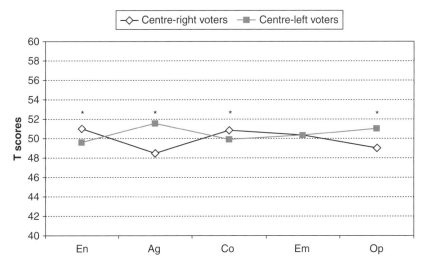

Note: A score of 50 indicates the average for the population. En = Energy/
Extraversion; Ag = Agreeableness; Co = Conscientiousness; Em = Emotional
Stability; Op = Openness. Data are from Caprara, Schwartz, Capanna, Vecchione
and Barbaranelli (2006). Asterisks are used to denote the traits that were
significantly different (p < .05) between centre-left and centre-right voters
(n = 3,044).

Figure 9.1. Voters' traits: findings from Italy

energy/extraversion – which consistently relate to a preference for the
centre-left and the centre-right respectively. As shown in figure 9.1, supporters who endorsed the platform of the centre-right coalition scored
significantly higher than their counterparts on energy/extraversion and
conscientiousness, whereas those who preferred the centre-left coalition
showed significantly higher degrees of agreeableness and openness
(Caprara, Schwartz, Capanna, Vecchione and Barbaranelli, 2006; see
also Caprara, Barbaranelli and Vicino, 1999; Caprara, Barbaranelli and
Zimbardo, 1999; Caprara and Vecchione, 2006). It has been reasoned that
energy/extraversion and agreeableness were the traits most congruent with
the distinctive ethos of the two main coalitions, and with the stereotypical
images of the respective leaders as conveyed by the media. The centre-right
coalition campaigned mostly on entrepreneurship, individual freedom
and achievements and was headed by Silvio Berlusconi, an entrepreneur
who in his speeches and campaign propaganda attempted to cultivate
and convey the image of an active, energetic, charismatic leader. The
centre-left coalition mainly campaigned instead on a platform of solidarity
and social justice. Likewise, the personalities of both Romano Prodi and

Walter Veltroni, the two prominent leaders of the left, were mostly associated with agreeableness, tolerance and benevolence towards others (Caciagli and Corbetta, 2002; Ceccarelli, 2007). In Germany, Schoen and Schumann (2007) found that supporters of left-wing parties (i.e., Social Democratic Party, Left Party and Green Party) scored higher on openness and agreeableness, whereas supporters of right-wing parties (i.e., Christian Democratic Union/Christian Social Union and Free Democratic Party) scored higher on conscientiousness.

In summary, citizens who favour conservative and liberal leaders and their campaign platforms showed similar traits in Europe and the USA. Liberals and left-oriented electors scored higher on openness, while conservatives and right-oriented electors scored higher on conscientiousness. In both Europe and the United States, higher scores on conscientiousness went along with preferences for political programmes that promote individual entrepreneurship and belief in the virtues of a free market, whereas higher scores on openness went along with a preference for political programmes that encourage pluralism and multiculturalism. Effects of other personality factors were less robust and less generalisable across cultures and political contexts.

Similar results were found in a few studies conducted on political elites. An original study was conducted in Italy on a sample of 103 male politicians drawn equally from the European parliament, Italian parliament (Chamber and Senate), and the provincial councils of Turin, Rome and Catania (Caprara, Barbaranelli, Consiglio, Picconi and Zimbardo, 2003). All of the politicians completed a questionnaire measuring the Big Five factors (i.e., the same questionnaire used in the above study on voters' traits). While politicians scored significantly higher than the general population on both energy/extraversion and agreeableness, right-wing politicians showed higher scores in energy/extraversion and conscientiousness than left-wing politicians, in accordance with findings from voters and with the centre-right's emphasis on the promotion of individuals' initiative and merit, industriousness and order. No significant differences between political groupings were found in agreeableness, openness and emotional stability (see figure 9.2).

A second study was conducted on a sample of 106 women members of the Italian parliament (Caprara, Francescato, Mebane, Sorace and Vecchione, 2010) which replicated the findings from voters, showing significant covariations between individual differences in traits and ideological affiliation, in accordance with the policies of the respective coalitions. Politicians affiliated to left-wing parties scored higher than centre-right politicians on openness and agreeableness traits. In contrast, politicians affiliated to right-wing parties scored higher than centre-left politicians

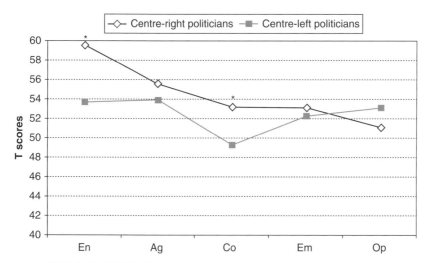

Note: A score of 50 indicates the average for the population. En = Energy/ Extraversion; Ag = Agreeableness; Co = Conscientiousness; Em = Emotional Stability; Op = Openness. Data are from Caprara, Barbaranelli, Consiglio, Picconi and Zimbardo (2003). Asterisks are used to denote the traits that were significantly different ($p < .05$) between centre-left and centre-right politicians ($n = 103$).

Figure 9.2. Politicians' traits: findings from Italy

on energy/extraversion and conscientiousness. Results from this study suggest that the congruency among self-reported traits and political choice fits better with politicians than voters, as traits contributed to the political affiliation of politicians much more than to the political orientation of voters. In particular, the percentage of variance in political choice accounted for by politicians' traits was surprisingly much higher than that accounted for among voters. However, it cannot be disregarded that concerns over self-presentation are much stronger in politicians than in voters, as they are expected to behave in accordance with the programmes they voice more so than voters. Nor can one exclude the possibility that predispositions exert a much more crucial influence in sustaining the political engagement of politicians than the voting preference of the electorate.

The role of values in determining political choice

Understanding the important role of traits in the process of personalising politics is complemented by a fuller appreciation of the contributions of values as key predictors of voting behaviour, as value-based judgements of policies and candidates may govern voting preferences to a considerable extent (Caprara and Zimbardo, 2004). Both earlier and contemporary scholars emphasised the central role of values in political judgement and choice (Barnea and Schwartz, 1998; Feldman, 2003; Schwartz, 1994), arguing that 'underlying all political belief systems are ultimate terminal values that specify the end states of public policy' (Tetlock, 2002, p. 247). Empirical studies have shown that personal values relate systematically to political choice across cultural contexts and political systems, suggesting that individuals tend to vote for parties whose platform or image suggests that electing them would promote attainment or preservation of those individuals' cherished, personal values (Barnea, 2003; Barnea and Schwartz, 1998; Caprara *et al.*, 2006). Most recent studies have adopted Schwartz's ten basic personal values: an established taxonomy that has paved the way for systematic international comparisons on the impact that values exert on political preferences (Schwartz, 1992). The ten values include: power, achievement, hedonism, stimulation, self-direction, universalism, benevolence, tradition, conformity and security. The theory specifies the structure of their dynamic relationships, assigning the values positions around a circle according to their compatibility. The values are organised into four higher-order-level value types, each including basic values:

(a) openness to change (self-direction, stimulation), which encourages independence of thought, feeling and action; receptiveness to change;
(b) conservation (conformity, tradition, security), which calls for submissive self-restriction, preserving traditional practices and protecting stability.
(c) self-transcendence (universalism, benevolence), which emphasises accepting others as equals and concern for their welfare;
(d) self-enhancement (power, achievement), which encourages pursuing one's own relative success and dominance over others.[1]

Even more so than traits, values accounted for a significant proportion of variability in voting, over and above the contribution of socio-demographic characteristics. Barnea (2003) related personal values to voting behaviour in fourteen democratic countries chosen to represent culturally distinct regions of the world. Whereas personal values discriminated significantly between supporters of different political parties in every country, the particular value dimension that structures ideological discourse depended upon the issues that are central in a given political context. Where political competition revolved around issues of national

---

[1] Hedonism values share elements of both openness and self-enhancement.

security versus equal rights and freedom for all, the key values influencing voters' preferences tended to be security and conformity as opposed to universalism and self-direction. Where the focus of political competition revolved around the distribution of material resources, the key values tended to be universalism and benevolence rather than power and achievement (Barnea, 2003). In the Israeli political arena of 1988, where protection of religious practice competed with free expression of a secular lifestyle, the key values that differentiated party supporters were tradition versus self-direction (Barnea and Schwartz, 1998). In the 2001 Italian elections, voters who attributed higher importance to universalism than to security values tended to vote for left-wing parties, which emphasise solidarity and pluralism. Right-wing voters, instead, assigned priority to security values, while scoring lower in universalism values than left-wing voters (Caprara *et al.*, 2006). Centre-left parties in Italy include traditional left-wing movements inspired by either Catholic or Marxist doctrine, which advocate social welfare, concern for social justice, equality, pluralism and tolerance of diverse groups. Such policies are most representative of universalist values. Centre-right parties instead praise the merits of tradition, community and family ties while promoting order, stability and security. Thus, the greater importance attributed by centre-left voters to self-transcendence values and by centre-right voters to conservation values is congruent with their ideological orientation. Figure 9.3 shows right- and left-wing voters' mean scores on Schwartz's ten value-types.

The same distinctive pattern of covariation between self-reported values and political choice has been found in a highly politically sophisticated group of women politicians (Caprara *et al.*, 2010). Members of the Italian Parliament completed the Portrait Values Questionnaire (i.e., the same questionnaire used in the above study on voters' values). Women politicians of opposite coalitions showed distinctive values that were congruent with their ideologies, in parallel with findings from a group of women voters taken from the general population (figure 9.4). Politicians affiliated to left-wing parties scored higher than centre-right politicians on the value of universalism. In contrast, politicians affiliated to right-wing parties scored higher than centre-left politicians on security, tradition, conformity and power values. Self-reported values accounted for a notable portion of politicians' ideological affiliation, much beyond what has been previously found among voters, further corroborating the Congruency Model of Caprara and Zimbardo (2004). This is particularly noteworthy in consideration of the characteristics of the examined population, namely top women politicians with high levels of education, expertise and political sophistication, all factors

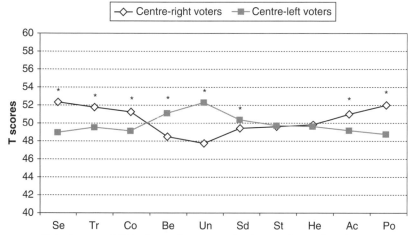

Note: A score of 50 indicates the average for the population. Se = Security; Tr = Tradition; Co = Conformity; Be = Benevolence; Un = Universalism; Sd = Self-direction; St = Stimulation; He = Hedonism; Ac = Achievement; Po = Power. Data are from Caprara *et al.*, 2006. Asterisks are used to denote the values that were significantly different ($p < .05$) between centre-left and centre-right voters ($n = 3044$).

Figure 9.3. Voters' values: findings from Italy

that are well known to increase ideological coherence (Jost, 2006). In particular, these results accord with findings from other studies (Tetlock, 2005), in which measures of cognitive styles have proven to be considerably more tightly connected to political ideology in elite samples than in mass samples. It is likely that values and political affiliation have dynamic and reciprocal influences: values orient towards certain political choices and careers, endorsing given ideologies and promoting programmes which reinforce politicians' choices and thus contribute to shaping their personalities. The more politicians promote and advocate the virtues and merits of their ideology, the more their behaviour and values are congruent with the principles they endorse in public, and the more likely they are to internalise the same principles. As social pressure requires that politicians present themselves in accordance with the ideological principles that they advocate, the match between ideological placement and self-reported values becomes reinforced over time through mechanisms aimed at avoiding the discomfort of dissonance (Fiske, 2004).

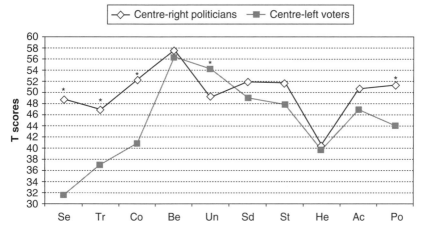

Note: A score of 50 indicates the average for the population. Se = Security; Tr = Tradition; Co = Conformity; Be = Benevolence; Un = Universalism; Sd = Self-direction; St = Stimulation; He = Hedonism; Ac = Achievement; Po = Power. Data are from Caprara, Francescato, Mebane, Sorace and Vecchione (2010). Asterisks are used to denote the values that were significantly different ($p < .05$) between centre-left and centre-right politicians ($n = 103$).

Figure 9.4. Politicians' values: findings from Italy

The joint contribution of traits and values to political affiliation

Traits and values are distinctive components of personality that play different roles in individuals' functioning, and that may account for political behaviour and voting to varying degrees. A comprehensive theory capable of explaining how traits and values operate in concert and reciprocally influence each other is critical to understanding the psychological structures that account for voting. To this aim, Caprara *et al.* (2006) assessed the relative contributions to voters' choices made by traits (using the Five Factor Model and the Big Five Questionnaire (BFQ), Caprara *et al.*, 2006), by a standard set of demographic variables, and by personal values (using Schwartz's theory of basic values and his Portrait Value Questionnaire [PVQ]; Schwartz, 1992). Data from 3,044 voters in the Italian national election of 2001 showed that values explained substantial variance in past and future voting and in the change of political choice, over and above personality traits. Similar results emerged in another study in which voters' values accounted for a significant portion of variance in voting, greater than voter's traits and demographic characteristics (Caprara *et al.*, 2008). While the importance of traits was much less than that of values, they were nonetheless more influential than socio-demographic variables (gender, age, educational level, income, profession and marital status). This finding fits with a view of personality as a proactive self-regulating, agential system operating in the pursuit of one's goals (Bandura, 1997, 2000; Caprara and Cervone, 2000). As people weigh alternatives and their implications in light of the personal standards that guide their behaviour, values take primacy over traits in predicting choices such as voting, which typically entails conscious consideration between alternatives (Caprara *et al.*, 2006).

Whereas the above findings assign primacy to values over traits in predicting political choice, other studies assign basic traits a crucial role in making sense of people's preferences, revealing that values which are decisive in political choices are rooted in individuals' predispositions. As argued by Rokeach (1973), traits can be viewed as stable personality features that serve as antecedents to values, which can in turn be reprioritised on the basis of experience and social expectations. A recent longitudinal study provides evidence of the mediational role of personal values in linking basic traits to voting and political ideology (Caprara, Vecchione and Schwartz, 2009). Traits measured during late adolescence, before the age of voting, contributed indirectly to later political orientation, through the effect of basic values. More specifically, conscientiousness was positively related to conservation values, in accordance with Tomkins' (1963) finding that conservatives are more motivated than liberals by norm attainment, rule following and orderliness. Agreeableness was positively related to self-transcendence values and negatively related to self-enhancement values. Openness was positively related to self-transcendence values and negatively related to conservation values, while energy/extraversion was positively related to self-enhancement values. Values fully mediated the influence exerted by the above traits on political orientation (Caprara *et al.*, 2009). Another longitudinal study (Block and Block, 2006) suggests that personality differences between liberals and conservatives begin in early childhood and affect political orientations throughout life. It is likely that basic dispositions, along with socialisation experiences, set the stage for ideological orientation whereas values mediate the influence of both on political choice.

A similar pattern was found in a further study of politicians (Caprara *et al.*, under review). As for voters, openness and conscientiousness traits contributed indirectly to political affiliation of politicians, through the mediation of values. These are also the traits that have shown robust and stable effects on political orientation across countries and political contexts. However, contrary to findings about voters, energy/extraversion and agreeableness have shown a direct effect on political affiliation, over and above the contribution of values. These are also the traits in which Italian politicians scored significantly higher than the general population. In this regard, the possibility cannot be excluded that energy/extraversion and agreeableness play a critical role in predisposing an individual to become involved in politics, more so than values. Also, one may speculate that a kind of self-presentation strategy leads politicians to convey an impression of their own person-alities that accords most with the attributes people appreciate in political actors, or with the attributes that conform directly to party policy and with the image conveyed by their leaders. Figure 9.5 summarises the mediational role of values in linking traits to the political preferences of both voters and politicians.

Although most of the findings have been shown to be consistent across samples of different ages and nationalities, the contribution of personality to ideology and political choices may vary significantly across political

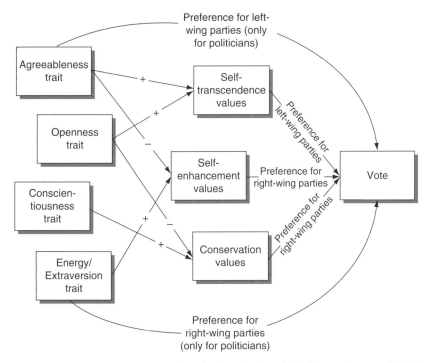

Figure 9.5. The mediational role of values in linking traits to political preference of voters and politicians

contexts. Whereas traditional ideologies like liberal and conservative or left and right may have different meanings at different latitudes, the strength of basic personal values as predictors of political orientation may depend upon cultural, economic and social factors. Barnea (2003), for example, reported that personal values are more relevant to political choice and group identity, and identification is less relevant, in autonomous and egalitarian cultures where people are encouraged to express their unique, personal preferences. Moreover, the patterns of covariation of traits and values with ideology may vary across political systems as a function of the status of political rights and of the specific content of political and ideological arguments (e.g., religion, civil liberties or economic security).

Politicians' traits and values as determinants of voters' preference

Numerous studies conducted in diverse linguistic and cultural contexts have shown that people's judgements of themselves as well as of others are usually traced back to the Big Five personality factors. However, the traditional five-factor distillation of traits does not accord with voters' typical appraisals of politicians (Caprara, Barbaranelli and Zimbardo, 1997, 2002; Caprara, Barbaranelli, Fraley and Vecchione, 2007). In reality, when judgements of politicians' personality are made from ratings of a list of adjectives including markers of the Big Five, voters' appraisals are typically traced back to only two factors.

Voters in Italy and the United States simplified their personality judgements of candidates in ongoing election campaigns (Bill Clinton and Bob Dole in the USA; Silvio Berlusconi and Romano Prodi in Italy) by compressing the usual five factors into a blend of only two. The collapsed factors included one blending energy/extraversion with openness and the other combining agreeableness, conscientiousness and emotional stability. Energy/extraversion and agreeableness served as primary anchors or 'attractors' for personality appraisals of politicians, as they subsumed the other dimensions of the Big Five. These two blends correspond notably with Digman's (1997) alpha and beta second-order factors and can be easily related to Bakan's (1966) and Wiggins' (1991) agency and communion dimensions, as well as to those reputed to count more highly among electorates in the Western democracies, namely leadership (or competence) and integrity (Chemers, 2001; Halpin and Winer, 1957; Jones and Hudson, 1996; Kinder and Sears, 1985; Popkin, 1993).

A follow-up study replicated earlier findings when voters were asked to evaluate the personality of Berlusconi when he was the leader of the opposition and of Prodi when he was prime minister, along with the personalities of two well-known Italian politicians: D'Alema (secretary of the Democratic Left) and Fini (secretary of the National Alliance) (Caprara, Barbaranelli and Zimbardo, 2002). About ten years on from the first study, a further sample of voters was asked to evaluate the personality of Prodi when he was the president of the European Commission, and that of Berlusconi when he was the Italian prime minister (Caprara, Barbaranelli *et al.*, 2003). Findings replicated the two personality factors, which were virtually the same as in 1997, although the same politicians were serving in different roles, suggesting that perceptions of political personalities tend to remain remarkably stable across several years (Miller, Wattenberg and Malanchuk, 1986). The simplification effect has been found also in Greece (Moustaka, 2008), where personalities of both main party leaders Kostas Karamanlis (New Democracy) and George Papandreou (PASOK) were assessed a few weeks after the 2007 parliamentary elections. Findings replicated the reduced factor structure found in most of the previous research, with energy/extraversion and agreeableness traits serving as anchors for personality appraisals of both politicians.

Similar findings emerged from data collected via the internet on a considerable number of US voters during the 2004 presidential election in which the Democratic candidate John Kerry opposed the Republican president George W. Bush (Caprara, Barbaranelli, Fraley and Vecchione, 2007). This study is novel in suggesting a unique perceived personality structure for Bush, whereas for Kerry the two personality factors were nearly identical to those previously found in Italian and American politicians. Bush's perceived personality was just as restricted as that of the other politicians, but the two factors represented a different combination of the Big Five traits. Adjectives typical of openness (e.g., informed and imaginative) loaded mainly onto the first calculated factor; furthermore, this personality factor showed high loadings on most descriptors of conscientiousness and some descriptors of agreeableness. Adjectives typical of energy/extraversion (e.g., happy and determined) and stability (e.g., self-confident and optimistic) loaded mainly onto the second calculated factor.

In summary, findings from diverse studies have demonstrated that voters organise their judgements of politicians along two, rather than five, dimensions. This simplification operates either in ongoing election campaigns or long afterwards and across different political offices. Findings were replicated also cross-culturally (Italy, US and Greece) and between participants' political preferences, using evaluations of voters for and against the candidate as well as non-voters (Caprara, Barbaranelli *et al.*, 2007). Yet, they seem limited to the political domain, as the same simplification was not observed when the same adjectives were used to evaluate voters' self-reported personalities, nor when voters evaluated the personalities of famous celebrities or athletes, such as basketball player Magic Johnson (Caprara *et al.*, 1997). In all such personality judgements the standard rule of five traits prevailed. Thus, fame is not the critical cause of simplification; more likely the quantity, complexity and often contradictory information about politicians from multiple media sources (e.g., negative campaigning), together with the need to reach a dichotomous voting decision, induce voters to use mental shortcuts they would not otherwise employ.

A similar simplification occurred when judgments were made of politicians' values, using the Schwartz (1992) theory of basic personal values and the Portrait Value Questionnaire (Caprara *et al.*, 2008). Whereas perceived traits are behavioural tendencies that one can observe, attributed values represent intended priorities that can be only inferred. Although voters discriminated the usual ten values in describing themselves, when they were asked to evaluate the values of Prodi and Berlusconi, they collapsed their evaluations into two broad dimensions: firstly 'concern for others' (as opposed to the self), which balanced values of benevolence and universalism against power and achievement respectively. Secondly the value of 'excitement' (versus caution) balanced stimulation and hedonism with aspects of conformity, security and tradition. Thus, parsimony apparently operates to manage complexity in estimating politicians' value structures, just as they do when judging politicians' personality traits. As shown in figure 9.6, voters perceived Berlusconi as possessing a stronger leadership trait whilst scoring lower than Prodi on integrity. Moreover, voters perceived Berlusconi as endorsing 'excitement' values more than Prodi, and Prodi as endorsing 'concern for others' more than Berlusconi. These perceptions largely correspond to the media stereotype of the two politicians.

What about the predictive value of both perceived traits and attributed values? As for traits, voters prefer politicians to whom they can attribute both leadership and integrity traits, as both are desirable. However, perceived integrity was more important in the case of Berlusconi and perceived leadership was more important in the case of Prodi. Political analysts note that few people doubt Berlusconi's leadership, though many question his integrity (Lane, 2005; *The Economist*, 2001); in contrast, many worry about Prodi's leadership, but few question his integrity (Caciagli and Corbetta, 2002). Thus, the more decisive perceived trait for political preference is the trait on which voters generally perceive the politician as weaker, as voters attach more weight to the trait about which they have reason to worry. This conforms with a common finding in the perception literature that negative traits and events have a stronger impact on judgements. Therefore the negative effect associated with the

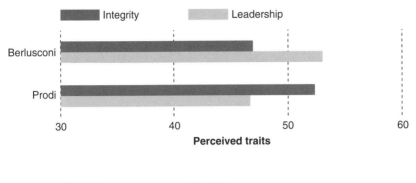

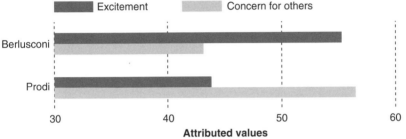

Note: For each variable, a score of 50 indicates the sample mean. Data are from Caprara *et al.*, 2008; n = 1164.

Figure 9.6. Perceived traits and attributed values of Berlusconi and Prodi (T scores)

lack of an attractive trait affects voting intentions more than the positive effect associated with the possession of an attractive trait (Baumeister, Bratslavsky, Finkenauer and Vohs, 2001; Peeters and Czapinski, 1990). Likewise, perceiving a candidate as valuing concern for others more, and excitement less, related positively to the intention to vote for Prodi's coalition. This is consistent with frequent findings in the literature, as people in the vast majority of cultures consider the values of concern for others (universalism and benevolence) more important than those of concern for the self (power and achievement), as well as prioritising the values of caution (security and conformity) over those of excitement (stimulation and hedonism) (Schwartz and Bardi, 2001).

Are perceived traits or attributed values more predictive of the political preferences of the electorate? Findings suggest that perceived traits explain substantially more variance in voting intention than attributed values, though both contribute significantly. It is likely voters trust perceived traits more than attributed values as they can directly assess candidates' traits by observing their speeches, actions, emotional expression and other behaviours, whereas they may only have access to candidates' values indirectly, through inference from the content of their communications (Caprara and Zimbardo, 2004). Thus, while voters' self-reported values have primacy over self-reported traits, as they have direct access to their own values, voters' perceptions of politicians' traits have primacy over attributed values, as these traits may serve as the anchors from which voters may infer politicians' values, motives and intentions (Caprara *et al.*, 2008).

Dispositional and likeability heuristics

Cognitive theorists argue that individuals navigate through the complexity of their political environments by using heuristics as efficient mental shortcuts for organizing information and guiding their dichotomous choices, given that ultimately they must translate complex perceptions and preferences into a simple behavioural act of voting for one particular candidate (Sniderman, Brody and Tetlock, 1991). Previous findings point to a kind of schematic knowledge that is conducive to anchoring voters' impressions and inferences about politicians' intentions to the traits that they most care for and expect from politicians at a given time in a given context, even at the cost of sacrificing a more detailed, fine-grained evaluation of the candidates' personalities (Conover and Feldman, 1986; Funk, 1999). Ultimately, the use of dispositional heuristics, while summarising a variety of sensations and perceptions and carrying specific attributions about politicians' motives and intentions, provides parsimonious ways to organise knowledge and potentially extend voters' control over politicians' future performance, on the common assumption that personality traits are relatively stable (Caprara and Zimbardo, 2004).

Another strategy that individuals use more or less unconsciously is a kind of likeability heuristic by which choices between people are weighted (Sniderman *et al.*, 1991). The more a candidate is liked, the higher his/her probability of gaining votes. As people tend to like people who they perceive as similar to themselves, voters will like and therefore vote for candidates they consider most similar. Thus, similarity promotes likeability which in turn affects political judgements and choices. Earlier studies have shown that voters prefer candidates with personal attitudes akin to their own on several policy issues (Crano, 1997; Lehman and Crano, 2002; Leitner, 1983; Piliavin, 1987; Quist and Crano, 2003). Recent studies extend the similarity–attraction relationship at the more basic level of traits, revealing that voters perceive politicians for whom they vote as being most like themselves with respect to a variety of personality characteristics. This effect has been shown in a study of the 2004 presidential elections in the USA and Italy (Caprara, Vecchione, Barbaranelli and Fraley, 2007). In the United States, people who planned to vote for Kerry saw themselves as more similar to Kerry than Bush. The opposite pattern of relation was found for people who planned to vote for Bush (figure 9.7a). In Italy, centre-right voters were more likely to see themselves as similar in traits to Berlusconi, the leader of the centre-right, than to Prodi, the leader of the centre-left. The opposite pattern of relation was found for centre-left voters (see figure 7b). These results were further corroborated by a study conducted in Spain during the 2008 parliamentary election, which revealed that people who voted for the Spanish Socialist Workers' Party were more likely to see themselves as similar to its leader Zapatero than to Rajoy, the leader of the opposition party (Vecchione, Gonzàlez Castro and Caprara, 2011). Likewise, people who voted for the Popular Party saw themselves as more similar to Rajoy than Zapatero (see figure 7c). Findings from each study showed that the similarity which counts is that of the trait which discriminates most between leaders and voters of opposite coalitions. In the USA for example, John Kerry was unanimously appraised to be more open-minded than George W. Bush, and Kerry's supporters showed significantly higher levels of openness than supporters of Bush. In addition, similarity between Kerry and his voters was particularly high for markers of openness (e.g., sharp, informed). In Italy, Silvio Berlusconi was unanimously appraised as more active, energetic and dynamic than Romano Prodi. Centre-right voters scored higher in energy/extraversion than centre-left voters and similarity between Berlusconi and his voters was particularly high for markers of energy/extraversion (e.g., active and dynamic) (Caprara et al., 2008). The similarity between Zapatero and his voters was particularly high in markers of openness, the most distinctive trait of Zapatero's personality according to the appraisal of voters, and of the self-reports of his supporters.

Whereas similarity is associated with political preference, there are no findings that allow us to fully clarify the mechanism by which similarity operates and the extent of its impact on voting. One may surmise that voters either project onto their preferred candidates their own most distinctive personality characteristics that they are likely to value most, or that voters are attracted by candidates displaying personality characteristics they hold dearest. One cannot say whether perceived similarity is most influential in voting or whether voting ultimately determines perceived similarity. Both hypotheses and alternative paths of influence are plausible and compatible. In reality, the similarity effect cannot be considered only due to pre- or post-voting projection, since other findings, such as those discussed above, have shown that self-reported politicians' personalities are more like the personalities of their voters than the personalities of their

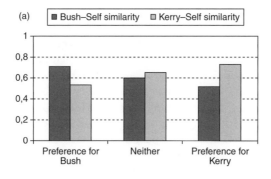

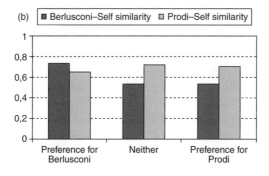

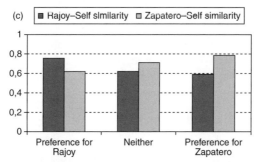

Note: Higher values indicate greater perceived similarity. To measure similarity, firstly the generalised Euclidean distance between the personality ratings of the voter and those of the politician they evaluated was calculated across a set of adjectives. Next, Euclidean distance was rescaled in a range of 0 to 1. These distances (or dissimilarity scores) were then converted into similarity scores by subtracting the normed index from 1. Italian and US data are from Caprara *et al.*, 2007. Spanish data are from Vecchione *et al.*, 2011.

Figure 9.7. Similarity between the perceived personalities of voters and those of Italian, US and Spanish politicians as a function of candidate preference

opponents' voters. Ultimately, whatever the source of perceived similarity, one cannot doubt the function that it exerts in building and keeping consensus. The more voters acknowledge in their leaders the same personal qualities that they use to characterise themselves, the easier it will be for voters to infer that their leader will act on their behalf and in accordance with a shared worldview.

Conclusions and directions for future research

The study of personality, as a reflexive and purposive system, may play a critical role in making sense of political judgements and choices. People do not just register, but also construe, select and prioritise information to which they are exposed, in accordance with personal goals and criteria. This chapter has presented the principal findings of a research programme aimed at understanding how, and to what extent, major individual differences in traits and values, two distinctive components of personality, may contribute to our understanding of political processes, and in so doing, has drawn upon the distinction between two major perspectives from which one may view the personalisation of politics.

By focusing on the role of voters' and politicians' personalities in making sense of their own preferences, findings from diverse countries highlight the distinctive patterns in self-reported traits and values of right-wing (conservative) and left-wing (liberal) voters, which mirror the traditional distinctions between the ideology of the respective political views. These results corroborate the hypothesis of a kind of congruency between self-presentation and political preferences, in accordance with a perspective of voters as reflexive and purposive agents who make political choices in line with habitual behaviours and basic principles that guide their lives (Caprara and Zimbardo, 2004). In reality, it is a property of our self and a necessity of our social life to preserve a certain level of consistency between what we declare, what we do and how we present ourselves. Patterns of congruity between thoughts, emotions and actions are at the core of our identity as they become associated with the experience of unity and continuity and allow us to make sense of others' behaviours, feelings and thoughts on the assumption that what accounts for oneself also accounts for others.

It remains to be clarified the extent to which the congruency among traits, values and political preferences reflect not only individuals' needs but also social roles and scripts that shape personal identities in accordance with the principles that govern social systems at different times and in different cultural contexts. As values remain at the core of both personal and social identities (Hiltin, 2003) they attest both to individuals' degrees of freedom in choosing the kind of person they become as well as to the pervasive influence of socialisation practices on individual development. Social theories focusing on the special properties of human agency view individuals as imbued with broad degrees of autonomy in selecting environments, activities and people, in pursuing goals that accord with their own values and in advocating a unique sense of one's own self. Yet other social theories which focus on the influence that membership of families, groups, class, and communities exert on individuals' development and functioning, view self-beliefs, attitudes and values as largely dictated by shared social conventions as well as by the place people occupy in society. In this regard, it is likely that 'a more or less' view seems more appropriate than an 'either or' perspective in addressing the congruency between values, habits and political preferences and in distinguishing which part of voting is due to the combination of idiosyncratic attributes of an individual or the result of his or her affiliations and memberships. In reality, personal and social identities are inextricably linked and as such, contribute to political preference.

One should also clarify the extent to which values that are decisive in political orientation are rooted in individuals' predispositions as well as in the nature of these predispositions. Evidence for the long-term persistence of political preferences has led a number of scholars to argue that political leanings result from acquired attitudes infused through early socialisation and crystallised over the course of one's life (Sears and Funk, 1999). Others argue that basic traits are at the root of any behavioural tendency, including attitudes and values. They point to the Big Five traits as the genotype of personality (McCrae and Costa, 1999). Recent findings suggest that genetics may play an important role in moulding political ideologies as they do in shaping other social attitudes and personality features (Alford, Funk and Hibbing, 2005; Bouchard and Lohelin, 2001; Hatemi, Medland, Morley, Heath and Martin, 2007). However, current progress in molecular genetics, while emphasising the pervasive influence of 'gene × environment' interactions, points to a kind of genetic probability rather than genetic determinism. Genes, in fact, do not work in isolation but influence the extent to which organisms are responsive to particular environments (Cicchetti, 2007). Thus, one may presume that genes account for a certain predisposition towards conservative or liberal ideologies, but environmental considerations are crucial in turning this into stable preferences and behavioural tendencies.

Focusing on the role of leaders' personality characteristics as inferred by voters, findings suggest that people use dispositional and similarity heuristics as efficient ways to organise personal information about political candidates. The use of these heuristics is likely to provide voters with a way both to simplify the available personal information about candidates and to anchor their judgements in a few basic personal characteristics thought to be relatively consistent across contexts and stable over time. The simplified perceptions of the personalities of political leaders may derive from a variety of strategies that people use to make reasonable choices, given their bounded rationality (Delli Carpini, Huddy and Shapiro, 1996; Popkin, 1991; Simon, 1985) and therefore correspond to a cognitively efficient strategy that voters adopt to cope with the massive amount of daily information to which they are exposed from multiple media sources about issues, candidates, parties, appeals and negative campaigns. In other words, likely simplification can help to extract coherence and congruency from very diverse and competing sources of political information.

There is substantial evidence from different countries that leadership and integrity are the traits that voters most care about and desire from politicians (Jones and Hudson, 1996; Popkin, 1993). However, findings warn against the simple assumption that the same personality descriptors always carry the same connotations when used to describe the personalities of politicians as they do for descriptions of non-politicians. Rather, it is critical to identify the personal dimensions that, at a certain time and in a certain context, serve to anchor the impressions voters form and the judgements they make about politicians' personalities. Future studies should clarify the extent to which similar restrictions in the number of categories used for such descriptions take place in domains other than politics, as well as the extent to which the meaning of words used to describe personality can vary across targets, contingencies or goals.

Findings from the above studies further corroborate the role of traits in organising political knowledge and preferences. It is likely that traits are the units that allow voters to organise their impressions of politicians and to link politicians' perceived personalities to their own and that these represent the elements through which both dispositional and likeability heuristics operate in politics. In the case of values, based on a single study in Italy, we do not yet know whether the 'concern for others' and 'excitement' value dimensions would emerge in other countries, although one cannot doubt that concern for others is what politicians mostly claim to possess and voters mostly expect from a politician. Moreover, there is as yet no evidence that simplifying attributed values applies only in the case of politicians and not in descriptions of third-party values. Future studies will have to clarify whether these or other combined dimensions of attributed values emerge in alternative political contexts and whether the simplification of attributed values is restricted to the political domain.

Both perceived traits and attributed values provide a unique contribution to political preferences, although their importance may depend on the particular candidates and their relative media exposure, on the specific traits or values that characterise them, or on the values of voters to which they appeal. Further research with other candidates in other contexts should seek to specify the conditions in which these or other factors increase or decrease the relative importance of candidates' personalities in political choice. Research on perceived similarity highlights a match between voters' self-reported personalities and the perceived personalities of preferred politicians. In this regard, both dispositional and likeability heuristics provide consistency. In reality, above findings attest to a congruency principle operating at different stages of political transactions to reduce uncertainty and to extend personal control. In particular in most western democracies, where political choices depend increasingly on voters' reasons, and voters' reasoning depends increasingly on self-reflection, this principle represents a unifying thread able to integrate and organise political knowledge and preferences in the political arena. First, the congruency principle operates in matching the self-reported personalities of voters and politicians with the ideology and programmes of their preferred coalitions. Next, congruency operates in how voters appraise politicians' personalities, selecting those attributes that they value most and that they believe to be most relevant to the political office. Ultimately, it operates in how voters perceive politicians as like themselves, either because politicians and voters of the same coalitions share similar values and habits, or because politicians tend to convey images that highlight traits most congruent with the political views they advocate. While congruency attests to the commonality of feelings, thoughts, habits and ideals among partisans and accentuates the contrast with opponents, the image that people have and cultivate of themselves serves as a compass that grants coherence to their own preferences and helps them make sense of politicians' behaviour.

References

Adorno, T. W., Frenkel-Brunswik, E., Levinson, D. J. and Sanford, R. N. (1950). *The Authoritarian Personality*. New York: Harper.

Alford, J. R., Funk, C. L. and Hibbing, J. R. (2005). Are political orientations genetically transmitted? *American Political Science Review*, 99, 153–67.

Altemeyer, B. (1981). *Right-Wing Authoritarianism*. Manitoba: University of Manitoba Press.

(1996). *The Authoritarian Specter*. Cambridge, Mass.: Harvard University Press.

(1998). The other 'authoritarian personality'. *Advances in Experimental Psychology*, 30, 47–92.

Bakan, D. (1966). *The Duality of Human Existence: Isolation and Communion in Western Man*. Boston, Mass.: Beacon.

Bandura, A. (1997). *Self-Efficacy: The Exercise of Control*. New York: Freeman.

(2000). Exercise of human agency through collective efficacy. *Current Directions in Psychological Science*, 9, 75–8.

(2001). Social Cognitive Theory: an agentic perspective. *Annual Reviews of Psychology*, 52, 1–26.

Barbaranelli, C., Caprara, G. V., Vecchione, M. and Fraley, R. C. (2007). Voters' personality traits in presidential elections. *Personality and Individual Differences*, 42, 1199–1208.

Barber, J. D. (1977). *The Presidential Character: Predicting Performance in the White House*. 2nd edn. Upper Saddle River, N.J.: Prentice-Hall.

Barnea, M. F. (2003). Personal values and party orientations in different cultures. Unpublished doctoral dissertation. The Hebrew University of Jerusalem, Israel.

Barnea, M. F. and Schwartz, S. H. (1998). Values and voting. *Political Psychology*, 19, 17–40.

Baumeister, R. F., Bratslavsky, E., Finkenauer, C. and Vohs, K. D. (2001). Bad is stronger than good. *Review of General Psychology*, 5, 323–70.

Block, J. and Block, J. H. (2006). Nursery school personality and political orientation two decades later. *Journal of Research in Personality*, 40, 734–49.

Bouchard, T. J., Jr. and Lohelin, J. (2001). Genes, personality, and evolution. *Behavioral Genetics*, 31, 23–73.

Caciagli, M. and Corbetta, P. (eds.) (2002). Le ragioni dell'elettore. Perché ha vinto il centro-destra nelle elezioni italiane del 2001 [The voter's reasons. Why the center-right won the Italian elections in 2001]. Bologna, Italy: Il Mulino.

Campus, D. and Pasquino, G. (2004). Leadership in Italy: the changing role of leaders in elections and in government. The Association for the Study of Modern Italy (ASMI) conference. London, 26 and 27 November 2004. 'The Second Italian Republic'.

Caprara, G. V., Barbaranelli, C., Consiglio, C., Picconi, L. and Zimbardo, P. G. (2003). Personalities of politicians and voters: unique and synergistic relationships. *Journal of Personality and Social Psychology*, 84, 849–56.

Caprara, G. V., Barbaranelli, C., Fraley, R. C. and Vecchione, M. (2007). The simplicity of politicians' personalities across political context: an anomalous replication. *International Journal of Psychology*, 42, 393–405.

Caprara, G. V., Barbaranelli, C. and Vicino, S. (1999). Personalità e politica [Personality and Politics]. *Giornale Italiano di Psicologia*, 26, 505–29.

Caprara, G. V., Barbaranelli, C. and Zimbardo, P. (1997). Politicians uniquely restricted Personalities, *Nature*, 385, 493.

(1999). Personality profiles and political parties. *Political Psychology*, 20, 175–97.

(2002). When parsimony subdues distinctiveness: simplified public perceptions of politicians' personality. *Political Psychology*, 23, 77–96.

Caprara, G. V. and Cervone, D. (2000). *Personality: Determinants, Dynamics and Potentials*. Cambridge University Press.

Caprara, G. V., Francescato, D., Mebane, M., Sorace, R. and Vecchione. M. (2010). Personality foundations of ideological divide: a comparison of women Members of Parliament and women voters in Italy. *Political Psychology*, 31, 739–62.

Caprara, G. V., Schwartz, S. H., Capanna, C., Vecchione, M. and Barbaranelli, C. (2006). Personality and politics: values, traits, and political choice. *Political Psychology*, 27, 1–28.

Caprara, G. V., Schwartz, S. H., Vecchione, M. and Barbaranelli, C. (2008). The personalization of politics: lessons from the Italian case. *European Psychologist*, 3, 157–72.

Caprara, G. V. and Vecchione, M. (2006). Le ragioni degli elettori: tratti, valori e stabilità del voto [The reasons of voters: traits, values and stability of vote]. *Giornale Italiano di Psicologia*, 33, 501–22.

Caprara, G. V., Vecchione, M., Barbaranelli, C. and Fraley, R. C. (2007). When likeness goes with liking: the case of political preference. *Political Psychology*, 28, 609–32.

Caprara, G. V., Vecchione, M. and Schwartz, S. H. (2009). The mediational role of values in linking personality traits to political orientation. *Asian Journal of Social Psychology*, 12, 82–94.

Caprara, G. V. and Zimbardo, P. (2004). Personalizing politics: a Congruency Model of political preference. *American Psychologist*, 59, 581–94.

Carney, D. R., Jost, J. T., Gosling, S. D., Niederhoffer, K. and Potter, J. (2008). The secret lives of liberals and conservatives: personality profiles, interaction styles, and the things they leave behind. *Political Psychology*, 29, 807–40.

Ceccarelli, F. (2007). La parabola del buonismo [The parabole of 'goodism']. *La Repubblica*, 27 June.

Chemers, M. M. (2001). Leadership effectiveness: an integrative review. In M. A. Hogg and R. S. Tindale (eds.), *Blackwell Handbook of Social Psychology: Group Processes* (pp. 376–99). Oxford: Blackwell Publishers.

Cicchetti. D. (2007). Gene–environment interaction. *Development and Psychopathology*, 19, 957–9.

Conover, P. J. and Feldman, S. (1986). The role of inference in the perception of political candidates. In R. R. Lau and D. O. Sears (eds.), *Political Cognition*. (pp. 127–55). Hillsdale, N.J.: Lawrence Erlbaum.

Costantini, E. and Craik, K. H. (1980). Personality and politicians: California party leaders, 1960–1976. *Journal of Personality and Social Psychology*, 38, 641–61.

Crano, W. D. (1997). Vested interest, symbolic politics, and attitude–behavior consistency. *Journal of Personality and Social Psychology*, 72, 468–91.

Delli Carpini, M. X., Huddy, L. and Shapiro, R. Y. (1996). *Research in Micropolitics: Rethinking Rationality*. Greenwich, Conn.: JAI.

Di Renzo, G. (1963). *Personalità e potere politico* [Personality and political leadership]. Bologna, Italy: Il Mulino.

(1977). Politicians and personality. a cross cultural perspective. In M. G. Hermann (ed.), *A Psychological Examination of Political Leaders* (pp. 147–204). New York: Free Press.

Digman, J. M. (1990). Personality structure: emergence of the five-factor model. *Annual Review of Psychology*, 41, 417–40.

(1997). Higher-order factors of the Big Five. *Journal of Personality and Social Psychology*, 73, 1246–56.

The Economist (2001). *Why Silvio Berlusconi Is Unfit to Lead Italy*. 28 April.

Elms, A. C. (1976). *Personality in Politics*. New York: Harcourt Brace Jovanovich.

Emler, N., Renwick, S. and Malone, B. (1983). The relationship between moral reasoning and political orientation. *Journal of Personality and Social Psychology*, 45, 1073–80.

Etheredge, L. S. (1978). Personality effects on American foreign policy, 1898–1968: a test of interpersonal generalization theory. *American Political Science Review*, 72, 434–51.

Eysenck, H. J. (1954). *The Psychology of Politics*. New York: Routledge, Chapman and Hall.

Feldman, O. (1996). The political personality of Japan: an inquiry into the belief systems of Diet Members. *Political Psychology*, 17, 657–82.

Feldman, S. (2003). Values, ideology, and structure of political attitudes. In D. O. Sears, L. Huddy and R. Jervis (eds.), *Oxford Handbook of Political Psychology* (pp. 477–508). New York: Oxford University Press.

Fiske, S. T. (2004). *Social Beings: a Core Motives Approach to Social Psychology*. Hoboken, NJ: John Wiley.

Frenkel-Brunswik, E. (1948). A study of prejudice in children. *Human Relations*, 1, 295–306.

    (1949). Intolerance of ambiguity as an emotional and perceptual variable. *Journal of Personality*, 18, 108–43.

Funk, C. L. (1999). Bringing the candidate into models of candidate evaluation. *Journal of Politics*, 61, 700–20.

George, A. L. and George, J. L. (1998). *Presidential Personality and Performance*. Boulder, Colo.: Westview Press.

Gerber, A. S., Huber, G. A., Raso, C. and Ha, S. (2009). *Personality and Political Behavior*. Working Paper, ISPS Yale University.

Gosling, S. D., Rentfrow, P. J. and Swann, W. B., Jr. (2003). A very brief measure of the Big Five personality domains. *Journal of Research in Personality*, 37, 504–28.

Gough, H. G. (1960). The Adjective Check List as a personality assessment research technique. *Psychological Reports*, 6, 107–22.

Greenstein, F. I. (1975). Personality and politics. In F. I. Greenstein and N. W. Polsby (eds.), *The Handbook of Political Science* (vol. II, pp. 1–92). Reading, Mass.: Addison-Wesley.

Halpin, A. W. and Winer, B. J. (1957). A factorial study of the leader behavior descriptions. In R. M. Stogdill and A. E. Coons (eds.), *Leader Behavior: Its Description and Measurement* (pp. 39–51). Columbus, Ohio: Bureau of Business Research.

Hatemi, P. K., Medland, S. E., Morley, K. I., Heath, A. and Martin, N. C. (2007). The genetics of voting: an Australian twin study. *Behaviorial Genetics*, 37, 435–48.

Hiltin, S. (2003) Values as the core of personal identity: drawing links between two theories of the self. *Social Psychology Quarterly*, 66, 118–37.

Jones, P. and Hudson, J. (1996). The quality of political leadership: a case study of John Major. *British Journal of Political Science*, 26, 229–44.

Jost, J. T. (2006). The end of the end of ideology. *The American Psychologist*, 61, 651–70.

Jost, J. T., Glaser, J., Kruglanski, A. W. and Sulloway, F. J. (2003). Political conservativism as motivated social cognition. *Psychological Bulletin*, 129, 339–75.

Kinder, D. R. and Sears, D. O. (1985). Public opinion and political action. In G. Lindzey and E. Aronson (eds.), *Handbook of Social Psychology*. 3rd edn, vol. II, pp. 659–741). New York: Random House.

King, A. (ed.). (2002). *Leaders' Personalities and the Outcomes of Democratic Elections*. Oxford University Press.

Lane, D. (2005). *L'ombra del potere* [The shadow of power]. Bari, Italy: Laterza.

Lehman, B. and Crano, W. D. (2002). The pervasive effects of vested interest on attitude-criterion consistency in political judgment. *Journal of Experimental Social Psychology*, 38, 101–12.

Leitner, L. M. (1983). Construct similarity, self-meaningfulness, and presidential preference. *Journal of Personality and Social Psychology*, 45, 890–4.

McCrae, R. R. (1996). Social consequences of experiential openness. *Psychological Bulletin*, 120, 323–37.

McCrae, R. R. and Costa, P. T. (1999). A five-factor theory of personality. In L. A. Pervin and O. P. John (eds.), *Handbook of Personality: Theory and Research*. New York: Guilford Press.

Miller, A. H., Wattenberg, M. P. and Malanchuk, O. (1986). Schematic assessments of presidential candidates. *American Political Science Review*, 80, 521–40.

Mischel, W. and Shoda, Y. (1998). Reconciling processing dynamics and personality dispositions. *Annual Review of Psychology*, 49, 229–58.

Moustaka, E. (2008). La personalizzazione della politica: uno studio in Grecia [The personalisation of politics: results from Greece]. Unpublished doctoral dissertation. 'Sapienza', University of Rome.

Peeters, G. and Czapinski, J. (1990). Positive–negative asymmetry in evaluations: the distinction between affective and informational negativity effects. *European Review of Social Psychology*, 1, 33–60.

Piliavin, J. (1987). Age, race, and sex similarity to candidates and voting preference. *Journal of Applied Social Psychology*, 17, 351.

Popkin, S. (1991). *The Reasoning Voter*. Chicago University Press.

(1993). Information shortcuts and the reasoning voter. In B. Grofman (ed.), *Information, Participation and Choice* (pp. 17–35). Ann Arbor: University of Michigan Press.

Prost, J. M. (ed.). (2003). *The Psychological Assessment of Political Leaders*. Ann Arbor: University of Michigan Press.

Putnam, R. (1973). *The Beliefs of Politicians*. New Haven: Yale University Press.

Quist, R. M. and Crano, W. D. (2003). Assumed policy similarity and voter preference. *The Journal of Social Psychology*, 143, 149–62.

Ricolfi, L. (2002). *La frattura Etica: la ragionevole sconfitta della sinistra* [The ethical rift: the reasonable defeat of the left]. Naples, Italy: L'Ancora del Mediterraneo.

Rokeach, M. (1973). *The Nature of Human Values*. New York: Free Press.

Rubenzer, S. J., Faschingbauer, T. R. and Ones, D. S. (2000). Assessing the U.S. presidents using the revised NEO Personality Inventory. *Assessment*, 7, 403–20.

Schoen, H. and Schumann, S. (2007). Personality traits, partisan attitudes, and voting behavior: evidence from Germany. *Political Psychology*, 28, 471–98.

Schwartz, S. H. (1992). Universals in the content and structure of values: theoretical advances and empirical tests in 20 countries. In M. Zanna (ed.), *Advances in Experimental Social Psychology* (25, 1–65). Orlando, Fla.: Academic Press.

Schwartz, S. H. (1994). Are there universal aspects in the structure and contents of human values? *Journal of Social Issues*, 50, 19–45.

Schwartz, S. H. and Bardi, A. (2001). Value hierarchies across cultures: taking a similarities perspective. *Journal of Cross Cultural Psychology*, 32, 268–90.

Sears, D. O. and Funk, C. L. (1999). Evidence of the long-term persistence of adults' political predispositions. *The Journal of Politics*, 61, 1–28.

Sidanius, J. (1978). Intolerance of ambiguity and socio-politico ideology: a multidimensional analysis. *European Journal of Social Psychology*, 8, 215–35.

(1985). Cognitive functioning and sociopolitical ideology revisited. *Political Psychology*, 6, 637–61.

Simon, H. A. (1985). Human nature in politics: the dialogue of psychology with political science. *American Political Science Review*, 79, 293–304.

Simonton, D. K. (1986). Presidential personality: biographical use of the Gough Adjective Check List. *Journal of Personality and Social Psychology*, 51, 149–60.

(1988). Presidential style: personality, biography, and performance. *Journal of Personality and Social Psychology*, 60, 607–19.

(1990). Personality and politics. In L. Pervin (ed.), *Handbook of Personality* (pp. 670–92). New York: Guilford Press.

(2006). Presidential IQ, openness, intellectual brilliance, and leadership: estimates and correlations for 42 U.S. chief executives. *Political Psychology*, 27, 511–26.

Sniderman, P. M., Brody, R. A. and Tetlock, P. E. (eds.) (1991). *Reasoning and Choice: Explorations in Political Psychology*. Cambridge University Press.

Tetlock, P. E. (1983). Cognitive style and political ideology. *Journal of Personality and Social Psychology*, 45, 118–26.

(1984). Cognitive style and political belief systems in the British House of Commons. *Journal of Personality and Social Psychology*, 46, 365–75.

(2002). Social functionalist frameworks for judgment and choice: intuitive politicians, theologians, and prosecutors. *Psychological Review*, 10, 451–71.

(2005). *Expert Political Judgment: How Good Is It? How Can We Know?* Princeton University Press.

Thoemmes, F. and Conway, L. G., III. (2007). Integrative complexity of 41 U.S. presidents. *Political Psychology*, 28, 193–226.

Thorisdottir, H., Jost, J. T., Liviatan, I. and Shrout, P. (2007). Psychological needs and values underlying left–right political orientation: cross-national evidence from Eastern and Western Europe. *Public Opinion Quarterly*, 71, 175–203.

Tomkins, S. S. (1963). Left and right: a basic dimension of ideology and personality. In R. W. White (ed.), *The Study of Lives: Essays in Honor of Henry A. Murray*. Chicago: Aldine-Atherton.

Van Hiel, A., Kossowska, M. and Mervielde, I. (2000). The relationship between openness to experience and political ideology. *Personality and Individual Differences*, 28, 741–51.

Vecchione, M., Gonzàlez Castro, J. L. and Caprara, G. V. (2011). Voters and leaders in the mirror of politics: similarity in personality and voting choice in Italy and Spain. *International Journal of Psychology*, 46, 259–70.

Wiggins, J. S. (1991). Agency and communion as conceptual coordinates for the understanding and measurement of interpersonal behavior. In W. M. Grove and D. Ciccetti (eds.), *Thinking Clearly about Psychology,* vol. II: *Personality and Psychopathology* (pp. 89–113). Minneapolis: University of Minnesota Press.

Winter, D. G. (1987). Leader appeal, leader performance, and the motive profiles of leaders and followers: a study of American presidents and elections. *Journal of Personality and Social Psychology*, 52, 196–202.

   (1992). Content analysis of archival data, personal documents and everyday verbal productions. In C. P. Smith (ed.), *Motivation and Personality: Handbook of Thematic Content analysis* (pp. 110–25). New York: Cambridge University Press.

Winter, D. G. and Stewart, A. J. (1977). Power motive reliability as a function of retest instructions. *Journal of Consulting and Clinical Psychology*, 45, 436–44.

10 Where red dictators coexist with promising democrats: the conceptualisation of politicians in post-communist Ukraine

Pavlo D. Frolov, Olha V. Petrunko and Dmitriy V. Poznyak

Overview

The collapse of the USSR revamped the political landscape of post-Soviet countries. The instant spread of new ideologies and development of multi-party systems caused the number of political leaders to skyrocket and the explosion of alternative media outlets challenged local electorates, with no prior experience, to choose between ideologies, parties and candidates. The superficial nature of voting in Soviet Union with a 'one candidate, one ideology' principle did not require complex decision making and had kept citizens detached from politics. Far from being a race, elections provided no agenda for the Soviet media or public scrutiny. As early as 1990–1 during the first democratic parliament and presidential elections, Ukrainian citizens had to choose between multiple candidates representing different ideologies and party affiliations. The choice voters had to make was not at all easy as a brand new political, social and media context required a completely different cognitive approach. What one could call 'communist' cognitive structures were ill-suited to the new realities and were to undergo substantial changes. The specific socio-political context in the USSR impacted on the political cognition of Soviet voters and began the development of specific political schemas. In this chapter it is argued that this process led to an overlap in old and new schemas over a period of time and here the cognitive structures of post-Soviet voters are assessed with an emphasis on the coexistence of schemas of both 'communist' and 'democratic' leaders.

Introduction

Since the inception of systematic voting research in the 1940s, scientists have attempted to describe voting behaviour in terms of social factors.

Lazarsfeld canvassed the field with the so-called sociological or Columbia model (1944) stressing the importance of social factors in voters' decision making. Campbell, Converse, Miller and Stokes (1960) went beyond this and put psychological factors, like early-learned social identifications with the party, at the core of their 'funnel of causality' model, also known as the social-psychological or Michigan model of voting. The rational choice approach, sometimes referred to as the Chicago model, was brought to political science by Downs (1957), describing voting as value-maximising 'rational calculus', where voters weigh the pros and cons of each candidate based on their self-interest.

Although each of these approaches established its own paradigm in voting behaviour research, long before the cognitive revolution in psychology in the late 1970s/early 1980s, they did not include one of the key variables in decision making, i.e., the processing of political information. As Herstein (1981, p. 844) concludes, these traditional political science models of voting are cognitively impractical as they fail to account for 'mental processes that accompany a vote'. With the cognitive revolution, the direction of voting behaviour research changed as well. From the early 1980s the primary focus shifted to the schematic perception of political leaders (see Kinder, Peters, Abelson and Fiske, 1980; Fiske and Linville, 1980; Lodge and Wahlke, 1982; Conover and Feldman, 1984; Lau and Sears, 1986; Miller, Wattenburg and Malanchuk, 1986; Kuklinski, Luskin and Bolland, 1991; Lau and Redlawsk, 2006).

The advantage of schema theory for political psychology was that it picked up research right where past models of voting behaviour had failed. Particularly, it seemed to have answered a lasting question posed by Converse in 1964 – how do people make quite logical decisions if they only have limited knowledge of, and interest in, political events? According to Rosch (1975) exposure to an overload of information leads people to rely on cognitive structures which serve as mental shorthand, minimising cognitive burden by organising, storing and processing information more effectively. These structures called *cognitive schemas* develop over time through people's repeated experience with others, objects, situations or events and organise the way they perceive the environment (Shaw, 1990). Schema theory established an original view of people as 'cognitive misers' sparing the efforts they need to process, interpret and understand complex social information (Augoustinos and Walker, 1996).

Borrowing an elaborate definition from Lau and Sears (1986, p. 349), 'a schema is a hierarchical organization of knowledge in a particular domain'. For example politics contains a category label (politicians), its general description (typically elected middle-aged or older males), higher- and lower-order categories (broad categories at the top vs. particular instances at the bottom), and inter-correlations between them (Barrack Obama is liberal – liberals are for social welfare policies and universal healthcare).

One way to illustrate how a schema simplifies perception is to use the analogy of a postal code. A worker at the sorting station does not need to read all the information to sort the letters properly, as s/he only has to read a code containing the necessary information in a fairly straightforward way (Shaw, 1990). However there is a shortcoming – a postal code only refers to a respective geographic unit, but it does not contain the name and exact address of the receiver. In a similar fashion, cognitive schemas only give a 'ballpark estimate' of a person or object although this is usually enough to successfully make decisions without digesting excessive amounts of information. After all, as 'cognitive misers', or 'motivated tacticians', we do not need a precise reconstruction of social objects at the cost of extensive and impractical cognitive efforts. Instead, the purpose of schemas is to minimise our cognitive efforts by providing hypotheses about incoming stimuli, which include plans for interpreting and gathering further information (Taylor and Crocker, 1981). In the context of political psychology, simple examples of leader-related schemas can include such broad dimensions as charisma, competence and physical attractiveness, or more narrow ones like communist or democrat.

Cognitive schemas also contain sets of prototypes that summarise the most typical characteristics of an object. Thus we may consider the prototype an average default setting of the schema. Considering the schema of a general politician, a prototypical political leader will perhaps be a respectable mid-aged male, wearing a suit and driven in a limousine. Depending on people's experience, a prototype may then include other more abstract properties like attractive and charismatic, or dishonest and corrupt. As schemas and prototypes develop based on past experience, a prototypical political leader for US voters could be a member of the Democratic or Republican Party, while for Chinese and Cuban voters s/he will perhaps be a communist.

In reality, people do not deal just with the average properties of social objects. Hence schema develop from the experience of dealing with particular exemplars (Stillings *et al.*, 1995). While a prototype is the average representation of a schema, an exemplar is its specific example. The schema of a 'charismatic politician' may contain such vivid exemplars as Franklin Roosevelt, Winston Churchill or Charles de Gaulle, while a 'communist leader' schema may have exemplars of Vladimir Lenin, Mao Zedong or Fidel Castro. For a 'democrat' schema, American voters may hold an exemplar of John Kennedy or Barack Obama, whereas for the post-Soviet electorate, most Western leaders and not necessarily those belonging to a left or centre party would fulfil this role. Likewise, Western

Europeans and Americans might consider Mikhail Gorbachev an outstanding democratic leader (Harris Interactive/*Financial Times*, 2006) while post-Soviet citizens would regard him as a failed pro-reform communist (Public Opinion Fund, 2006).

Before a schema can be applied to any person, inclusive of political leaders, they first need to be categorised. Categorisation is a fundamental characteristic of human perception and occurs whenever people identify or label a given individual, whether a political leader or a taxi driver (Augoustinos *et al.*, 2006). The categorisation process is closely linked to the prototypes and schemas people store in memory.[1] In fact a prototype contains features or categories used to define an object (Anderson, 1995). Therefore, objects are categorised around prototypes, or with prototypical features in mind, in order to confirm whether a new instance fits the 'schema average'.

Let us suppose that the prototype of the 'charismatic politician' schema will be an attractive leader with outstanding speaking abilities and a talent to inspire and lead people. Supposedly, the most salient features or attributes voters will use to categorise leaders as charismatic will be attractiveness, communication skills and the abilities to persuade and lead. Then, if a certain leader matches a prototype stored in memory, s/he will be categorised as a charismatic politician. If a leader exhibits traits and behaviours that do not fit any existing schema, this will possibly lead to schema assimilation or adaptation.

As one can see, schema theory provides a convenient framework to study voting behaviour. However, this approach in political psychology receives less attention due to the need for a level of research complexity. Unfortunately, public opinion polls with closed-ended questions, which serve as bread and butter for behavioural researchers, do not allow for the modelling of cognitive processes. Schema studies usually require multistage handcrafted designs, typically with open-ended questions, quasi-experiments and a mixed-method approach incorporating qualitative techniques such as focus groups and cognitive interviews, alongside survey research. To a certain extent Miller *et al.*'s observation made back in the 1980s regarding the state of schema research still seems relevant: 'candidate evaluations are one of the most important but least understood facets of American voting behavior' (Miller *et al.*, 1986, p. 521).

Miller's statement highlights one more important idea: most schema research has a distinct American flavour and thus findings cannot be generalised to other societies with different political systems and cultures. At the same time, the state of corresponding studies in Europe is limited, but

---

[1] When describing categorisation processes here we refer to theories of 'categorisation by prototype' or 'categorisation by schema' (Lane and Nadel, 2002).

not due to lack of interest, studies or data. Schema research in the United States is simply more feasible because of the bi-party model as well as the stability and succession of a political system deeply rooted in social life.

Yet, as we move into the post-communist world, studying the voters' cognitive system becomes even more complicated. With passive and atomised political culture (Chudovsky and Kuzio, 2003), citizens' political apathy, the predominance of survivalist and materialist cultural values (Inglehart and Welzel, 2005), a mix of ideologies, social cross-pressures and the perpetual change of political and electoral systems over two decades, the cognitive system of post-Soviet voters must substantially differ from that inferred by research in traditional democracies. As an illustration, throughout the 1990s voters in post-communist Ukraine were typically choosing from over thirty parties and dozens of candidates. Taking into account a classic thesis that voters are not fools (Key, 1966) then a primary question of interest for political psychologists is what their choices are based upon. This chapter will attempt to answer this by examining the cognitive system of post-Soviet voters in the mid- to late 1990s.

Cognitive schemas and conceptualisation of politicians in a post-Soviet context

Due to insufficient previous research on the political cognition of post-Soviet voters, an inductive approach appeared more feasible for the construction of relevant theory. Firstly, several research questions concerning voters' conceptualisation of politics arising from socio-political changes in the former USSR in the early 1990s are highlighted. Next, plausible answers are sought by blending together research findings from American, European and post-Soviet studies.

Acknowledging the role of the unique social-political environment in which post-Soviet voters found themselves in the 1990s, the first question is how this new context impacted on their conceptualisation of politics and politicians. A second question naturally arises from the fact that the political experience of post-Soviet voters was characterised by two distinct periods either side of the fall of the USSR. Referring to schema change theories, the key problem here is how pre-existing schemas of leaders were affected during voters' resocialisation in the late 1980s–1990s. Thirdly, taking into consideration a chaotic mix of communist and post-communist ideologies after the collapse of the USSR, it is very likely that schemas of existing leaders adjusted to fit the new types of emerging politicians. Additionally it is not known on which basis – ideological, party identification, professional or personal characteristics – these types were developing.

The changing political context and conceptualisation of political leaders

From the standpoint of many paradigms in social cognition, whether taking Heider's attribution-based 'consistency seeker' as one of the oldest (Heider, 1958), or Fiske and Taylor's information-processing 'motivated tactician' as one of the most recent (Fiske and Taylor, 1991), the problem of voters' choice is viewed similarly, as prior to decision making, images of candidates must be identified and interpreted by the voters. The peculiarities of this decision-making process are subject to varying views within different paradigms, but research from the last few decades converges on the idea that it involves two key phases: 'categorisation', i.e. reconstruction of a candidate's image using salient or primed classification criteria, and 'comparison' of retrieved images with pre-existing information already stored in the memory. In modern cognitive social and political psychology this pre-existing information is generally known as schemas (Piaget, 1926; Axelrod, 1973; Anderson, 1981).[2]

Following Fiske and Taylor's cognitive miser paradigm, the number of voters' schemas should be quite limited: a finding which has been repeatedly confirmed in empirical studies (Kinder *et al.*, 1980; Miller *et al.*, 1986). The reason is that the level of schema development and abstraction depends on the political sophistication of the voters (Lau and Sears, 1986). However, as much as voters are cognitive misers they are also 'not fools' as Key previously suggested. This should mean that the number of voters' schemas must be sufficient to effectively process political information and eventually make a choice. Along with Caprara, Barbaranelli and Zimbardo (2002) we believe that schematic perception can be interpreted in terms of parsimony. Parsimony in this context implies that 'voters reduce complex political environments and develop uniquely simplified perceptions of political candidates during campaigns' (Caprara *et al.*, p. 72). If we describe schematic perception as the reduction of '*N*' actual political characters to '*n*' broad universal types already existing in voters' memories, then it begins to resemble a sampling procedure which, based on a limited number of representative observations called schemas, voters can generalise their predictions to the entire target population of political leaders.

The idea of parsimony in schematic perception has found numerous empirical verifications. In the study by Kinder *et al.* (1980), leader schemas tended to be clustered around two broader dimensions: candidate's

---

[2] For an alternative view of the schema as the reworking of an attitude model, see the excellent critique by Kuklinski, Luskin and Bolland (1991).

character and performance. Miller *et al.* (1986) identified five factor-schemas that activate during candidates' evaluation: competence, integrity, reliability, charisma and personal attributes, which may be similarly grouped in character and performance clusters. Alongside these, Lau (1986) pinpointed issues, group relations, candidate personality and party identification schemas. As described, the range of identified leader schemas can be reduced to a limited number of dimensions.

Extrapolating the idea of schematic parsimony to post-Soviet realities, we argue that several factors make the perception of political leaders in newly emerged democracies such as Ukraine quite distinct. This is due to a number of factors. Firstly, because of the diverse political landscape in times of transition post-Soviet voters probably developed a number of leader prototypes to account for newly emerging types of politicians. Secondly, since the cognitive system of post-Soviet voters represents a mix of abstract democratic and authoritarian concepts (Diligenski, 1994) it is also expected that leader schemas encompass both communist and post-communist elements. Modern cognitive psychology describes several modes of schema transformation. Schemas can alter gradually with the receipt of new discordant information, change completely when incongruent information exceeds a certain threshold or develop hierarchies by accommodating new subtypes. To find an appropriate model fitting post-Soviet realities, further consideration of schema transformation is required.

Theories of political schema change and their applicability to the post-Soviet context

It is generally assumed that once developed and validated, schemas function as fairly stable and static cognitive structures (Fiske and Taylor, 2008, p. 81). How does this correlate with the political (re)socialisation of a typical adult voter in the former USSR, first during communism and then in the course of democratisation following the collapse of the USSR?

Modern research shows that schemas are indeed very stable if there are no motivations for their change (Fiske and Taylor, 2008) – that is if voters face a fairly constant and predictable political environment. If, however, such an environment undergoes substantial changes, such as the transformation of a social and political system, pre-existing schemas will cease to perform their main function and will either disappear or transform (e.g., Conover and Feldman, 1984). A vivid example often employed in sci-fi literature is the failure of astronauts' Earth-based schemas to successfully recognise objects on a newly 'inhabited' planet. Similarly we may rely on old schemas even in unusual circumstances, for example, when searching for a dining place in an exotic country. One possible option may be lunch at a well-known international chain restaurant where we already know what to expect. However, we may need to go beyond what our schemas can envisage, by exploring local cuisine. In this case, our schemas will have to adapt to the new environment. It is an accepted view that schemas can change (Fiske and Taylor, 2008), although the mechanisms and magnitude of this change is subject to discussion.

The 'Book-keeping' or 'Fine-tune' model assumes that people gradually adjust existing schemas with each piece of information they receive. The scale of such changes may vary depending on the level of inconsistency between existing schema and new data, but it is assumed that change will occur incrementally with the accumulation of knowledge that contradicts existing schema (Rumelhart and Norman, 1978). We believe that this model does not fit post-Soviet realities as it implies a rather slow and stepwise change over a lengthy time period, while the nature of socio-political changes would dictate a different pace of change. Additionally, taking into account political transformations in the former USSR, it is reasonable to expect the development of new subcategories within existing schemas rather than their modification.

The 'Conversion model' implies that while minor inconsistencies between schema and incoming data are tolerated, changes occur when this inconsistency exceeds a threshold of subjective tolerance, or simply when inconsistency is large enough (Rothbart, 1981). While major transformations occurring in the former USSR in 1990s may indirectly support this model we believe that dramatic 'all-or-none' conversion would mean the disappearance of old schemas where instead the development of new subcategories to fit new types of politicians would be expected. Additionally, it was shown that this model predicts more change in the presence of a single contradictory effect rather than consecutive partially-contradictory instances (Weber and Crocker, 1983), which was more characteristic of the Perestroika period.[3]

The 'Subtyping model' focuses on the hierarchical structure of schemas, with superordinate categories on top and subordinate ones at the bottom. While subordinate schemas accommodate exceptions in respect of any discrepancy between schema and data, superordinate schemas remain intact (Weber and Crocker, 1983). Contrasting with the previous model, the Subtyping model does predict more schema change when disconfirming information is spread rather than concentrated in a few cases. Furthermore, there is empirical evidence that this model provides a

---

[3] The Perestroika period refers to the post-1986 era of restructuring which heralded the introduction of contested elections.

better overall picture of the process of schema change (Webber and Crocker, 1983). If we assume that the Subtyping model provides the best explanation of changes in the cognitive system of post-Soviet voters then we should expect schemas to respond to political changes by relegating disconfirming instances (e.g., new political types) to new subcategories (Augoustinos and Walker, 1996). This would indicate the development of a hierarchical structure of leader-related schemas with virtually intact superordinate schemas on top and more specific subcategories below – most likely referring to types of politicians.

The basis for the development of leader schema subtypes

If one subscribes to the Subtyping model of schema change then it should be accepted that due to changes in political system after the collapse of the USSR, the voters' cognitive systems must have accommodated a number of new leader schema subtypes. Therefore during the transition period of the 1990s these included a mixture of fading communist and emerging post-communist types of political leaders. This coexistence of subtypes represents a peculiar political-psychological phenomenon yet to be studied and described.

As studies show, the development of political schemas typically positively correlates with political sophistication. Thus experts in any field will have more elaborate, structured and easily activated schemas than novices (Luskin, 1987; Lau and Sears, 1986). However, this does not mean that a broader range of leader subtypes indicates high political sophistication among post-Soviet voters. Instead, we argue that most post-Soviet voters are in fact what Lau and Sears (1986) call political novices and their development of new subtypes is rather based on stereotypical features of politicians than on available rational information. Although this hypothesis has yet to be empirically tested, lines of thought are presented here which suggest low levels of political sophistication among post-Soviet voters.

Firstly, as the transition from communism to democracy in the 1990s was only in its embryonic stage, it is reasonably hard to expect political expertise from voters with no prior experience of democracy in any of its manifestations. Returning to a previous metaphor, it would be equally naive to expect high sophistication from astronauts dealing with an alien planet's environment.

Secondly, Adorno's 'Authoritarian personality' studies repeatedly demonstrated the psychological rigidity, conformity and dogmatism of the communist outlook (Eysenck and Coulter, 1972). An analysis of European Value Studies (EVS) shows that post-Soviet nations possess among the lowest tolerance scores along with some of the highest levels of protest activity (Bishop and Poznyak, 2008). Although one may argue that these characteristics refer rather to personality than cognition, ideological content has repeatedly been found to positively correlate with political sophistication. For instance, Tetlock's (1986) Value Pluralism theory assumes that unsophisticated or monistic ideologies, including communism, are indicators of low political sophistication.

Thirdly, Fiske, Lau and Smith's (1990) scale of political sophistication is based on general political knowledge, political activity, media usage (electronic and printed) and politically-related schema (e.g., ideology, general interest and perceived importance of politics). According to these criteria and data obtained from Ukrainian studies, the majority of the post-Soviet electorate when faced with fragmented political knowledge, unrefined political activity and quite low media usage, would be placed in the category of low-sophisticates (Frolov, 1998, 1999, 2002). Finally, patterns of answering political questions by post-Soviet samples demonstrate only a limited understanding of relevant issues (Bishop and Poznyak, 2008; Frolov, 2002). This, as Carnaghan (2007) argues, can also be used as a direct measure of political sophistication.

In order to provide a more tangible benchmark of 'low political sophistication' it is helpful to refer to another model of schema elaboration developed by Taylor and Winkler (1980). This model includes four stages of schema sophistication, i.e., novice, stereotypical, relative expertise and true expertise. Our past research suggests that the schema development of post-Soviet voters would best fit the stereotypical phase characterised by the development of generalised attributes which define a candidate (Frolov, 1998, 1999, 2002). In this case schema accommodation and the development of new subtypes can occur through a number of often subtle contextual variables that emphasise the link between a schema and a new category (Rothbart, 1996). The question is what these contextual variables could be.

Studies demonstrate that sophisticated voters have a more coherent and abstract network of schemas while less politically sophisticated individuals are typically aschematic (Hamill and Lodge, 1986). Naturally the latter does not mean that voters will have no schemas at all, rather it implies that their schemas will be simpler and will rely on more accessible cognitive cues, such as party affiliation and the personal and professional characteristics of a candidate (Pierce, 1993). Lau and Redlawsk (2001) showed that voters compensate for a lack of knowledge of politics by using the most accessible information shortcuts known as heuristics. In terms of the American bi-party political system such shortcuts may be obvious party and ideological heuristics (Lau and Redlawsk, 2006). However, given low political sophistication, the chaotic mix of multiple ideologies and the large number of parties and leaders, we expect that such schemas would rely not on political criteria *per se*, i.e., ideology, party, issue position, etc., but on more accessible and less abstract criteria primarily associated with the personality and performance of political leaders, such as attractiveness, charisma, competence and trust. These criteria are not necessarily linked to more complex political schemas and as such are less challenging for the voters (Pierce, 1993). This assumption also aligns with our schema change model, since in terms of social and political instability, people would rather rely on more robust criteria like personal and professional characteristics than on context-dependent and political-ideological factors which are prone to change.

Measuring political schemas

A common problem in political cognition research is how to introduce schematic concepts into empirical analysis. There have been three dominant approaches to this in schema research. The first one stands on the grounds of experimental cognitive psychology and studies schematic processing in laboratory conditions using indicators like reaction time, i.e., true and false recognitions of schema-consistent information. One example of this approach is Hamill and Lodge's (1986) experiment on schema effects.

The second route deals with direct measurement of cognitive structures that presumably underlie political schemas (Conover and Feldman, 1984, 1989). Followers of this approach typically refer to Q-sort and similar or complementary techniques like thinking-aloud to study the organisational properties of schemas (Lau, 1986). Q-methodology is particularly advantageous for schema research by virtue of correlating respondents rather than variables and reducing individual viewpoints to a few dimensions which represent shared perceptions that in turn indicate underlying political schemas.

The third approach utilises data available from mass surveys. It functions by highlighting indicators of political schemas available from public opinion polls, such as the National Election Study (NES) or General Social Survey (GSS) in the US. The problem associated with this approach is that direct measurements of schemas are often too time-consuming to be used in large-scale surveys (Lau and Sears, 1986), hence researchers have to abandon closed-ended questions and deal with a handful of open-ended questions (Lau, 1986; Miller *et al.*, 1986). The advantage, however, is the ability to generalise findings to the entire target population.

In the studies described in this chapter, secondary data could not be used due to the absence of a comparable NES or GSS in the Ukraine, therefore the mass survey approach was not a viable option. This necessitated an approach to measuring cognitive schemas which followed either the first or second routes described above. Instead of a laboratory experiment that would certainly have narrowed the external validity of research into social cognition, we chose the Q-sort and thinking-aloud methods to study the cognitive system employed by Ukrainian voters.

Studying the cognitive systems of Ukrainian voters

A long-term project was carried out in Ukraine between 1995 and 1998, consisting of four consecutive cross-sectional studies (Petrunko, 2000). The first study (1995) was based on a nationally representative sample (n = 2005). A set of closed and open-ended questions were designed to elicit a political thesaurus from the Ukrainian electorate containing both an active and a passive vocabulary considered and/or used by voters to describe political leaders. The logic of this study was somewhat similar to the NES open-ended like–dislike questions for parties and candidates that underlie many studies on political schemas in the US. Another objective was to obtain a list of political leaders most familiar to Ukrainian voters at that time. Data were processed by content and frequencies analyses.

The next three studies shared both research goals and designs. They all drew from the political thesaurus and the list of political leaders obtained in the first study and each relied on similar research methods such as semantic differentials (Osgood, Suci and Tannenbaum, 1957), Q-methodology or Q-sorting technique (Brown, 1980; Conover and Feldman, 1984; McKeown and Thomas, 1988) as well as elements of cognitive interviewing such as thinking-aloud (Willis, 2004). These studies were conducted on relatively small non-probability quota samples, which, although arguably limiting the external validity of any findings, combined quantitative and qualitative methods which would not have been possible in a mass survey. Q-methodology, however, does not require large samples, focusing instead on the number of variables (Brown, 1980). Obviously, quota sampling shares drawbacks with all non-representative designs, including an inability to estimate how well it represents the population; however, studying psychological concepts like cognitive schemas does not necessarily require the precision and data-fit of representative samples. Also, the choice of a non-probability design served the additional purpose in three somewhat similar studies of

Table 10.1. *Research design and methodology used with Ukrainian voters*

Study	Sample size	Year	Objective	Method	Data analysis
1	2005	1995	Voters' political thesaurus and stimulus objects	Open-ended questions	Content and frequency analyses
2	114	1996	Dimensions of leader categorisation	Modified semantic differential	Exploratory factor analysis
3	56	1996	Leader schemas and prototypes	Q-sort and thinking-aloud	Cluster analyses
4	40	1998			

controlling for the reliability of findings while manipulating research methods. All three studies shared the research objective of modelling how Ukrainian voters conceptualise political leaders.

In the second study (1996; n = 114) we employed modified semantic differentials (Osgood *et al.*, 1957) and analysed data with exploratory factor analysis (EFA). Our main objective here was to reveal the major dimensions of political leader categorisation. In the third (1996; n = 56) and fourth studies (1998; n = 40) we combined Q-sort with thinking-aloud technique and analysed data with EFA and hierarchical cluster analysis (HCA). These two studies differed in the list of stimuli objects (political leaders) offered to respondents as well as in sampling. In the fourth study, the list was expanded by including notable politicians from the past and a sample of voters with a particular interest in politics was recruited. An additional goal for these studies, aside from eliciting Ukrainian voters' leader schemas and prototypes, was to compare the conceptualisation of political leaders by 'political novices' and 'relative experts'. Table 10.1 provides a summary of the overall research design.

A political thesaurus of Ukrainian voters

While many studies on political cognition have used open-ended questions about parties' and candidates' characteristics from mass surveys, there was no comparable NES or GSS in the Ukraine in the mid-1990s. Thus a bespoke method somewhat similar to NES open-ended questioning was devised with the purpose of reconstructing a 'political thesaurus' of Ukrainian voters' language when describing political leaders.

For this purpose, we designed a relatively short and simple question-naire containing two groups of similarly worded open-ended questions. The first group of questions was as follows:

1. Which modern Ukrainian politicians do you know?
2. Who do you consider the best Ukrainian politician? Why?
3. What should an ideal political leader be?
4. What should an ideal political leader not be?
5. Into which groups could you subdivide all the political leaders you know?

Answers to the first and second questions were used to obtain a list of political leaders to act as stimuli for the ensuing studies.[4] Answers to the third and fourth questions were content analysed and frequency sorted in order to highlight the most identified characteristics Ukrainian voters use when describing political leaders. Answers to the fifth question facilitated our understanding of how Ukrainian voters explicitly classify known political leaders and upon which criteria these classifications rely.

Arguably, the most interesting finding of this study is the political vocabulary of Ukrainian voters. It contains more than 600 words, among which the following were used most frequently to describe political leaders.

Characteristics of an ideal political leader ('An ideal political leader should be'):

1 – Honest; 2 – Smart; 3 – Decent; 4 – Compctent; 5 – Even-handed; 6 – Determined; 7 – Brave; 8 – Insistent; 9 – Assured; 10 – Purposeful; 11 – Self-controlled; 12 – Independent; 13 – Optimistic; 14 – Educated; 15 – Intelligent; 16 – Energetic; 17 – Industrious; 18 – Good speaker; 19 – Reputable; 20 – Rich; 21 – Sincere; 22 – Sympathetic; 23 – Promising; 24 – Principled; 25 – Attractive; 26 – Kind; 27 – Inspiring; 28 – Strong; 29 – Able to lead; 30 – Has political vision.

Characteristics of a non-ideal political leader ('An ideal political leader should not be'):

1 – Promise-breaker; 2 – Law-breaker; 3 – Dishonest; 4 – Dodgy; 5 – Bribe-taker; 6 – Weak; 7 – Feckless; 8 – Indeterminate; 9 – Unprincipled; 10 – Businessman; 11 – Careerist; 12 – Incompetent; 13 – Concerned With Own Wallet; 14 – Pessimist; 15 – Populist; 16 – Unpatriotic; 17 – Irresponsible; 18 – Deceiver; 19 – Mercenary; 20 – Churlish loner; 21 – Drinker; 22 – Manipulated; 23 – Unjust; 24 – Unsure; 25 – Lightweight; 26 – Lacking own thought; 27 – Poor economist; 28 – Ill-behaved; 29 – Purposeless; 30 – Short-tempered.

---

[4] As the list contains leaders mostly unknown to the audience outside of Ukraine their names are omitted, but can be supplied by the authors upon request.

Frequency analysis showed that respondents most commonly refer to the personal characteristics of political leaders with an approximate ratio of 3:1 personal to political and ideological characteristics. This is consistent with other studies indicating that person-related characteristics dominate voters' knowledge of candidates, a phenomenon which Sears (1969) defined as the 'personalization of politics'. Based on this list we selected twenty-six of the most frequently used characteristics which arguably provide the most rounded description of a political leader.

Based on the analysis of respondents' subjective classifications of political leaders (fifth question) we identified fifty-six political types highlighted by respondents:

1 – Patriot; 2 – Charismatic leader; 3 – Dissident; 4 – Demagogue; 5 – Dilettante; 6 – Marionette; 7 – Symbol of the past; 8 – Dictator; 9 – Fanatic; 10 – Psychopath; 11 – Unsympathetic; 12 – Adventurer; 13 – Politically bankrupt; 14 – Separatist; 15 – Fascist; 16 – Careerist; 17 – Red leader; 18 – Professional; 19 – People's favourite; 20 – Smart Guy; 21 – Time-server; 22 – Reliable; 23 – Populist; 24 – Reformer; 25 – 'One of us'; 26 – Idealist; 27 – Dark Horse; 28 – Liberal; 29 – Right-wing; 30 – Hard worker; 31 – Radical; 32 – Leftist; 33 – Member of Parliament; 34 – State clerk; 35 – Practitioner; 36 – Manager; 37 – Cabinet minister; 38 – Communist; 39 – Socialist; 40 – Party leader; 41 – 'Power-man' (coming from one of the armed forces: militia; army; intelligence services, etc); 42 – Federalist; 43 – Pro-Western; 44 – Democrat; 45 – Centrist; 46 – Presidential supporter; 47 – Power-hungry; 48 – Neo-imperialist; 49 – Workhorse; 50 – Inactive; 51 – Nationalist; 52 – Theorist; 53 – Intellectual; 54 – Oddball; 55 – Economist; 56 – Fighter.

Dimensions of political leader categorisation

The objective of the second study (n = 114) was to reveal the most typical way respondents think about political leaders. Here we attempted to find what are called 'dimensions of political leader categorisation'. These dimensions represent chunks of categories revealing particular aspects of political leaders' personalities, for example, competence, charisma and personal attractiveness (Miller et al., 1986).

Respondents were asked to evaluate thirteen prominent Ukrainian politicians according to the twenty-six adjectives which appeared most frequently in the first study. With the focus on the meaning respondents assign to stimulus objects (political leaders), semantic differential scales were used. These featured a seven-point scale which permitted a neutral opinion (middle point), provided robust and meaningful data and yet was not too tedious to complete.

The data was processed by EFA with maximum likelihood extraction and orthogonal Varimax rotation providing uncorrelated factor solution.[5] EFA, also known as R-methodology (Brown, 1980) reduces the variables to meaningful factors and provides a summary of classification criteria respondents use to categorise political leaders. In line with Miller *et al.* (1986) these are termed criteria dimensions of political leader categorisation. Although these dimensions are related to cognitive schemas, as far as categorisation activates a schema in memory, we are

Table 10.2. *Dimensions of political leader categorisation in the Ukraine (Study 2)*

Dimensions of political leader categorisation	Proportion of variance explained	Hypothesised leader prototype[6]
1. **Political aptitude (competence, efficacy and charisma)** *competent (.879), educated (.864), smart (.840), self-assured (.815), industrious (.774), good speaker (.772), purposive (.737), principled (.718), discreet (.712), inspiring (.699), able to lead (.683), has political vision (.615)*	47.8%	Competent or expert; efficient; charismatic (well-educated, smart, hard-working, inspirational, able to lead, having political vision)
2. **Reliability** *brave (.831), determined (.817), persistent (.771), active (.737), independent (.670)*	7.8%	Reliable leader (strong, determined, and hard-working)
3. **Integrity** *understanding (.751), intelligent (.749), sincere (.740), honest (.705), just (.699), decent (.661)*	5.9%	Moral leader (empathic with the people, sincere, honest and just)
4. **Affluence** *rich (.865), resourceful (.863)*	3.3%	Business leader (taking advantage of politics to profiteer)
5. **Image / Personal characteristics** *optimistic (.696), pleasant (.655), kind (.627), attractive (.605)*	3.2%	Popular leader (crowd-puller, 'charged', attracting people)

Note: The numbers in brackets (factor loadings) are Pearson correlation coefficients of a variable with the dimension.

---

[5] Kaiser-Meyer-Olkin measures of sampling adequacy and Bartlett sphericity coefficients were well above the thresholds of acceptability. The number of factors was selected based on Keiser-Gutman stopping criterion ('scree-plot') with eigenvalues $\geq$ 1. Descriptors (variables) correlating with factors at less than .3 were excluded from further analysis.

[6] Although the authors have no empirical evidence of schemas and prototypes underlying these categorisation dimensions, the most suitable prototypes have been hypothesised.

reluctant to simply derive corresponding schemas based on the meaning of achieved dimensions, since the semantic differential technique used here is not suitable for this purpose.

The first and most important dimension of political leader categorisation has been termed *political aptitude*. This dimension accounts for roughly half of the total variation and has a rather complex meaning. Visual inspection of this factor indicates that political aptitude encompasses competence, efficacy and the leadership abilities of politicians. Indeed, second-level factor analysis performed on this factor shows that political aptitude further splits into *competence* (competent, self-assured, educated and smart), *efficacy* (industrious, purposive and principled) and *charisma* (discreet, good speaker, inspirational, able to lead and possesses political vision).

The second dimension has been defined as *reliability*. If competence deals mainly with leadership potential, reliability has applied relevance to a leader's determination and capacity for work. Reliability also implies the trust people put in political leaders based on their capability, decisiveness and bravery. The reliability factor consists of two major sub-categories: activity (brave, active, and independent) and strength of mind (determined and persistent).

The *integrity* dimension reflects the idea of trustworthiness, represented by such categories as empathy, sincerity, honesty and decency. Similar to the reliability dimension, integrity also deals with the confidence one puts in political leaders whilst implying a quite different aspect of trust. By specifying a different factor solution and extracting a different number of factors, the single factor which can be defined as *trust* straddles both reliability and integrity dimensions. As Miller *et al.* (1986) put it, reliability is trust in a political leader in terms of their capabilities rather than honesty, while integrity is based on the truthfulness of a leader. Therefore it may be argued that reliability may refer to whether a leader can be trusted from a professional perspective while integrity rather implies interpersonal trust.

If the previous dimensions are commonly found in similar studies using different samples (Miller *et al.*, 1986), the fourth dimension, *affluence*, arguably represents a post-Soviet artefact. It appears to reflect the method of entry to politics from business or using politics as a source for self-enrichment. Following the collapse of the USSR, getting into politics was almost an end in itself for a number of newly wealthy Ukrainians as it provided a convenient way to sustain and boost their own businesses whilst holding legal inviolability as elected deputies. Finally, the fifth dimension is a leader's *image* or *personal characteristics*. This factor resembles the likeability dimension found in other studies and reflects respondents' personal likes and dislikes in politicians (Rosenberg, 1977; Miller *et al.*, 1986).

This analysis confirms our assumption that post-Soviet voters mainly refer to personality characteristics rather than political-ideological criteria when considering images of political leaders.

The conceptualisation of political leaders by Ukrainian voters

In the previous study the semantic differential technique was combined with EFA to obtain dimensions of categorisation referred to by respondents when processing information about political leaders. However, alternative methodology is required to move from categorisation to political leader schemas and prototypes. A combination of Q-methodology and qualitative techniques, such as the thinking-aloud technique, provides an insight, albeit based on explicit comments, into how political leaders are linked in respondents' memories, while cluster analysis helps to confirm the underlying structure. An alternative view to this approach is to consider what can possibly 'glue' certain politicians together in the respondent's memory. By processing the aggregate Q-sort matrix it is possible to discover *how* political leaders are linked together, which leads to consideration of *what* links them together. We argue that the reason for these links is that they fit the same cognitive schema which already exist in respondents' memories. To this end schemas referring to both quantitative (multivariate statistical analysis) and qualitative (thinking-aloud characteristics) criteria are defined.

In the third study respondents were invited to sort cards carrying the topical names of domestic and foreign leaders into an arbitrary number of groups whilst commenting on the logic applied in the sorting task as well as defining and describing the respective groups. Hierarchical cluster analysis was used to process the data. This combination of Q-sort and cluster analysis aimed at grouping objects based on their semantic proximity enabled us to define a taxonomy of political leaders, where each cluster is presumably underpinned by cognitive schema.

The analysis of data collected from this sample of 'typical voters' yielded a four-cluster solution. The first cluster groups leaders characterised as unknown, unremarkable and average as well as those opposite to them in nature – i.e., successful and mature leaders holding political office. We believe that the cognitive schema underlying this cluster is *political potential* and it includes the criteria of leadership abilities, charisma and political viability. Due to the nature of cluster analysis, the political aptitude dimension elicited in the previous study could not be correlated with the schema of political potential, but further analysis based on thinking-aloud comments indicates their relatedness. However, the political potential schema has a somewhat narrower connotation with the focus on the political abilities and viability of a politician, rather than on his or her competence and efficacy. In voters' memories potential is represented by two subtypes of politicians – *mediocre politicians* (average and unpromising domestic politicians) and *successful politicians* (mature, successful, already realising their potential in politics and serving in office).

The second cluster groups Western leaders (Bill Clinton, François Mitterrand and John Major) whom Ukrainian respondents defined as real professionals. Although this cluster has a somewhat complex meaning, i.e. foreign leader, competent and successful, the accompanying thinking-aloud characteristics enable the conclusion to be drawn that the underlying cognitive schema may be defined as *competence*, with the respective leader prototype described as *professional* or *expert*. Arguably, this is a characteristic respondents struggled to find among domestic leaders during the 1990s, recalling the saying that no man is a prophet in his own country, especially during crises. However, this characteristic was attributed to prominent foreign politicians, who benefited from association with the prosperity of their respective countries. It is illustrative that respondents' thinking-aloud responses implied that 'their' (foreign) political leaders are much better, more professional, discreet, moral and patriotic than 'ours' (domestic).

The third cluster contains active Ukrainian politicians who did not enjoy public confidence and whose names were disgraced. According to thinking-aloud responses they define Ukrainian politics and possess real power, but at the same time are characterised as untrustworthy and anxious about advancing their own careers and making a profit. Such a combination of characteristics makes this cluster rather hard to define. This represents what Anderson (1996) calls a 'tangled network' of concepts linked together in a system without a predetermined hierarchy. Apparently recognition of politicians here is based on a *formal status* criterion which in turn is linked to the criteria of *reliability* (dependability) and *trustworthiness* (integrity or morality). In a sample of typical voters, (considered here as political novices) this combination of formal status and trustworthiness schemas yields three political types: *symbol of the past* – an orthodox communist exemplified by 'old school' Soviet politicians who do not want to adjust to the new social and political realities; *dilettante* – lacking professionalism and competence; *careerist* – abusing politics as a tool with which to serve their own interests.

Table 10.3. *Voters' conceptualisation of Ukrainian political leaders (Study 3)*

# Cognitive schema	Implied leader prototype	Thinking aloud characteristics
1 **Political potential** (leadership abilities, charisma and political viability)	Mediocre politician	Average, mediocre, inexperienced, unpromising
	Successful politician	Plays leading roles in politics, successful, has real status, holds office
2 **Competence** (professionalism and expertise)	Expert	Ideal leader, political heavyweight, leader you can rely on
3 **Formal status and trustworthiness** (reliability and integrity)	Symbol of the past	'Old guard', out of date leader, untrustworthy, unreliable, has no understanding of the people
	Dilettante	Shoddy leader, breaks everything he tries, unprofessional, unreliable
	Careerist	Cunning, tricky, puppets, servers, easy to fail people's interests, immoral
4 **Political perspective** (Orientation on future vs. past)	Economist-reformer	Smart, forward-looking, reformer, expert in economics

The fourth and final cluster represents modern, progressive, experienced and up-and-coming politicians. Here the cognitive schema is defined as *political perspective* (past vs. future) and the underlying leader prototype as an *economist-reformer*, adhering to the most common characteristics attributed by respondents. Considering the economic situation in the Ukraine following the collapse of the USSR and widespread credence given to cure-all reformers, the identification of this political type should not seem strange. Assuming that political-ideological cues in terms of socio-political transformation were too abstract for the majority of Ukrainian voters, we believe that political orientation schema may serve as a proxy for ideology and party affiliation as well as helping voters develop a hypothesis of what to expect from a politician and forecast their political strategies.

In the fourth study forty respondents, who were identified as politically engaged opinion leaders were recruited. The criteria for respondents' selection were self-reported frequency of exposure to political information, an interest in politics and willingness to share their opinion with others; most respondents had completed a degree. To the expanded list of modern domestic and foreign leaders were added a number of historically prominent politicians, and respondents were instructed to divide them into an arbitrary number of groups and give characteristics to respective groups, explaining the reasons for inclusion of certain leaders in each group. Similar to the previous study the data were cluster analysed.

Analogous with the third study, the first cluster combines political leaders according to their *political potential*. Likewise, this schema also includes the criteria of leadership ability, charisma and the political viability of a politician. However, relative political experts have a more developed conceptualisation of leaders, as this cluster further splits into four distinct sub-clusters, each representing a specific type of leader. The first sub-cluster almost entirely overlaps with the *mediocre politician* type defined in the previous study and includes politicians whom respondents define as average and unpromising. The second sub-cluster groups politicians similarly characterised as mediocre with little or no political experience, but who are nevertheless considered quite competent in their field, mostly economics. This subtype was defined as *skilled professional but poor leader*. Ironically the subsequent Ukrainian president Viktor Yushchenko and then a chief of a national bank fell into this sub-cluster. The third sub-cluster brings together well-known leaders like Adolf Hitler, Joseph Stalin, Vladimir Lenin, Saddam Hussein, Mikhail Gorbachev and Boris Yeltsin. Taking into account thinking-aloud characteristics, this subtype was defined as *power-hungry* or *dictator*. As far as Gorbachev and Yeltsin seem to deviate from the conception of what one could call true dictators, it is appropriate to re-emphasise the sample selection in this study. Some respondents would have characterised Gorbachev or Yeltsin as democrats or reformers, while it is quite possible that for more politically sophisticated respondents they were 'dictators in disguise' or, in other words, authoritarian leaders with a democratic image. Finally, the last sub-cluster combines Ukrainian and Russian politicians whom respondents considered quite successful but played only secondary roles in politics. We believe that this classification is represented in respondents' memories as *weak politicians*.

The second overall cluster represents a group of mostly, but not exclusively Western political leaders such as Margaret Thatcher, Bill Clinton, Helmut Kohl, John Major, Jacques Chirac and Yitzhak Rabin and the first president of the Ukraine in 1918, Mykhailo Gryshevskyi. They were characterised as competent professionals, pragmatists, smart, well-educated, and successful politicians. Similar to the previous study, we defined the cognitive schema underlying this cluster as *competence*, with the respective prototype of *expert*. Apparently the categorisation criteria respondents might use here are also similar to those described in the previous study, i.e., professionalism, expertise and competence. The competence cluster contains two sub-clusters defined as *expert-pragmatist* and *expert-intellectual*.

Similar to political novices, the sample of more politically experienced voters yields a third cluster containing the phenomenon of a tangled schema network. As before a *formal status* schema acts in conjunction with *reliability* and *trustworthiness*. Quite possibly this tangled network may encompass other more abstract schemas, such as personal characteristics, competence, populism and orientation to the past or future. This complex cluster contains six sub-clusters representing particular types of political leaders. These types were defined as *modern professional* and *dilettante* (based on the competence criterion), *careerist* and *businessman* (integrity criterion), and *demagogue* and *political bankrupt* (reliability criterion). The modern professional type is characterised as signifying the 'new school', smart and up to date, a leader in contrast to the incompetent dilettante who plays supporting roles in politics. *Careerist* and *businessman* types are both regarded as unsympathetic to people and pursuing their own interests. The difference between them is that while one struggles at first to advance his/her own political status, politics is later used as a source for self-enrichment. *Demagogue* and *political bankrupt* are both defined as inefficient and unreliable types where the first one, as respondents put it, 'talks a lot but does nothing', and the latter is disgraced through wrongdoing in the past. A good illustration of respondents' attitudes to Ukrainian politicians is that five out of these six types are characterised negatively.

The fourth cluster represents a new generation of Ukrainian and Russian leaders whom respondents define as promising and forward-looking but who have not yet achieved substantial successes and realised themselves in politics. Paraphrasing Taylor and Crocker (1981), this may be a type of leader for whom respondents have not yet fully developed hypotheses for further interpretation. Consequently, such leaders are defined as modern and promising but at the same time as unfamiliar to respondents. The underlying leader schema here was interpreted as having a *political perspective (with an orientation to the future)*. This cluster consists of three sub-clusters representing leader prototypes: *dark horse* – political leaders whom voters characterise as promising but almost completely unknown to them; *economist-reformer* – believed to be competent in the market economy but yet to achieve visible success; and *modest professional*, whom voters regard as experts in their own field (like banking or industry) but who have not yet become sufficiently well known to set out a political agenda.

Finally, the fifth cluster groups politicians bearing characteristics of old school Soviet-style leaders. Based on the analogy of the fourth cluster, we interpreted the respective schema as *political perspective (with an orientation to the past)*. This cluster has two sub-clusters that represent corresponding

Table 10.4. *Conceptualisation of leaders by respondents with political knowledge (Study 4)*

#	Cognitive schema	Implied leader prototype(s)	Thinking-aloud characteristics
1	**Political potential** (leadership abilities, charisma and political viability)	Mediocre politician	Average, mediocre, inexperienced, unpromising
		Skilled professional but poor leader	Average politician but good specialist
		Power-hungry or dictator	Large-scale, global ambitions, unconquerable will
		Weak	Small-scale, playing secondary roles
2	**Competence** (professionalism and expertise)	Expert	Professional, competent, pragmatist, intelligent, smart, successful, patriot
		Expert-pragmatist	Professional, democratic, educated, pragmatic, successful in practice
		Expert-intellectual	Professional, intelligent, educated, good theorist but not successful in practice
3	**Formal status and trustworthiness** (reliability and integrity)	Modern professional	Professional, smart, modern
		Dilettante	Semi-professional, average, playing secondary roles in politics
		Careerist	Pursuing own career interest, not caring about people, selfish, aspiring to advance own status, carpetbagger, crook
		Businessman	Smart and far-sighted
		Demagogue (populist)	Professes too much; all talk no action, unreliable, never keeps promises, chatterbox
		Political bankrupt	Disgraced, compromised, unreliable, cannot be trusted, futureless
4	**Political perspective** (Orientation to the future)	Dark horse	Dark horse, promising, stranger, as yet unrealised
		Economist-reformer	Smart, professional, businesslike; as yet unrealised
		Modest professional	Competent, honest, decent, lacking leadership skills, as yet unrealised
5	**Political perspective** (Orientation to the past)	Symbol of the past	'Old guard', obsolete, double-minded, unreliable, populist
		Apparatchik or state clerk	Time-server, chameleon, average leader, untrustworthy

prototypes defined as a *symbol of the past* and *apparatchik* or *state clerk*. The first is characterised as an obsolete and unchanged bureaucrat with a Soviet mindset, while the second is viewed as a 'chameleon' who has successfully adjusted to the new political reality. As can be seen here, a more general political perspective cluster found in a sample of typical voters splits into two more narrow clusters indicating politicians' orientations to the past versus the future. As one would expect, political sophisticates have also developed a more detailed classification of types of leader.

Conclusions

Our studies shed some light on the problem of voters' perceptions of politicians following the collapse and disappearance of communist rule in the Ukraine. Unfortunately, due to the absence of corresponding research prior to the fall of the Iron Curtain, the opportunity to reconstruct how people organised their beliefs about politics and politicians during communist rule is not feasible. As our research only captures subsequent changes in citizens' cognitive systems without referring to their previous state, these conclusions will in one way or another bear this limitation.

It is nevertheless clear that the cognitive system of post-Soviet voters indeed underwent significant changes following the collapse and split of the Soviet Union. The best evidence for this is the development of brand new political prototypes that certainly reflect the post-communist *zeitgeist*. An alternative way to understand changes in citizens' conceptualisation of politicians is through the *political perspective* schema. It is likely this schema developed alongside political transformations following Perestroika and captured the orientation of politicians drifting from communism to radical reforms. In terms of rapidly changing ideologies and development of a multi-party system in the Ukraine, the *political perspective* schema appeared to be both a simpler and more reliable substitute for ideology and party affiliation schemas relevant to voters in stable political systems like the US, but not yet developed by Ukrainian voters.

The studies described here confirm that post-Soviet voters do think about politics in terms of a limited number of categories but the way they organise their knowledge is reminiscent of other findings, closely resembling those from studies on non-Ukrainian samples. At least three dimensions of categorisation were repeatedly elicited from studies which used similar methodology, e.g., Miller *et al.*, 1986: reliability, integrity and personal attributes. In fact, taking into account the broad political aptitude dimension consisting of competence, efficacy and charisma, the model derived from our studies almost entirely overlaps with the competence, charisma, integrity, reliability and personal dimensions found by Miller *et al.* (1986). This gives rise to the possibility of a fairly stable set of cross-cultural cognitive criteria relatively unaffected by nuances of political systems. Put simply, these criteria constitute a universal standard for the ideal political leader and provide a benchmark for further evaluation of political candidates.

Although post-Soviet voters may in many ways have similar standards for judging political leaders, they cannot avoid certain important distinctions. A remarkable example is an affluence dimension in the categorisation system of Ukrainian voters, which carries a unique post-Soviet connotation. This criterion may serve to explain the latent motivation of candidates, such as a focus on personal profit or gain, as well as describing the route into politics which is often from business. Survey research suggests that in Ukrainian public consciousness the affluence of politicians is often viewed in two conflicting ways. The first one bears a somewhat utopian assumption that a wealthy candidate can help voters (in the Ukraine this was at least partially true during election campaigns), while the second view is that 'a leopard cannot change his spots' and those with new-found wealth do not follow altruistic goals in politics (Petrunko, 2000). Notwithstanding this distinction, in most other respects the way post-Soviet voters organised their knowledge of political leaders and candidates was as expected. This is evidenced both by the structure of politician-related schemas and by embedded leader prototypes. Furthermore the combination of mass survey, Q-methodology, multivariate statistical modelling and projective methods elicited a stable set of cognitive schemas through which citizens organise their knowledge about politicians. In both less and more politically sophisticated voters a four-dimensional model was derived, which included political potential, competence, formal status and trustworthiness and political perspective.

It is important to emphasise that the categorisation dimensions achieved by applying a semantic differential approach do not entirely overlap with the schema structures elicited using Q-methodology. This is particularly evident with the affluence and personal characteristic dimensions although these criteria are apparently incorporated into other schemas and were made explicit by respondents in thinking-aloud comments. There are two possible reasons for this inconsistency. The first, and perhaps most plausible, is the difference in research methodology, i.e., semantic differential versus Q-sorting. Somewhat less likely is objective change in respondents' cognitive systems explained by an eighteen-month interval between the two studies. However, virtually identical solutions using samples of less and more politically sophisticated voters were obtained using Q-sort methodology, which suggests time lag was not the issue.

As the Subtyping model of schema change suggests, political leader schemas held by Ukrainian voters do accommodate a broad number of subtypes in order to account for the wide range of candidates. Although it is not possible to retrace their development, it is likely that by the mid-1990s a *communist leader* type – presumably dominant prior to Perestroika – was not most salient for Ukrainian voters. Moreover, this and similar political types (the orthodox communist *symbol of the past* and political *apparatchik*) were more defined by the criteria of obsolescence and orientation to the past than by the ideology to which they adhered. In the absence of more elaborate political and ideological schemas, the orientation of politicians towards the future or past played an apparently important role in helping citizens develop basic expectations of their elected representatives.

This does not mean, of course, that voters were not detecting a 'legacy of communism' in Ukrainian politics in the 1990s. It is more likely that due to the exodus from the Communist Party and divergence from prevailing ideology the presumed communist leader type transformed in the public consciousness into others, for example to dilettante, career-ist, demagogue or politically bankrupt, as all of these at least partially comprise former members of the Communist Party. The rapidly grow-ing and chaotic political scene witnessed the spread of numerous ideol-ogies and the entry of fresh political players, which in turn led to the development of new leader prototypes in the cognitive system of voters. However, most of these new types carry negative connotations as described above and these reflect fairly well the prevalent attitude of Ukrainian voters to domestic politics and politicians. The reason for this could be attributed to a huge economic crisis and the deterioration of living standards in the Ukraine after the fall of the USSR. In comparison, the relative prosperity of Western nations led Ukrainian respondents to recognise Western leaders as uniformly credible, competent and expe-rienced politicians.

Our findings suggest that in terms of social-economic instability the major call of Ukrainian respondents was not only for a trustworthy and competent leader but also for the economist-reformer type able to cope with crisis. This type summarised the conception of an ideal Ukrainian politician in the 1990s. Paraphrasing Kinder *et al.* (1980), this conception may stem from widely shared beliefs about 'cure-all' modern reformers fuelled by the media and politicians, when in reality their ability to cope with such a crisis, as well as the limitations of current politicians, led many to fall short of this standard.

Somewhat contrary to our expectations, respondents with relative political expertise essentially have the same set of leader schemas as political novices. Similarly to Pierce (1993), we find that sophisticated voters do not differ from novices in their use of less abstract personal and performance characteristics of politicians. Also contrary to what was expected, political sophisticates did not appear even partially to organise information about politicians based on ideological criteria. There is, however, a substantial difference between sophisticates and novices in the effective number of political subtypes they develop, store and apply in considering political leaders. Those with relatively more political expertise seem to have a more developed conceptualisation of political leaders though, once again, these political subtypes essentially fit the same leader schemas. Nevertheless it is also possible that eliciting more leader subtypes can be partially attributed to the expanded list of politicians suggested to respondents in the final study. While flaws in design cannot be completely ruled out, thinking-aloud protocols collected from the politically aware sample do indicate an increased abstract knowledge of politics.

Our findings confirm the assumption that in the course of social and political transformations following the collapse of the USSR, voters developed relatively simple cognitive schemas relying on personal and professional characteristics: likeability, charisma, competence and reliability as well as politicians' orientation to the past or future. In terms of socio-political changes and ideological chaos in Ukraine in the 1990s, these cognitive categories were proven to be more robust and less prone to change as they focused on stable and fundamental characteristics instead of more complex and malleable political-ideological criteria.

As our studies have been inductive and exploratory in nature, it is important to point out certain theoretical and methodological limitations. Given a limited set of studies on voters' cognitive system in the post-communist states we had to rely on assumptions rather than established views in our theoretical framework. Due to the absence of specifically designed mass surveys in Ukraine we devised our own methodology for the empirical part of the study. Nevertheless, our studies shed some light on the cognitive system of Ukrainian post-Soviet voters shortly after the collapse of the USSR, which have been and largely remain *terra incognita* for political psychologists. We believe that future studies may find it interesting and practical to focus on further dynamic changes in cognitive schema during the late 1990s and 2000s. This, in its turn, necessitates mobilisation of methods typically used in political schema research, as outlined in this chapter.

References

Anderson, J. R. (1981). Concepts, propositions, and schemata: what are the cognitive units? In J. Flowers (ed.), *Nebraska Symposium on Motivation*. Lincoln: University of Nebraska Press.

(1995). *Cognitive Psychology and Its Implications and Scientific American Explores the Hidden Mind*. New York: Worth Publishers.

(1996). *The Architecture of Cognition*. Mahwah, N.J.: L. Erlbaum Associates.

Augoustinos, M. and Walker, I. (1996). *Social Cognition: an Integrated Introduction*. London: Sage Publications.

Augoustinos, M., Walker, I. and Donoghue, N. (2006). *Social Cognition: an Integrated Introduction*. London: Sage Publications.

Axelrod, R. (1973). Schema theory: an information processing model of perception and cognition. *The American Political Science Review*, 67 (4), 1248–66.

Bishop, G. F., and Poznyak, D. (2008). Social-democratic tolerance in forty-seven nations. Paper presented at the World Association of Public Opinion Research, New Orleans, 13 May.

Brown, S. R. (1980). *Political Subjectivity: Applications of Q-methodology in Political Science*. New Haven, Conn.: Yale University Press.

Campbell, A., Converse, P., Miller, W. and Stokes, D. (1960). *The American Voter*. New York: John Wiley and Sons.

Caprara, G. V., Barbaranelli, C. and Zimbardo, P. G. (2002). When parsimony subdues distinctiveness: simplified public perceptions of politicians' personality. *Political Psychology*, 23, 77–95.

Carnaghan, E. (2007). *Out of Order: Russian Political Values in an Imperfect World*. University Park: The Pennsylvania State University Press.

Chudovsky V. and Kuzio T. (2003). Does public opinion matter in Ukraine? The case of foreign policy. *Communist and Post-Communist Studies*, 36, 273–90.

Conover, P. J. and Feldman, S. (1984). How people organize the political world: a schematic model. *American Journal of Political Science*, 28 (1), 95–126.

(1989). Candidate perception in an ambiguous world: campaigns, cues and inference processes. *American Journal of Political Science*, 33 (4), 912–40.

Converse, P. (1964). The nature of belief systems in mass publics. In David Apter (ed.), *Ideology and Discontent* (pp. 206–61). New York: Free Press.

Diligenski, G. G. (1994). *Socialno-Politiceskaja Psihologija (in Russian)*. Moscow: Nauka.

Downs, Anthony. (1957). *An Economic Theory of Democracy*. New York: Harper.

Eysenck, H. J. and Coulter, T. J. (1972). The personality and attitudes of working-class British Communists and Fascists. *Journal of Social Psychology*, 87, 59–73.

Fiske, S. T. and Linville, P. W. (1980). What does the schema concept buy us? Symposium on social knowing, *Personality and Social Psychology Bulletin*, 6, 543–57.

Fiske, S. T., Lau, R. R. and Smith, R. A. (1990). On the variety and utility of political knowledge structures. *Social Cognition*, 8, 31–48.

Fiske, S. T. and Taylor, S. E. (1984). *Social Cognition*. Reading, Mass.: Addison-Wesley.

(1991). *Social Cognition*. 2nd edn. New York: McGraw-Hill.

(2008). *Social Cognition: from Brains to Culture*. Boston: McGraw-Hill Higher Education.

Frolov, P. D. (1998). Voters' fears on the eve of president elections. Unpublished manuscript (in Ukrainian).

(1999). Voters' perceptions of ideal and real candidates for Ukrainian president (based on the 5–14 August 1999 study). Unpublished manuscript (in Ukrainian).

(2002). Monitoring and forecasting of people's beliefs about Ukrainian political system functioning. Unpublished manuscript (in Ukrainian).

Hamill, R. and Lodge, M. (1986). Cognitive consequences of political sophistication. In Richard R. Lau and David O. Sears (eds.), *Political Cognition: the 19th Annual Carnegie Symposium on Cognition* (pp. 69–94). Hillsdale, N.J.: L. Erlbaum Associates.

Harris Interactive/*Financial Times* (2006). Retrieved on 11 January 2010 from www.harrisinteractive.com/NEWS/allnewsbydate.asp?NewsID=1072.

Heider, F. (1958). *The Psychology of Interpersonal Relations*. New York: Wiley.

Herstein, J. (1981). Keeping the voters' limits in mind: a cognitive process analysis of decision making in voting. *Journal of Personality and Social Psychology*, 40, 843–61.

Inglehart, R. and Welzel, C. (2005). *Modernization, Cultural Change, and Democracy: the Human Development Sequence*. Cambridge University Press.

Key, V. O. (1966). *The Responsible Electorate: Rationality in Presidential Voting, 1936–1960*. Cambridge, Mass.: Belknap Press of Harvard University Press.

Kinder, D. R., Peters, M. D., Abelson, R. P. and Fiske, S. T. (1980). Presidential prototypes. *Political Behavior*, 2, 315–38.

Kuklinski, J. H., Luskin, R. C. and Bolland, J. (1991). Where is the schema? Going beyond the 'S' word in political psychology. *The American Political Science Review*, 85 (4), 1341–56.

Lane, R. D. and Nadel, L. (2002). *Cognitive Neuroscience of Emotion* (Series in Affective Science). Oxford University Press.

Lau, R. R. (1986). Political schemata, candidate evaluation and voting behavior. In Richard R. Lau and David O. Sears (eds.), *Political Cognition: the 19th Annual Carnegie Symposium on Cognition* (pp. 95–126). Hillsdale, N.J.: L. Erlbaum Associates.

Lau, R. R. and Redlawsk, D. P. (2001). Advantages and disadvantages of cognitive heuristics in political decision making. *American Journal of Political Science*, 45, 951–71.

(2006). *How Voters Decide: Information Processing during Election Campaigns*. Cambridge University Press.

Lau, R. and Sears, D. O. (1986). Political schemata, candidate evaluation, and voting behavior. In Richard R. Lau and David O. Sears (eds.), *Political Cognition: The 19th Annual Symposium on Cognition*. Hillsdale, NJ: Erlbaum Associates.

Lazarsfeld, P. F., Berelson, B. R and Gaudet, Hazel (1944). *The People's Choice: How the Voter Makes Up His Mind in a Presidential Campaign*. New York, Duel, Sloan and Pearce.

Lodge, M. and Wahlke, J. C. (1982). Politicos, apoliticals, and the processing of political information. *International Political Science Review*, 3: 131–60.

Luskin, R. C. (1987). Measuring political sophistication. *American Journal of Political Science*, 31, 856–99.

McKeown, B. and Thomas, D. (1988). *Q Methodology*. (Quantitative Applications in the Social Sciences). London: Sage Publications.

Miller, A. H., Wattenberg, M. P. and Malanchuk, O. (1986). Schematic assessments of presidential candidates. *The American Political Science Review*, 80 (2), 521–40.

Osgood, C. E., Suci, G. and Tannenbaum, P. (1957). *The Measurement of Meaning*. Urbana: University of Illinois Press.

Petrunko, O. V. (2000). Implicit leadership typologies of Ukrainian voters. Unpublished doctoral dissertation, Institute for Social and Political Psychology, Kiev, Ukraine (in Ukrainian).

Piaget, J. (1926). *The Child's Conception of the World*. London: Routledge and Kegan Paul.

Pierce, P. A. (1993). Political sophistication and the use of candidate traits in candidate evaluation, *Political* Psychology, 14 (Spring), 21–36.

Public Opinion Fund (2006). *Mikhail Gorbachev, the President of USSR* (in Russian). Retrieved 11 January 2010 from http://bd.english.fom.ru/report/cat/az/D/democracy/ed003209.

Rosenberg, S. (1977). New approaches to the analysis of personal constructs in person perception. In J. K. Cole and A. W. Landfield (eds.), *Nebraska Symposium on Motivation* (pp. 179–242). Lincoln: University of Nebraska Press.

Rosch, E. (1975). Cognitive representation of semantic categories. *Journal of Experimental Psychology*, 104 (3), 192–233.

Rothbart, M. (1981). Memory processes and social beliefs. In D. Hamilton (ed.), *Cognitive Processes in Stereotyping and Intergroup Perception*. Hillsdale, N.J.: Lawrence Erlbaum.

    (1996). Category-exemplar dynamics and stereotype change. *International Journal of Intercultural Relations*, 20 (3–4), 305–21.

Rumelhart, D. and Norman, D. (1978). Accretion, tuning and restructuring: three modes of learning. In. J. W. Cotton and R. Klatzky (eds.), *Semantic Factors in Cognition*. Hillsdale, NJ: Lawrence Erlbaum.

Sears, D. O. (1969). Political behavior. In Gardner Lindzey and Aronson Elliot (eds.), *Handbook of Social Psychology*, 2d edn, vol. V. Reading, Mass.: Addison-Wesley.

Shaw, J. B. (1990). A cognitive categorization model for the study of intercultural management. *Academy of Management Review*, 10, 435–54.

Stillings, N. A., Weisler, S. W., Chase, C. H. Feinstein, M. H., Garfield, J. L. and Rissland, E. L. (1995). *Cognitive Science: An Introduction*. Cambridge, Mass.: The MIT Press.

Taylor, S. E. and Crocker, J. (1981). Schematic bases of social information processing. In E. T. Higgins, C. P. Herman and M. P. Zanna (eds.), *Social Cognition: the Ontario Symposium* (pp. 89–134). Hillsdale, N.J.: Lawrence Erlbaum.

Taylor, S. E. and Winkler, J. D. (1980). The development of schemas. Paper given at the 88th annual convention of the American Psychological Association, Montreal, Canada.

Tetlock, P. E. (1986). A value pluralism model of ideological reasoning. *Journal of Personality and Social Psychology*, 50, 819–27.

Weber, R. and Crocker, J. (1983). Cognitive processes in the revision of stereotypic beliefs. *Journal of Personality and Social Psychology*, 45, 961–77.

Willis, G. B. (2004). *Cognitive Interviewing: A Tool for Improving Questionnaire Design*. London: Sage Publications.

Index